SERIES IN
CITIZENSHIP STUDIES

....

SERIES EDITORS

Marc W. Kruman

Richard Marback

ACTS OF ANGRY WRITING

ACTS OF ANGRY WRITING

....

On Citizenship and Orientalism in Postcolonial India

ALESSANDRA MARINO

Wayne State University Press
Detroit

Manufactured in the United States of America.

19 18 17 16 15 5 4 3 2 1

ISBN 978-0-8143-4057-8 (cloth); ISBN 978-0-8143-4058-5 (ebook)
Library of Congress Control Number: 2015950435

Designed by Bryce Schimanski
Typeset by Keata Brewer, E.T. Lowe Publishing
Composed in Adobe Caslon Pro

I want freedom, the right to self-expression,
everybody's right to beautiful,
radiant things

Emma Goldman, *Living My Life*

CONTENTS

Map of India. Copyright www.mapsofindia.com.

INTRODUCTION

Just Anger

> [Borderlands are] never a comfortable place to live in . . . hatred, anger and exploitation are prominent features of these landscapes.
>
> Gloria Anzaldúa

> I am not asking you to feel my anger. Understand it, and respect it.
>
> Arundhati Roy

Booker prize winning author Arundhati Roy is eloquently outspoken on the relation between poverty, capitalist development, and the exploitation of resources in developing countries. Labeled a "word warrior" by Naomi Klein (A. Roy and Barsamian 2004, vi), Roy sees her writing and activism as equally powerful ways of speaking truth to power. By maintaining that public intellectuals have a duty to denounce injustice and reveal hidden stories of discrimination and abuse against the poor, Roy has tied her name to a number of famous protests and resistance movements, including the anti-dam campaign carried out since the 1980s in the Narmada Valley and Maoist guerrilla struggles. In the introduction to *Field Notes on Democracy: Listening to Grasshoppers*, her collection of essays interrogating the meaning of democracy in neoliberal times, Roy states that the volume was "written in anger, at moments when keeping quiet became harder than saying something" (A. Roy 2009, xi).

Roy identifies people's indignation at dispossession and social inequality as the motivation for fighting against the forceful acquisition of farmland and tribal land.[1] In places such as Singur and Nandigram (West Bengal), where the violent unrest against the land grab resulted in police opening fire and killing fourteen farmers in 2007, the anger of poor villagers confronted the rising alliance between the interests of the government and international corporations. Recognizing that liberalizing the Indian economy meant increasing pressure on marginal citizens to give up natural resources and make way for new industrial plants and infrastructure projects, Roy voices her anger at a system in which "a citizen's rights are such a fragile thing" (A. Roy 2008, 73).

Roy's outcry against the attack on unarmed people in Nandigram joined the protestations of many activists, including the leader of the Narmada Bachao Andolan, Medha Patkar, and such intellectuals as the film director Aparna Sen and the writer Mahasweta Devi (see Chakravorty et al. 2007). Devi is a prominent Bengali author and winner of the Jnanpeeth Award; she is widely known for her lifelong commitment to tribal rights. Devi's writing and activism have the effect of directing regional, national, and international attention toward the deprivation and inhuman living conditions experienced by Adivasis all over India.[2] When she received the Yashwantrao Chavan National Award in 2010, the jury statement read, "She writes with a pen dipped in fire and a heart full of anger and sorrow."[3] Anger, as Devi herself admits, is the motivation for taking up writing as a weapon to fight injustice: "Language is a weapon; it's not for shaving your armpits" (Taldukar and Devi, 2001).

In a similar vein, the recent autobiography of Sampat Pal, the leader of a female gang known as the Gulabi Gang, has excited international debate about gender and caste subjection in rural India. The book powerfully describes Pal's engagement in social and political disputes as angry reactions against institutional gender oppression; the writer is cast as a forgotten hero whose support to the nation's poorest citizens deserves wider recognition.

Motivated by these examples of intertwining social and literary activism, in *Acts of Angry Writing* I consider anger as a trigger for political writing and see literature as one of the battlefields where struggles for basic rights of indigenous people and lower castes are fought. My aim is to show not only how the affective work that traverses the actions of political associations inspires new cultural and literary creations but also that literature has the power to bring about a material transformation of reality, because it activates reactions for or against a particular case and triggers the mobilization of an audience. The expression of anger in literary works can generate and motivate new manifestations of fury.

This book is divided into four parts, the first three of which deal with different authors and examples of activism. Three women and their acts are at the center of my critical investigation: Roy, Devi, and Pal. In the last part I present a theoretical reflection on the relation between the ethical call that initiates acts of social protest and writing. By looking at literature as a performative activity, I trace its relation to citizenship movements that are active in contemporary rural India.

The first two parts of the book focus on Devi and Roy, and I analyze how their works relate to some of the most famous actions of social protest in which they have been involved. In particular, I examine Roy's participation in the struggle of the Narmada Bachao Andolan (NBA) movement in the Narmada Valley and explore Devi's practices of legal activism in Purulia (West Bengal), where she has long been a member and supporter of an association fighting for the rights of the Kheria Sabar tribe. I use the phrase "acts of writing" to refer to the process of creation of works such as Roy's "Greater Common Good" (reprinted in A. Roy 1999) and Mahasweta Devi's *Chotti Munda and His Arrow* (2003), which were born out of specific social and environmental struggles and need to be looked at in their context. These acts reveal the performative quality of literature, which can shape the language that fuels social protests and creates a path for their dissemination. Moreover, thinking about these acts of writing motivated by anger at oppression invites us to focus on how postcolonial women writers manifest the sense of responsibility they feel toward their times and society.

In the third part of the book I examine the representation of anger as a productive emotion in *Warrior in a Pink Sari*, the autobiography of Sampat Pal. In her memoir the leader of the Gulabi Gang, based in Uttar Pradesh, describes herself as a tireless soldier who has dedicated her life to fighting against injustice and gender violence. Following the publication of the book, Pal gained considerable fame and, as a consequence, more power in her local community. Originally published in Hindi and translated into several languages, the memoir provides me with a telling example of the close relation between literature, the social reality, and ongoing political debates. I analyze Pal's story and the movement she founded in relation to the sociopolitical context of Bundelkhand.

In the fourth and final part of *Acts of Angry Writing*, I discuss the performative quality of literature and the relation between anger and activism. The life and writing of Devi, Roy, and Pal reveal that anger, literature, and activism are entangled in a virtuous cycle: Anger is the fundamental condition for writing and activism, but these two together disseminate and generate more anger at exploitation and injustice. Feminist criticism, and in particular the works of women of color, opposes the dismissal and criminalization of anger as an unproductive or purely harmful emotion. In contrast to the rationalist tradition that informs Western philosophy and social sciences, in this book I cast anger and literature as fundamental elements for discussing political and activist work.

From Aristotle to Seneca, anger was categorized as aggressive behavior, incompatible with rational conduct. Considered an illogical emotion, anger was then associated with femininity and its flaws. In *Just Anger*, which explores depictions of anger in early modern women's writing, Gwynne Kennedy traces a different Western genealogy of philosophical representations of anger, rooted in the thinking of Thomas Aquinas. For Aquinas, anger can be motivated by reason and, in some cases it can carry beneficial consequences (Kennedy 2000, 11).

Taking up the baton of Kennedy's attempt to break free of a rationalist line of philosophical inquiry, I reclaim for this book a lineage of feminist, postcolonial, and antiracist critical works that have seen anger as a justified reaction to injustice. This genealogy, positively consecrating anger as a feminist emotion, includes the works of Audre Lorde, Elizabeth Spelman, Marilyn Frye, Kathleen Woodward, Sara Ahmed, and Sue Kim.

With *On Anger* (2013), Kim provides an extensive and up-to-date analysis of works of feminist cultural studies that discuss anger as a productive feeling. Her book also highlights that the feminization of anger should not be dissociated from its reconfiguration as an attribute of the racialized other of the so-called third world: "Works on anger in ethnic and postcolonial studies have largely involved reclaiming and exploring the ideological validity of emotion, as well as interrogating characterization of minorities in the West and Third World peoples as pathological, volatile, and irrational in their anger" (Kim 2013, 49). Kim shows how representations of feminine and emotional actors are at odds with Western definitions of political subjectivity, whose rationality leaves no space for affects and feelings. Contemporary political theory thus appears to be unable to describe the political work of women who live, fight, and write angrily in a former colonial space and in the global cultural sphere. Some of these women are the subjects of my analysis. Their acts have inspired the interrogation of the Western and imperial lineage of citizenship that is part of this book. Kim makes a powerful case for the oppressor-oppressed paradigm being key for resignifying anger as a weapon of political struggles rather than a signifier for the lack of rationality (Kim 2013, 47).

Highlighting the importance of locating one's position in a system of gender, class, and racial oppression, Audre Lorde's "Uses of Anger" remains fundamentally inspiring in its assertion that there is reason in anger, or anger has it reasons. Lorde maintains that her feminist rage is a legitimate response to racism and reveals that from the perspective of marginalized social groups, anger is a crucial tool for creating alliances against institutionalized and hegemonic forms of violent discrimination (Lorde 1984, 129–33).

Anger is a collective weapon. In this spirit, Roy speaks of an angry "we," whose reasons clash with the machinations and objectives of governments and oligarchs: "Why should we be scared of being angry? Why should we be scared of our feelings, if they're based on facts? The whole framework of reason versus passion is ridiculous, because often passion is based on reason. . . . Anger is based on reason" (A. Roy 2008, 70).[4] Giving shape to her anger through writing, Roy explores the possibility of nurturing the creation of a broader community of committed readers who can share the resistance of the portrayed angry subject(s).

bell hooks's *Killing Rage, Ending Racism* (1995) sees the expression of anger from the space of the colonized as an act of survival. Referring to Toni Morrison's *The Bluest Eye* (1970), she argues that anger allows an expression of subjectivity that does not merely accommodate itself to one of the roles prescribed to the people of color by the colonizers. In Morrison's first novel, *The Bluest Eye*, her narrator says of the dehumanized colonized little black girl Pecola that there would be hope for her if only she could express her rage, because, "Anger is better, there is presence in anger. Perhaps then it is that 'presence,' the assertion of subjectivity that colonizers do not want to see, that surfaces when the colonized express rage" (hooks 1995, 12). The rage of the colonized is subversive because it is tangibly present in the book.

Anger can be touched, despite falling outside the spectrum of what the white man can or wants to hear.

In *Acts of Angry Writing* I register the reasons for anger formulated by Lorde, hooks, and other women of color and question the Western and masculine bias that underpins contemporary conceptions of the political subject and its relation to emotions. I follow Kim in her definition of the four axioms that summarize the feminist scholarship on anger. She claims that anger is (1) cognitive, so it is not opposed to reason; (2) individual, collective, and intersubjective; (3) gendered, raced, and classed; and (4) historical and thereby ideological and political (Kim 2013, 68–69). This book exemplifies all four of these points. Dealing with anger as a trigger for activism and writing in rural India, I consider anger a legitimate response to gender, class, and caste oppression. Moreover, I argue that anger is the link between the writing individual and a protesting collectivity; as Kim writes, "Not only are emotions produced by a group, but also groups are produced by emotions" (Kim 2013, 68). The intersubjective aspect of anger allows the creation of resistance through acts of reading literary works. Finally, I read narrations of anger in their specific contexts to show how particular books relate and contribute to ongoing ideological and material struggles.

Writing women's anger at exploitation emerges as a way out of the binarism, established by colonial ideology, between criminalizing and romanticizing "oriental" and "native" subjects. In the following sections I outline my theoretical trajectory, drawing on postcolonial and cultural studies, political theory and literary theory, and the approach used to connect the main themes of this book: anger, narratives, and citizenship. I maintain that anger, a feminized and orientalized emotion, can be a useful lens to shed new light on contemporary citizenship struggles. Political literature fueled by anger at injustice here becomes an instrument to understand the ways in which marginalized citizens rewrite the modern nation.

ANGRY AGAINST THE NATION: WOMEN AND TRIBAL GROUPS

Political literature and anger are indissolubly tied up, because this literature is the result of a process, or a reflection on the process, of questioning the conditions of living in a specific world or in a given society. These reflections deal with order, power, and justice. Immediately after World War II and the loss of the empire, anger famously defined a group of English playwrights and novelists: the Angry Young Men. The main concern of the Angry Young Men was to voice the sense of dissatisfaction that working people felt against the country's traditional powers; these young intellectuals scorned England for its loss of global primacy after the war and rebelled against the persisting class divisions. John Osborne's *Look Back in Anger* is one of the most famous examples of the way in which English theater in 1956 captured the changing social dynamics of the time and allowed the working-class character Jimmy Porter to express his bold and bitter rage against higher classes. A brief look at this drama, which reveals the crisis that followed the loss of the empire, highlights two issues that are central to my investigation: first, that anger has a deeply ideological meaning; and second, that recent literary works that view anger as a response to class oppression reiterate violent oppression against women.

Look Back in Anger dramatizes Jimmy's rejection of middle-class values against the backdrop of the changing European political arena, represented by the Spanish Civil War and the fall of the British Empire. Jimmy's father fought on the losing side of the Spanish Civil War, together with other anti-fascists, whereas Jimmy's father-in-law, whom he despises, served all his life as a colonel in British India. Jimmy's anger at the endless and unchanging marginalization of the poor clashes with the melancholic perspective of the colonel, who realizes that for him everything has changed. Interpreter of these divided worlds is Jimmy's wife, Alison, who bluntly says to her father, "You're hurt because everything is changed. Jimmy is hurt because everything is the same. And neither of you can face it. Something's gone wrong somewhere, hasn't it?" (Osborne 1994, 70). Alison occupies a space in-between her father's self-pity and her husband's fury, but she pays the price for her liminality by becoming estranged from her family and becoming the main target of Jimmy's misogynistic and violent language. What appears to be the rise of a new class consciousness goes hand in hand with a shift in gender relations, where women's increasing independence from domestic life opens up a space of contestation.

Michelene Wandor's *Look Back in Gender: Sexuality and the Family in Post-War British Drama* (1987) sees the shift from wartime to post-wartime Britain as the moment when women became more self-sufficient, partly as a consequence of being forced to work during the war, and men became less patriarchal, or even more feminized. What Osborne puts on stage, though, exposes verbal and physical violence as the price women had to pay for the establishment of this new social configuration. The young man's anger here is a weapon of political rebellion for the poor white urban character who finds a way to express his discontent in the wider political scene; but it is also a tool for gender oppression.

Conscious that men's anger has been complicit in women's oppression in patriarchal societies, in *Acts of Angry Writing* I focus on women's literary rebellions against the discrimination of poor and tribal communities in contemporary India, with the aim of enhancing our understanding of women's political acts in contemporary culture. *Look Back in Anger* is an example of how the conquest of a visible space by a marginalized group, such as poor workers, ended up overshadowing the claims of others to justice, creating new forms of domination. In a similar vein, I emphasize that the works of postcolonial theorists such as Partha Chatterjee (1993), Chandra T. Mohanty (2003), and Anupama Roy (2005), among others, denounced the effacement of the role of women in nationalist movements of liberation and highlighted the renewed gendered oppression that followed the victory of decolonization movements.

The victory of freedom fighters in India and their anger at the colonial system did not materialize into more social equality.[5] Women's experiences of Partition, including widespread rapes and abductions, provide us with an example of how gendered narrations of nationalist struggles challenge romanticized accounts of the acquisition of freedom and equality.[6] Ritu Menon's collection of testimonials of women who survived the horrors of Partition demonstrates that female citizens are stranded in the space between the old colonial oppression and the violence of independence. Although independence created citizenship, establishing specific rights for citizens, the violence that populated the history of the separation of India from Pakistan and Bangladesh pushed women into a new space of vulnerability. From the moment of its foundation, India has been a "no woman's land," as the title of Menon's book suggests (Menon 2004).

Women's narrations of the borders, questioning the ways in which they were created, explore the shifting grounds of national identity. In this book I look at various ways in which literature and autobiographical accounts criticize the very meaning of being Indian. I explore the work of women such as Arundhati Roy and Mahasweta Devi, who dwell on the fences of mainstream culture. Roy affirmed that she was ready to secede from a country that takes pride in its nuclear activities (A. Roy 1999, 119); on many occasions

Devi rejected the notion that India is a free and egalitarian democracy, highlighting that the tribal groups do not yet enjoy basic citizenship rights. They live in borderlands that, in Gloria Anzaldúa's words, are "never a comfortable place to live in," because "hatred, anger and exploitation are prominent features of these landscapes" (Anzaldúa 1987, 19). Anger and exploitation, or anger at the exploitation of the poor, are fundamental reasons for these Indian women's writing and activism.

While listening to these women's angry narratives, I also zoom in on the heroes of their stories to highlight how Adivasi women, in particular, live in the borderlands of the nation. Metaphorically, they are caught between the private and the public sphere of marginalized communities. Physically, tribal areas are located geographically at the borders of different states and far from the urban centers. This peripheral position is reflected in Adivasis' invisibility in the political sphere. Their long history of discrimination was marked by the passing of colonial acts, such as the Criminal Tribes Act (1871), which declared some Adivasi groups to be criminal. In accordance with a Utilitarian ideology, indigenous people were considered backward and dangerous, permanently trapped in a state of nature. In the first two chapters of this book I deal directly with the relation between the colonial legal and cultural framework of the nineteenth century and its heritage.

In contemporary India, Adivasis' condition of marginalization determines their poverty, and poverty contributes to their marginalization; their labor is often exploited and underpaid, if paid at all. Moreover, their lack of education makes them vulnerable to the abuses of the police and upper castes. The political invisibility of indigenous people in India prevents them from enjoying de facto the rights that were granted to them de jure with the constitution. In reaction to the expropriation of resources and exploitation of their bodies and labor, Adivasis have angrily taken up different forms of resistance, some peaceful and others violent. The case of Maoist guerrilla groups paradigmatically exposes the transformation of tribal groups into national enemies or anticitizens; since 2011, the government has waged a massive war operation against them, called Operation Green Hunt. Several activist organizations have described the operation as genocide or an instance of civil war.

Arundhati Roy's essay "Walking with the Comrades," in *Broken Republic*, describes the writer's stay with a Maoist group for three weeks in an attempt to get a grip on who the Maoists are, where they live, and what their aims are. She sheds light on the large number of women participating in acts of extreme violence and listens to their stories, which are often full of memories of rape, abduction, and atrocious police violence. Anger and desperation pervade the text, accompanied by a sense that there is nothing else to do but keep on struggling. After the publication of the essay, Roy was accused of sympathizing with the motivations and the methods of the guerrilla army. She did not deny feeling a sense of solidarity. The essay is important for this book because in it Roy attempts to desacralize the importance of neutralizing these allegedly fierce enemies of the nation.

While writing this book, I became increasingly aware that anger could give rise to different responses to the feeling of being wronged but also that anger is not a prerogative of minorities and can be a means of oppression, as *Looking Back in Anger* exemplifies. But rather than providing an atlas of anger, in its multiple scales and shades, I decided to examine how anger originating in specific spaces of marginality and exploitation, such as rural India, can trigger the production of creative acts that denounce injustice. These acts of accusation of the empty promises of democracy, as I will show, rewrite the language of citizenship rights.

POSTCOLONIAL NARRATIVES OF INDIAN CITIZENSHIP

More than sixty years after independence, Indian citizenship is still a contested issue. In civil society and in academia, battles for the acquisition or the enactment of rights are fought under the banner of citizenship. Writers, but also eminent scholars such as Rajeswari Sunder Rajan (2003) and Niraja Gopal Jayal (2013), highlight the gap between the entitlement to citizenship rights and their actual enjoyment by the poor, rural villagers, Adivasis, and women.

This fundamental contradiction of modern Indian citizenship, which registers the substantial exclusion of tribal groups from their basic entitlements, is clearly highlighted by Jayal's *Citizenship and Its Discontents: An Indian History*. Jayal's book performs two important tasks. First, it traces the legacy of the language of colonial law within the philanthropic discourse of citizenship; and second, it presents an interesting argument on the failure of the group-differentiated strategy of citizenship. Jayal denounces the marginality of the tribal question in political and legal studies and compares the contemporary rhetoric of protectionism of indigenous rights with a colonial attitude: "The marginality of the so-called backward tracts in colonial discourse in late colonial India is paralleled by the marginality of the tribal question in mainstream nationalist discourse. The constitutional incorporation of the Scheduled Tribes after independence demonstrates some continuity with the colonial discourse of protection, though there was a remarkable ambivalence about how protection should be conceived" (Jayal 2013, 236).[7] Categories such as "backward classes" were created in an attempt to account for the complexity of Indian society in the race toward leveling class disparity. The attribute of backwardness echoes the colonial tag that identifies indigenous areas as "backward tracts" (The Government of India Act of 1919), but in the legislation of modern India, backwardness became an attribute of different communities, including untouchables, aboriginal people, and criminal tribes.

When drafting the constitution, the Constituent Assembly had the task of translating into laws the values of egalitarian freedom and justice for all, which summarized the aspirations of a free India. A model of group-differentiated citizenship, where citizenship was mediated by the community, was adopted with the aim of protecting civil and political rights of minority groups. Unfortunately, the creation of exceptional tags, such as Scheduled Tribes and Denotified and Nomadic Tribes, as a way of tackling inequality has proved woefully ineffective, as is clearly demonstrated by the social destitution of millions of citizens living below the poverty line. Jayal concludes that the failure of constitutional citizenship depends precisely on the chosen strategy of group-differentiated inclusion, which was dependent on the creation of new categories of exception, because "the very act of naming these categories for special provisioning ended up entrenching exclusions" (Jayal 2013, 18).

Jayal could be criticized here for conflating group-differentiated citizenship with class-stratified citizenship. As I demonstrate in Part I, the case of India is an example of class-stratified not group-differentiated citizenship.[8] But I want to highlight that Jayal touches on the performative role of ascriptive rather than descriptive legal categories. Law shapes subjectivities and traps them in discrete positions that may have the countereffect of confining them to the margins of mainstream society, as in the case of Adivasis. I interpret the emphasis Jayal seems to place on the performative power of law as an invitation to further investigate the relation between the production of law and the political and social context that shapes it.

Specific cultural settings, at given times, sustain the production of law and provide a justification for its principles. By the same token, cultural change urges legal change. In "Force of Law," Jacques Derrida shows that, contrary to the notion that the law gains its strength from a supposed universal applicability, legal codes in fact depend on the specific moment in which they are founded: "Each advance in politicization obliges one to reconsider, and so to reinterpret the very foundations of law, such as they had previously been calculated or delimited. This was true for example in the Declaration of the Rights of Man, in the abolition of slavery, in all the emancipatory battles that remain and will remain, everywhere in the world, for men and women" (Derrida 1990, 971). Struggles for emancipation, including the civil rights movement, have insistently questioned both the making of the law as an exercise of power and the broader cultural framework that sustains that power. Therefore, when the study of citizenship prioritizes legal principles over the linguistic, cultural, sexual, and affective level, it runs the risk of obliterating the complex dynamics that determine the process of political subjectivation, or the formation of the citizen.

One of my aims in this book is holding together numerous elements that make up the fabric of being a citizen, including language and affects. I am not alone in this undertaking and, in this section I present the intersection between different, and complementary, critical works on citizenship. A number of eminent theorists of citizenship have pointed out the significance of taking culture and language into account when considering such issues as the emergence of the political subject, nationalism, multiculturalism, and, more generally, belonging. In *Sources of the Self* (1989), Charles Taylor argues that language is the founding element of identity, because the "I" is constituted through a web of interlocutions. Despite agreeing on the significance of language in the construction of social networks and forms of cultural identification, critics such as Seyla Benhabib have noted that Taylor proposes a scenario in which the entitlement to recognition on the basis of the co-constitution of the self in communicative situations devoids the world of existing conflicts for primacy and normativity.

In *The Claims of Culture* (2002), Benhabib devotes particular attention to the role of women and minorities in the discourse of diversity. She endorses a "narrative view of actions and cultures" (5) according to which "we identify what we do through an account of what we do" (6). Benhabib sees culture as a set of complex and contradictory narratives that can be interpreted through an analysis of their textual network. Citizenship pertains to this domain, because it is one of the hegemonic narratives that "interpellate" the constitution of subjectivity. But the normative and legal aspect of citizenship, as Benhabib maintains, cannot overshadow its other dimensions, such as the identification with a collectivity and the entitlement to social rights: "We need to disaggregate the theory and practice of citizenship into these various dimensions and broaden our focus to include conditions of citizenship in sociologically complex, decentered, welfare-state democracies" (161). Benhabib suggests, then, that there is an alternative to the theoretical model that views citizenship as the formal entitlement to membership. Instead, she invites us to consider citizenship as a compound of practices and narratives. The claims to culture can be read as a step toward reading citizenship in relation to people's acts of making claims on the legal order.

By outlining the different interpretative keys used by political theory and sociology to study citizenship, Benhabib reveals a concern over the methodology needed to understand its social and narrative aspects. In *Becoming Imperial Citizens* (2010), Sukanya Banerjee provides a persuasive argument to stop looking at citizenship as an object of analysis and start considering the ways in which claims to citizenship *ante-litteram* were formed and started to circulate in the colonial spaces, forging an idea of the citizenship to come. This change of perspective is significant; by looking at official documents, political speeches, and literary works that constituted the political scene in which rights and belonging were challenged in colonial India, Banerjee shows that citizenship can be considered a discursive field that instantiates itself imaginatively as much as normatively. The claims to citizenship and equal rights that fueled the struggles of anticolonial movements influenced the existing concept of citizenship and its relation to freedom. To grasp the interconnection of imaginative, social, and political dimensions, Banerjee promotes the textualization of citizenship as a method for tracing a genealogy of its coming into being.

> Tracing this genealogy requires a textualization of citizenship, a mode of enquiry that is sensitive to the narrative constituents of its claims as well as its statutory prescriptions, both of which speak to the imaginative framings through which the category of citizenship consolidates itself. Such an interpretative filter places emphasis on citizenship as "social practice," an aspect of citizenship which, Seyla Benhabib notes, remains underexamined in studies of citizenship that otherwise tend to ignore the "dialogical" and the "narrative" constructions of political selfhood. (Banerjee 2010, 5)

By revealing the existence of a discourse of citizenship at a moment when Indians were officially subjects of the empire, Banerjee locates citizenship "not so much in the realm of statutory enactment as in the cultural, imaginative, and affective fields that both engender it and are constituted by it" (Banerjee 2010, 5). This does not mean that the statutory dimension ought to be dismissed, but textualizing citizenship enables us to understand claims to citizenship both outside and in conversation with the legal framework.

Endorsing Banerjee's invitation to textualize citizenship, I inscribe affect and literature within an existing group of feminist critical studies of Indian citizenship, which have focused on how processes of subordination and resistance affect the way in which citizenship is experienced across different social groups. For example, in *The Scandal of the State: Women, Law, and Citizenship in Postcolonial India* (2003), Rajan analyzes contemporary cases of violence against women, including child marriage and prostitution, and argues that for women in India the entitlement to equal rights is often just an abstract ideal. Women, especially those who belong to lower castes, reveal an image of the nation that often clashes with the benevolent rhetoric of rights. Rajan evokes the estrangement of lower castes from the meaning of free India, quoting a passage from Mahasweta Devi's story "Douloti," in which a low-caste character, the washerwoman Rajbi, admits to not knowing the meaning of the terms "country" or "India" (M. Devi 1995, 41). Dealing with bonded labor and forced prostitution, "Douloti" shows that citizenship in India has a farcical aspect, because it does not prevent the continued exclusion of marginal subjects from politics.[9] Rajan says, "Citizenship may be a birthright, but its value and weight are produced only through exercising it" (Rajan 2003, 19). Like Rajan, I consider legal citizenship to be sterile if uncoupled from the performance of rights. My analysis of Devi's narrations, which questions the law in its universal aspiration and lack of relation with people's lives, does not approach citizenship only from its institutional and colonial roots; I also shed light on the experienced reality and acts of ordinary people.

ACTS, WRITING, AND AFFECT

In the panorama of recent criticism on citizenship, increasing attention has been dedicated to the importance of literature and affects for the definition of one's cultural and imaginative spheres of belonging. *Acts of Angry Writing* is born in dialogue with a wide range of works of cultural studies, psychoanalysis, and ethnography that focus on how artworks, and literature in particular, open the law to new angles of investigation and reveal its shortcomings. By focusing on the mundane aspects of citizenship, these works show how resistance to the normative aspect of law often takes place through everyday actions.

In this light, Juliana Chang's *Inhuman Citizenship: Traumatic Enjoyment and Asian American Literature* (2012) presents a Lacanian reading of works of popular culture to explore the trauma of migration in Asian communities in the United States. Chang's approach to citizenship reflects a preoccupation with the ordinary; instead of engaging with grand narratives of what citizenship is in the institutions, Chang looks at citizenship in its flesh and bones as the interconnection of the practices of survival and the cultural work emerging within marginal communities. Referring to the work of Lisa Lowe, Chang maintains that her main focus is on "immigrant acts"— that is, "the acts of labor, resistance, memory, and survival, as well as the politicized cultural work that emerges from dislocation and disidentification" (Chang 2012, 24).

In my view, Chang's aim of interpreting Asian American literature and film for their ability to capture immigrants' acts sets the scene for a more in-depth investigation of which acts are considered political or related to citizenship. Engin Isin and Greg Nielsen's *Acts of Citizenship* (2008), which problematizes the concept of citizenship as formal membership, is helpful in formulating an approach to citizenship that emphasizes how local and grassroots instances of political struggles call for a continuous revision of theories on political subjectivity and agency. In chapter 1 of the book, "Theorizing Acts of Citizenship," Isin uses the examples of migrants' demonstrations and the civil disobedience of the Montgomery boycott to show that acts of claiming rights or belonging do not depend on formal national inclusion and give birth to forms of citizenship to come.

Emphasizing the importance of keeping a tight focus on particular cases and instances of rights claiming, Isin also theorizes what constitutes an act as an act of citizenship. The main feature of acts is that they place an unexpected demand on existing regimes of citizenship. By questioning the divide between citizens and their others, a condition at the basis of national recognition, acts create a rupture in the current political and legal discourses. The main features of Isin's idea of acts can be summarized as follows: Acts produce creative breaks in the given political field; they are materially and symbolically constitutive, because the very enactment of an act gives rise to new forms of political subjectivity; they involve the transformation of a subject into a claimant; and finally, as in a domino effect, the act of claiming can produce other actors who become answerable to ideas of justice (Isin and Nielsen 2008, 10). Crucially, as happened with the fight of civil rights activists against discriminatory laws in the United States, acts of disobedience denounce injustice and effectively demand a change in the law. But instead of merely advocating an expansion of rights to more people, leaving the core of citizenship rights fundamentally unquestioned, acts radically interrogate law and citizenship as universal and natural realities.

It is significant to note that Isin's theory is underpinned by a narrative idea of the world, where the actors' verbal claim to justice is fundamental for the act to be registered as inherent to citizenship. Taking a cue from Isin's work, I use the expression "acts of writing" to investigate the cases in which literature participates materially and symbolically in ongoing political struggles. I analyze the writings of Roy, Devi, and Pal with regard to their political effects, their participation in tribal struggles, and their modes of dialogical or collaborative production. I look at how certain types of writing have mobilized people, spreading awareness of peripheral and often overlooked realities of deprivation. Acts of writing reveal that literature is an instrument of creation, not of mere representation. Literary works can fulfill both the creative and the transformative characteristics that Isin considers fundamental for theorizing acts. In this case, they help us to understand the performative nature of law and citizenship.

Literature poses a potential threat to the law by exposing its common textual composition. Because laws are texts to be interpreted and performed, their existence is not natural or universal. My work, like Isin's concept, is indebted to Jacques Derrida's idea of law and citizenship as founded on interpretable, or deconstructible, textual strata (Derrida 1990, 943): "Laws, constitutions, the declaration of the rights of man, grammar or the penal code are not 'natural realities' and they depend upon the same structural power that allows novelesque fictions or mendacious inventions and the like to take place. This is why literature and the study of literature have so much to teach us about right and law" (Derrida 1988, 134). Derrida refers to the performative quality of literature: "Literature can *play the law*, repeating it while diverting it or circumventing it" (216). The pun creates a double meaning: Literature can subversively impersonate the law, and by doing so, it mocks the law and its univocal authority.[10]

Derrida exposes the textual nature of literature and law and suggests that literature can interrogate the sacred role of law in the modern nation. Among the critical works that have recently looked at the possible intersections of literary and legal studies is Brook Thomas's *Civic Myths: A Law-and-Literature Approach to Citizenship* (2007). Thomas considers that literature can provide an insight into the cultural framework that underpins the making of the law; literature "can help us identify stories about national membership and national values that are only implied by citizenship laws" (13). Thomas maintains that literary works "dramatize various conflicts citizens subject to rule by law confront. If, unlike much political discourse, they do not resolve those conflicts by providing models of substantive, or even procedural justice, they do alert readers to the inevitable emotional as well as intellectual contradictions that citizenship entails" (216). Thomas's work neatly separates the normative dimension of law and the freedom that literature allows: Literature does not have the power to grant citizenship, and yet it provides a powerful critique of the law by revealing the emotional contradictions inscribed in its making.

The common denominator of these works is that literature appears to be capable of reaching what the law cannot grasp. *Narratives of Citizenship: Indigenous and Diasporic Peoples Unsettle the Nation-State*, edited by Aloys N. M. Fleischmann, Nancy Van Styvendale, and Cody McCarroll (2011), also infers that literature can fill the gap between citizenship as law and its performance in everyday practices. The book highlights the fact that official state documents, including surveys and the census, are important for our understanding of the relation between Canada and its indigenous population, but they are by no means exhaustive. Instead of being seen as the repositories of truthful facts, official narratives can be analyzed for their failure to capture the aboriginal experience in its private and public connotations. Instances of resistance to assimilative demands or paternalistic politics of minority protection take place "in both public and private spaces and across juridical, political and affective registers" (Fleischmann et al. 2011, xii). The difficulty of grasping the interconnection between the juridical and the experiential dimensions of citizenship is the reason that discussions on the subject often turn to the arts and narratives for insights into indigenous and diasporic resistance to universal citizenship: "The juridical and political dimensions of citizenship are inseparable from its affective aspects, just as the public spaces of its narrativization are bound up with its private articulations" (xii).

Whereas Thomas highlights the emotional contradictions that literature explores, Fleischmann and co-editors explicitly affirm that the private and the affective dimensions of citizenship have long been overshadowed by the hegemony of a legalistic and normative approach to the subject.

At the beginning of this Introduction, I reclaimed for this book a lineage of feminist, postcolonial, and antiracist critical works. This is particularly evident when one looks at the works concerned with the literary expressions of everyday experience and with the affective dimension of citizenship. In this sense, a relevant source of inspiration for me is anthropologist Renya Ramirez's book on Native American communities in the Silicon Valley, *Native Hubs* (2007), which suggests that the importance of the affective register for understanding citizenship has been highlighted in studies carried out by women of color. These works are strikingly different from mainstream studies of law and politics rooted in Eurocentric traditions, which promote objective observations in support of universal logics.

> The importance of affect in citizenship debates has not been seriously considered, because citizenship has been a white, male enterprise that emphasizes reason and rationality. White women and people of color are disenfranchised in the public sphere, because of the white, masculine notion that assumes subordinated groups cannot act with reason but only according to feelings. We cannot fully belong in the public domain, because the emotional state of disenfranchised groups will disrupt the rationality and reason that should control the public sphere. By contrast, I argue that affect assists in Native people's empowerment and struggle to belong. (Ramirez 2007, 19)

Like Ramirez, I am struck by the importance of affective glue in the construction and remodeling of social networks. For dispossessed indigenous people, who have lost their land or who nomadically follow the flows of seasonal labor, affective ties become essential in the definition of their space of belonging. Moreover, because in the life of marginalized groups governments figure only as abstract entities, it is the work of movements that creates the ground for them to speak about rights, contest unjust policies, and question the lack of implementation of laws passed in their favor.

A bias against indigenous and colonial subjects, considered to be backwardly organized around kinship and lacking the tools for developing modern forms of societal organization, inhabits the works of Western political theorists, from John Locke to Max Weber (Isin 2005, 39, 45–46). Isin considers this prejudice a form of political orientalization or a mode of "thought that grants the existence of citizenship only on condition of being found in a particular form in the occident" (Isin 2005, 42). Questioning the interpretative framework that deprives tribal groups of political subjectivity, I see literature as a tool for understanding people's actions in relation to forms of attachment to spaces, networks, and histories. Because literature is free from the rationalist imperative of political philosophy, it can give an account of citizenship struggles in rural India that is not merely informed by preconceived colonial ideas of who is a political subject.

In this light, my project of looking at acts of angry writing appears to be motivated by the political and intellectual task of challenging multiple forms of orientalist discrimination. The acts of angry writing carried out by Roy and Devi and through Pal's autobiography openly contrast with the labeling of tribal groups as backward and oppose the prejudice that links anger with a typically female and oriental lack of rationality. These works call for the deconstructive task of reconsidering modern citizenship in relation to the Western philosophical trajectory in which it originated and as a consequence of its dissemination through colonialist enterprises. Also, literature supplements this historical investigation with a creative project: By resignifying the language of rights, literary works compel us to imagine other ways in which people claim and envision citizenship. My attempt to "textualize citizenship" through literature, to borrow Banerjee's phrase, demonstrates that a novel approach to citizenship is possible if we overcome rigid disciplinary boundaries that confine law and literature to neatly separated domains. For this reason I present an interdisciplinary reading of Indian citizenship that weaves together works of cultural studies, gender studies, anthropology, literature, and critical legal studies. The aim is to shed light on how anger inspires performances of citizenship that reveal and resignify the colonial legacy that underpins contemporary citizenship. Then I also ask, What does citizenship look like once we bracket the traces of orientalism inscribed in its legal making and in the neoliberal imperative to development at the expense of the poor? Devi provided an implicit tentative answer to this question in her speech given at the Jaipur Literary Festival in 2013: "All my life I have seen small people with small dreams. It looked like they wanted to put them all in a box and keep them locked up . . . but somewhere, some of them escaped, as if there has been a jailbreak of dreams. Like the Naxalites. Their crime is that they dared to dream. And why shouldn't they?"[11] In the mainstream political discourse the Naxalites are anticitizens; they are a criminal guerrilla army against which the government has waged a war. For Devi, though, they are small people, whose small dreams of escaping poverty have fueled armed actions. Can their right to dream be considered a fundamental citizenship right? Devi clearly thinks so. By showing that the poetics of dreaming can carry a disruptive political force, literature opens up the cultural, imaginative, and affective fields of citizenship and disrupts the boundaries of legally instituted and policed national identities. In this spirit, in *Acts of Angry Writing* I explore how literary forms of social activism initiate, as Felman puts it, "a dynamic movement of modification of reality" (Felman 2003, 51).

1

Mahasweta Devi

1

POOR, NOT CRIMINALS

Devi Against Legal Orientalism

In November 1998, Budhan, a young man belonging to the Kheria Sabar tribe of Purulia (West Bengal), was found hanged in the local prison. His death, initially declared a suicide by the authorities, was further investigated by activists and village people, who uncovered a story of brutality, discrimination, and institutional violence. Then it became apparent that Budhan had been tortured and killed by the police, after being arrested as a suspected robber, a charge of which he was later declared innocent.

Only one year later, Bhadra, another young man from the same district, was the protagonist of an equally tragic story. Accused of having stolen three goats, some agricultural tools, and a fishnet, Bhadra was taken from his house by several village men and cruelly lynched. His wife promptly ran to the police station to ask for help, but the indolent officers did not prevent the drama from unfolding. By the time they arrived, Bhadra was already dead (see Kumar Roy 2011).

On November 16, 1999, Bengali writer Mahasweta Devi wrote to the Calcutta High Court demanding further investigation into Bhadra's death and asked the chief justice to file her letter as a petition in the name of the Sabar villagers. In the letter Devi mentioned Budhan's case, which she presented as a public interest litigation in 1998, as an example of the violence resulting from the prejudice that still affects indigenous people. "The conduct of the police authorities," Devi wrote, "is not only questionable but invites the attention of all prudent citizens whether rich or poor, upper caste or denotified tribe" (M. Devi 2011, 53). Devi called for the vigilance of all citizens, regardless of class and caste, because Bhadra's and Budhan's cases dramatically revealed how the "state and its machinery have failed to protect its citizens" (53).

In relation to Budhan's case, the High Court proclaimed that no person could be injured, tortured, or killed because of his or her identity. It also declared that tribal individuals were too often and deliberately the objects of violent discrimination.[1] These stories of everyday violence reveal the existence of a gap between Indian institutions and poor citizens, whose demands for justice and fairness seem destined to remain unattainable (M. Devi 2011, 53). Although the constitution of the modern state incorporates the promise of equal protection for all, equality for denotified tribes appears more like a distant ideological horizon than an actual right. Such fundamental inequity is the trigger for Devi's writing and activism.

In independent India, Devi was the first middle-class woman writer to devote her life and lend her pen to support Adivasis, participating in their struggles since the 1970s to sustain the political nature of their demands for civil rights. Gayatri Spivak's translations of Devi's work from Bengali into English greatly contributed to the fame of Devi's works in the Anglophone world. Spivak's seminal analyses of the writer's short stories and novels highlight that Devi's writing is specifically rooted in the tribal villages of West Bengal and its neighboring states, where the author traveled extensively to report on the living conditions of indigenous people. Devi's realistic portrayals of tribal life are inspired by an activist commitment to the project of social justice. In "A Literary Representation of the Subaltern," Spivak maintains that Devi's fictional technique produces a complex focus on the subaltern as an object of the historical gaze and a subject of literature and simultaneously questions the "truth effect" created by both fields. Devi's accuracy in reconstructing stories of subaltern oppression creates a form of realism that sustains the transformation of her characters into icons of class and gendered exploitation (Spivak 1987, 369). Such is the case of "Stanadayini," in which the professional wet nurse Joshoda, who develops breast cancer after years of feeding numerous children, is at the same time "a signifier for subalternity as such, as well as a metaphor for the predicament of the de-colonized nation-state India" (355). Marginalization and discrimination of the poor spread like a cancer in the body politic of independent India.

The fact that Devi's detailed representations of poor and marginalized Indian citizens are based on direct experience inspired scholars such as Kumum Yadav (2003) and Anjum Katyal (2002) to look deeper into the social realities of the tribes described in her stories. They highlight how Devi's fiction and nonfiction works engage with the colonial and recent histories of the Lodhas of Palamu and the Sabars of West Bengal. As Katyal explains, "Mahasweta Devi's experience of the rural condition is the base of what she writes about; her choice of what to depict and how to depict it is ideologically motivated. Her writing is activist; and her stance is unequivocal. She has taken sides and declared it, and her fiction takes sides as well" (Katyal 2002, 213). Devi's literary works originated from the same political commitment and militant activism that pushed her to become a journalist and the editor of her father's journal, *Bortika*, which she transformed into an open platform where peasants and tribals could write and share their stories.

Devi's most recent activist experience is closely tied to the association Paschim Banga Kheria Sabar Kalyan Samiti, of which she has been president since 1983.[2] Before then, Devi had worked among the Lodha communities in Palamu. Her commitment to the Sabars stimulated her reflections on the contemporary relevance of researching the history of "criminality by birth." As Devi reports, "Till 1983, few Kherias entered Purulia town as free citizens. Whenever they did, they were handcuffed and dragged by a rope around their waist" (Devi 1997, 183). Similarly, in an article that appeared in *India Together* in March 2002, Devi denounced the continuous repetition of episodes of violence against Adivasis in modern India: "Between 1979 and 1982, 42 denotified Lodha tribals were mob-lynched not for crimes committed, but for being born as 'Lodhas.' Between 1960 and 1998, more than 50 Kheria Sabars have been killed by the police, or mob-lynched. In the Lodha cases, police took no action" (M. Devi 2002). The number and the nature of the incidents listed by the author, in which Adivasis were victims of unjustified violence, are striking. Looking at Budhan's and Bhadra's deaths from this perspective, they do not appear as isolated events but as the symptoms of the ongoing discrimination and marginalization of denotified tribes in contemporary India.[3] Budhan's story is merely one of a series of unmotivated deaths revealing that for the Kheria Sabars "the curse of being a criminal still haunts their existence" (M. Devi 2002).

Gopi Ballava Singha Deo, founder of the Paschim Banga Kheria Sabar Kalyan Samiti in Purulia, West Bengal, the association of which Mahasweta Devi is honorary president. Heir to a royal family, Deo has sustained the Sabars and their rights for more than sixty years.

The school and headquarters of the Paschim Banga Kheria Sabar Kalyan Samiti in Purulia, West Bengal. In the foreground is Prasanta Rakshit, the main activist of the association.

In the center for Kheria Sabars of the Paschim Banga Kheria Sabar Kalyan Samiti, students are encouraged to read Mahasweta Devi's works.

Guided by Devi's work with indigenous groups and informed by legal studies and colonial historiography, in this chapter I examine the distinctive history behind the discrimination against the Sabars. Kheria Sabars were among the tribes outlawed by the Criminal Tribes Act (also known as CTA), passed by the British in 1871. This colonial law, which declared that some nomadic tribal groups were criminals, was repealed after independence (1949), and the affected communities were categorized as "denotified." To better understand the social mission of Devi's writing, I investigate the historical circumstances under which the CTA was passed and explore its relation to previous colonial provisions aimed at controlling the Indian territory. I highlight that Victorian moral values have significantly influenced the treatment of nomadism in the colony. After briefly discussing the legacy of the CTA, which produced a social stigma against tribal groups, I read the short story "Shishu" and ask how Devi's language counteracts the common assumption that Adivasis are backward and dangerous citizens.

Devi's journalistic pieces, legal letters, and creative works present a cross-fertilization of genres, styles, and content that responds to situations of political urgency. In the introduction to the English translation of the short story "Draupadi," Spivak lists "bureaucratic Bengali" among the other varieties of language, such as literary and street Bengali, that are part of Devi's linguistic collage (Spivak 1981, 384). As Budhan and Bhadra's cases suggest, law and its language are among the terrains where Devi acts politically and creatively. Her everyday activist practices involve engaging with the legal system through filing petitions and public interest litigations; but investigating law and its history, aims, and reach is also useful for unveiling the causes of the marginalization of the Sabars. By conjoining legal and aesthetic strategies, Devi's work prompts further investigation into the state of social destitution of denotified tribes.

As McCall has noted, Devi's work is particularly significant when considered as an analytical device: In relation to women and development, it poses crucial questions on the interpretative framework that failed to highlight the interconnections between bonded labor and the sex trade (McCall 2002). In an analytical spirit similar to McCall's, I look at how the legacy of colonial laws enforces the oppression of Adivasis. Devi's insistence on the detrimental effects of the CTA instigates a new reflection on how orientalism at work in the field of law sustains the equation between tribals and outlaws. In outlining the continuity between colonial and postcolonial legal frameworks, I incorporate Piyel Haldar's reading of Edward Said's *Orientalism* and propose looking at law as a device that governs subject formation.

CRIMINALIZATION, LAW, AND ORIENTALISM

As noted, Kheria Sabars are among the Adivasi groups declared criminals under the CTA. First enacted in the northern regions and extended to other presidencies in 1911, the CTA outlawed only smaller tribes, which had no "fixed place of residence" and no "lawful occupation" and whose declared means of living was "a pretence for the purpose of facilitating the commission of crimes" (Act XXVII of 1871, pt. I, sec. 4). Meena Radhakrishna's study on the criminal tribes highlights that nomadic tribes were considered more likely to elude the control of the colonial authority, because of their lack of a fixed habitation and their peripatetic wanderings through the forests. For this reason, they were brought under the strict yoke of law (Radhakrishna 2001, 5–9).

Devi recalls the issue of the CTA as a unique moment in Indian history that exposed the brutal effects of colonialism.

> It's very interesting, what you Europeans will not understand, because it has not happened—to my knowledge—in Europe: When the British were in power in India, they passed a terrible act, a Criminal Tribes Act. In India there are tribes—many tribes—and many of them are forest-living tribes. The forest-living tribes do not destroy the forest, but learn how to live in harmony with the forest and its trees. . . . Some of the tribes in West Bengal were condemned under this act. Two of them I knew very well: one is the Lodhas of Darjeelipur and Kheria Sabar of Purulia.[4]

The foreign rule swept away a preexisting culture in order to define the borders of modern Indian identity. Entire groups were thus stigmatized as dangerous, troublesome, and prone to illegal activities.

One of the common charges against the tribal groups was that, because they had not taken up cultivation and lived in the forests, their subsistence was related to dishonest activities, such as stealing. Budhan and Bhadra's stories highlight that the memory of this charge is still vivid in contemporary culture. Reacting against this prejudice, Devi highlights that the widespread distrust of indigenous people is, in part, a consequence of the colonial misinterpretation of their social and economic transactions. The lack of a cash economy in the villages and the recourse to the exchange of goods in the markets, where the exchange was often silently carried out by taking products away from the stands and leaving roots or leaves in their place, led to the translation by the British of this barter into theft. In *Imaginary Maps* Devi points out that "the British had isolated the small tribes. They were afraid to touch the majority tribes for fear of widespread havoc. They branded the small tribes as criminal tribes because they lived in the forest and they did not take to cultivation. These tribes had no concept of money. They would come out of the forest, go to the village market, place honey, leaves, roots, flowers and silently take away whatever they needed: rice, oil, spices. So they were thieves!" (M. Devi 1995, v–vi). The charge of theft reveals the colonial onslaught on indigenous economies and social organization. The assimilation of their radical otherness into the dominant culture enabled imperial subjugation by dispersing the traces of the subalterns' precarious subjectivity.

For Devi, the CTA exemplifies how law sustains the discursive power of the colonizer, enforcing rules and regulations over its subjects. The legal system forms part of what Spivak calls the "epistemic violence" of imperialism

In Budhan's village, his wife and other villagers dedicate themselves to arts and crafts. The manufacture of objects to be sold in the market is an important source of cash for Sabars.

(Spivak 1988, 281). The colonization of hearts and minds takes place via the legal field in two ways. On the one hand, it enables the formation of a series of governing institutions; on the other, it establishes norms and codes of social behavior while disseminating a discourse in support of the "colonizing mission." Law aims at taming native subjectivity. The inassimilable difference of the colonial other, which Edmund Burke famously labeled the Eastern "sublime," has to be aligned with the colonizer's expectations of imperial subjects. Haldar states, "Law inhabits the subject (or, colonizes the subject) as a site of civilized and civic pleasure as distinct from the supposed Oriental forms of surplus enjoyment. Colonialism offers us a history—a history of a legally instituted subjectivity" (Haldar 2007, 2).

Haldar describes the colonial legal enterprise as an orientalist project founded on the assumption that law contributes to reducing the insurmountable ontological gap between Western civilization and colonial subjects. Law, as Devi shows, institutes and reproduces the orientalist bias that sees civilization as a prerogative of the West and a capital to be exported.

T. B. Macaulay's widely quoted 1835 Minute, which embraced the possibility of transforming subjects who were Indian in blood and color into "English in tastes, in opinions, in morals and in intellect," introduced the cultural reforms that supported the legal restructuring of India (Macaulay 1862, 115).[5] Referring to the British enterprise of codification of Hindu law, Spivak remarks, "The education of colonial subjects complements their production in law" (Spivak 1988, 77).

Haldar's labeling of the legal enterprise as an orientalist project takes its cue from his revision of Edward Said's *Orientalism* (1978) and its view of the East as a discursive production sustaining the project of Western domination. Said's work has become central in questioning the relation between the representation of Indian subjectivities and their cultural production.[6] Images of colonial "others" as inferior, dangerous, and backward, globally circulating in various artistic forms, laid the groundwork for the enforcement of "the Utilitarian Victorian enterprise of 'improving' the natives through English education" through colonial policies (Niranjana 1992, 16–17).

Haldar's work revisits Said to bridge the gap between literature and legal theory. Haldar persuasively invites us to take law into account in the debates on orientalism and its reproduction, because law underpinned the circulation of colonial discourses and enabled their application. The enforcement of legal principles over colonized subjects shaped colonial subjectivity, and, in turn, the imposition of new rules, instances, and practices legitimized the patrolling function of Western legality. Paraphrasing Spivak, one could say that orientalism in law has the role of exporting the "subject of the west"—an occidentally instituted sense of inferiority—but also of keeping the "West as the Subject" of Universalist definitions of humanity and politicality (Spivak 1988, 66).

In brief, orientalism has the effect of inferiorizing native populations by erasing their political subjectivity. Haldar's point is particularly poignant in relation to the question of Adivasis, because the legal constraints of the British Empire underwrote the establishment of their subaltern position. The question of Adivasis in this critical framework, though, still remains to be explored. Sanjay Nigam, author of pivotal anthropological studies on the Criminal Tribes Act, refers to orientalism only briefly as "a political vision of reality" that sustains the production of types and racialized categories (Nigam 1990, 132), but he does not look at its long-term legal and cultural effects. On the other hand, Haldar's work, though groundbreaking for its angle of investigation, barely mentions that the incorporation of customary rights into the British code eventually led to the disavowal of Adivasis' culture and does not deal with the CTA or its consequences.

Devi, however, stubbornly insists on the importance of looking at this law as constituting Adivasis as exceptional subjects, different from mainstream Indian society. Her emphasis on the creation of the legal category of criminal tribes directs our attention toward a mechanism that, in keeping with Haldar's analysis, can be labeled "legal orientalism."[7] Far from merely representing tribal life, Devi's investigations, conceptualized in *Imaginary Maps* and in such articles as "The Slaves of Palamau" and "Lodhas of West Bengal" (M. Devi 1997, 16–22, 157–81), point to the historical and discursive construction of tribal backwardness and criminality.

In a similar analysis of the criminalization of indigenous groups, historian Crispin Bates sees modern understandings of Adivasi identity as deriving from their marginalization and land dispossession under British rule. Bates maintains that compartmentalizing Adivasis into a "criminal race" was underpinned by the orientalist view that they did not comply with Western systems of social life, because they did not hold a concept of private property and individual rights. Bates points to the role of anthropological knowledge in creating new social categories: "Theories about supposedly 'criminal' tribes and so-called 'martial' races (such as the Sikhs) facilitated the understanding and the administration of vast territories, which might otherwise have appeared utterly strange, chaotic and threatening" (Bates 1995a, 114). Bates also recognizes the need to identify possible allies and enemies of the British Empire as the rationale behind the criminalization of a number of tribes.

Devi's reflection expresses the same belief that colonial rulers feared that nomadic tribes could cause disorders and spread "havoc" throughout the colonized territories (M. Devi 1995, v–vi). A form of economic organization that did not rely on cultivation or permanent settlements was incompatible with a Western idea of society.

SEDENTARY VALUES AND VICTORIAN ANTHROPOLOGY

In her study on the "despotism of law," Radhika Singha (1993) emphasizes that social Darwinism, Victorian principles, and Utilitarian and liberal thought underpinned the framework of rational rule instituted by the British. Private property and individualism were enforced through a series of colonial legislations, of which the CTA was only one example. The Forest Acts (1878) promoted the consolidation and protection of forest covers and introduced new definitions of forest offenses. Disregarding the status of dependency of forest dwellers from their habitat, these laws effectively created an opposition between the environment and its inhabitants. The Land Acquisition Act allowed the confiscation of lands by the Crown; the acquisition of territories classified as wastelands benevolently covered the grab of fields that were vital sources of grazing and firewood for communal land administration (see chapter 5). Although these acts progressively pushed nomadic tribes out of the forests, the CTA actively criminalized entire groups perceived as a possible danger to colonial surveillance and its sedentary social order (see P. Roy 1998, 58).

However, the CTA presented a particular case among the laws just mentioned, because it overruled the principle of individual responsibility, which was a cardinal feature of British law, for determining the culpability of particular offenses. The rule of law of the British legal system allowed the introduction of exceptional legal measures of control. As Singha affirms, police instructions drew on widespread associations between a wandering lifestyle, low social status, and criminality to assess people's guilt. Their aggressive conduct against the tribals "indicated a greater ambition towards extirpating a certain way of life than is evident from the policies of indigenous regimes" (Singha 1998, 44).

Taking Singha's point further, one could say that despite the foundational character of the principle of individualism in British law, the CTA opened up a space of exception. Because orientalist perceptions and early anthropological classifications justified the view that Indians could be only community- or caste-based collectivities (Radhakrishna 2001, 157), wandering tribes were regulated as a collective rather than as individuals (Freitag 1991, 230).

In criminalizing entire communities, the CTA was modeled on an important precedent: the legislation on the bands of robbers and professional murderers known as Thugs or Thuggees.[8] Act XXX (1836) against Thugs had, in fact, maintained that criminal intention could be assessed not only as a result of a specific criminal act but also in relation to the characteristics of a collectivity.[9] Despite the enormous differences between Thug gangs and notified tribes, Act XXX and the CTA similarly saw criminal disposition as the heritage or the characteristic of specific, wandering communities.

In the light of Bates, Singha, and Radhakrishna's writings, it is not surprising that the CTA put particular emphasis on the regulation of movement.

The act not only established the creation of a register of criminal tribes but also specifically declared that "any tribe, gang or class, which has no fixed place of residence, may be settled in a place of residence prescribed by the local government" or "may be removed to any other place of residence" (Act XXVII of 1871, pt. I, secs. 13 and 14). When tribes were declared unlawful by means of public notification in the local gazette, members of notified groups had to register in police stations. They were fingerprinted and forced to present themselves weekly to official controls. They could not change residency without formal permission from the authorities and, if absent from their villages without a license or if they refused fingerprinting, were liable to be arrested and detained for up to three years (Radhakrishna 2001, 29). The CTA allowed arrest "without a warrant by any police officer or village-watchman" if people were caught beyond the territories to which their tribe was bound (Act XXVII of 1871, pt. I, sec. 20). Frequent arrests of male members of notified tribes and the use of custody as a precautionary measure took a significant toll on the social and economic organization of entire villages.

The colonial impulse to control people's movement ultimately led to the establishment of "reformatory settlements" (Act XXVII of 1871, pt. I, sec. 18) with the formal intent to assimilate the notified tribes into civilized society. In these detention camps, adults and youngsters were "supervised and controlled," as the law specified, while they embraced a sedentary lifestyle through Western education and trainings in factory jobs. Obliged to perform low-paid work, tribals were supplying British factories with cheap labor. In its updated version of 1911, the CTA specifically established the number of hours of daily work to be carried out in the settlements; adults were expected to work for more than eleven hours, and children under 14 years of age had to work for eight hours and devote two hours to school education. As a means of comparison, at the beginning of the twentieth century detainees in British jails were sentenced to work for eight hours a day and could enjoy Sundays off.

After 1908, the settlements were largely managed by the Salvation Army, and the ideas of its founder and first general, the Methodist preacher William Booth, played a primary role in guiding the administration of native populations. Radhakrishna notes that Booth's writings largely influenced common perceptions of immorality and criminality both in England and in the colonies. For Booth, "what constituted crime and immorality . . . was the inverse of what Victorian values conceded" (Radhakrishna 2001, 16). Booth's book *In Darkest England and the Way Out* (1890) contains a catalogue of types and grades of criminal offenses, for each of which Booth suggested specific treatments, strategies of prevention, or punishments. British policies in India assimilated not only Booth's classification of criminal acts but also the idea that immoral behavior could be cured with discipline. The reformatory settlements constituted an experiment aimed at rectifying delinquents according to the doctrine of "criminocurology" (Radhakrishna 2001, 16).

Nomadism and vagrancy are among the violations of Victorian social principles to which Booth makes explicit references. In the nineteenth century aimless movement was simultaneously constituted as a crime in the colonies and at home, where vagrancy laws targeted the gypsy, the vagrant, and the migrant (Radhakrishna 2001, xv). Although reformatory settlements were established in India for nomadic tribes, workhouses were created to force a sedentary lifestyle onto the English working classes (see Poor Law Amendment Act of 1834). Workhouses were a tool to facilitate the control of poor urban masses and the containment of their discontent. The English poor and the Indian native equally defied the Victorian ideal of reliable citizens, and representations of them were marked by similar references to an intrinsically inferior, deviant, or animal nature.

In *London Labour and the London Poor: Cyclopedia of the Condition and Earnings of Those That Will Work, Those That Cannot Work, and Those That Will Not Work* (1851), Henry Mayhew, who had worked for the East India Company in his younger years, proposed a neat division of contemporary English society into settlers and wanderers. Wanderers were clearly associated with low intellectual capacity and subhumanity.

> Whether it is that in the mere act of wandering there is a greater determination of blood to the surface of the body, and consequently a less quantity sent to the brain, the muscles being thus nourished at the expense of the mind, I leave physiologists to say. But certainly be the physical cause what it may, we must all allow that in each of the classes above mentioned (the pickpockets—the beggars—the prostitutes—the street-sellers—the street-performers—the cabmen—the coachmen—the watermen—the sailor), there is a greater development of the animal than of the intellectual or moral nature of man, and that they are all more or less distinguished for their high cheek-bones and protruding jaws—for their use of a slang language—for their lax ideas of property—. . . their repugnance for

> continuous labour—their disregard of female honour—their love for cruelty . . .—and their utter want of religion. (Mayhew 1851, 2–3)

Mixing biological and social arguments, Mayhew's hierarchy of civilization sees sedentary life as characteristic of the highest stage of human evolution. His view of the criminal underworld of London as "wandering classes" consecrates the equation between nomadism and lack of morality.

Moreover, Mayhew's representation of the core features of underclasses, including their simple and rudimentary language, religious predisposition, and disregard for labor and women, paves the way for a comparison with Eastern subjects. Mayhew and Binny's *Criminal Prisons of London and Scenes of Prison Life* (1862) makes this similarity explicit. In this text they affirm, "If Arabia has its nomadic tribes, the British Metropolis has its vagrant hordes as well. If the Carib islands have their savages, the English capital has types almost as brutal an as uncivilized as they. If India got its Thugs, London has its garrotte men" (Mayhew and Binny 1862, 5). In the colonies, the Middle East, India, or the Caribbean, nomadic hordes are examples of moral deficiency and disregard for social principles. Their predisposition to lawlessness has its visible traits in physical features, such as high cheekbones and protruding jaws. Mayhew and Binny refer to theories of criminal anthropology, including Cesare Lombroso's *Criminal Man* (1876), to maintain that the body carries physical markers of an immoral inclination. In agreement with the foundational principles of physiognomy and phrenology, Mayhew and Binny believed that unusual aspects of facial appearance and irregularities in the shape of the skull could reveal people's inclination to criminal behavior.

In the late nineteenth century anthropometric studies became crucial for classifying morphological differences among races and for categorizing Indian tribes and castes. James Wise compiled a catalogue of anthropometric data on Bengali people, including measurements of brain size and descriptions of skin color and orbitonasal indexes. As Bates notes, "This [catalogue] was combined with E. T. Dalton's work on the tribes of Chota Nagpur to produce a four-volume dictionary of the Tribes and Castes of Bengal, which was finally published in 1891" (Bates 1995b, 245). The classification of Indian races was strictly related to the definition of certain groups as criminals. Physical features became evidence of people's primitive, bestial, and dangerous nature. Because the emphasis was on the hereditary disposition of indigenous people, the CTA equally outlawed nomadic communities that were socially different, such as the gypsy-like Chharas of Ahmedabad, and small traders moving across large territories, such as the Koravas of the Madras Presidency. Against these groups loosely defined as criminal, colonial laws created a fluid space of prosecutorial license.

Budhan and Bhadra's stories, presented at the beginning of this chapter, show that widespread cultural prejudice and the stigma of thievery still implicitly authorize violence against indigenous people. Discrimination against tribes is also enabled by the continuity between the colonial legal apparatus and the penal code of the independent nation. The Habitual Offender's Act, passed by the government of India in 1949, preserved most of the provisions of the repealed CTA (Sharma 1979, 22). Listing denotified tribals among the habitual criminals, it endorsed the orientalist bias that underscored colonial legality.

Mahasweta Devi's distinctive role in contemporary Indian literature is clear when her works are read against this background of historical tribal marginalization and subjection. Her fiction and nonfiction works maintain that the colonial violence on indigenous subjectivity could not be undone by simply revoking the CTA and still needs to be counteracted. As Nigam puts it, "There is nothing essential or self-contained about the notion of criminal castes and tribes. It occupies a certain space within colonial discourse both politically and semantically, and the distinctions made between the criminal castes and tribes and the moral subjects are forever marked by their political origin" (Nigam 1990, 164). The main political and ethical goal of researching, and writing about, denotified tribal communities is to deconstruct the relation between criminality, nomadism, and indigeneity. Devi accepted the ethical responsibility of fighting against this form of essentialism and demonstrated a lifelong commitment to indigenous struggles, both as an activist and as a literary writer. Her creative works deconstruct the colonial nomenclature and oppose the ways in which, as Upendra Baxi revealed, the postcolonial discourse of development revived the trope of tribal criminality (Baxi 1994, 55–57).

THIEVES OR HEROES? READING "SHISHU"

In this chapter I have demonstrated how the equation between nomadic tribes, which used to live in the forests, and criminality was naturalized in law. I also have considered how anthropological and social theories supported the views that nomadism was a mark of backwardness and that the physical features of Adivasis were the bodily signs of their primitive and even criminal nature.

As highlighted in relation to the relevance of anthropology and physiognomy for the classification of tribes, until the early twentieth century it was common opinion that criminal communities looked different from ordinary human beings. In 1928 the British traveler W. J. Hatch, author of *Pirates of Land in India* (1928), "took it upon himself to assure his English readers that the physique of the criminal castes, when fed properly, differed very little from that of the other Indian castes: 'They do not have that flattened head with ears low down and long, which suggests a criminal'" (Radhakrishna 2001, 36). Without disputing the main thesis of criminal anthropology, Hatch tried to explain why tribals look different. He indicated that the most important causal relation to be unveiled is the one between endemic poverty and institutionalized discrimination.

Devi's short story "Shishu" (1998), translated as "Little Ones," puts the spotlight on these elements and unveils the triangular relation between ethnic differences, poverty, and criminality. The story deals with a tribal community whose members, because of malnourishment, have developed unusually small limbs. They are the Agariyas of Lohri (near Ranchi, modern Jharkhand), who traditionally made their living in the iron trade.[10] Agariyas were never seen again after losing a battle with the government to privatize the iron mines. The soil in Lohri is so dry and stony that agriculture is impossible and, having lost access to the mines, these tribals were doomed to starvation. Some of them abandoned the old villages and found refuge in the nearby forests, living off crops and hunting. Extreme poverty pushed them to steal as a means of survival. Both the Agariyas' criminal acts and the anomaly of their small bodies result from the progressive impoverishment of the forests and their inhabitants in modern India, but they are feared as inhuman creatures. Because this short story reads like mystery tale, the reader only gets to know the Agariyas' story at the end of the narration. In the meantime, mysterious thefts of rice carried out in the forest give rise to fear.

Devi's bare language evokes the dry and deserted land where Adivasis live and their stark condition of deprivation. The narrative point of view at the beginning of the story belongs to the young and good-intentioned relief officer, Singh, who is in charge of setting up a relief camp in Lohri. During his travels, he is promptly advised that his destination is "a damned terrible place. The inhabitants have no honest way of living" (M. Devi 1998, 1).

Adivasis are not honest because they do not comply with the moral demands of civilization or with mainstream middle-class values. Perceived as subjects in need of spiritual guidance, indigenous people have been for centuries the target of missionaries and religious staff, including the Salvation Army, which has taken up the job of rectifying their misconduct. The benevolence of charitable people, though, is not free from prejudice. The relief officer is also warned that those who come for relief are repelling "near-naked, shriveled, worm-ridden, swollen-bellied Adivasi men and women" (2).

The vocabulary of primitiveness, bestiality, and lack of civilization prevails in the first half of the story. Singh crosses Lohri in a jeep, and his driver comments that tribals are close to animals: "Animals all of them! . . . They're inhuman" (M. Devi 1998, 10). The jeep driver then states, "Listen to them sing! Would any civilized person sing like this at such a time?" (11). This curtain of prejudice in Lohri is thickened by fear. The nearby forests are the shelter for small and mysterious creatures that come out to steal at night: "Things get stolen. And those who do the stealing are not human" (14). The thieves have been seen but never caught, and all the eyewitness accounts agree on their minute and ghostly physical appearance. Another officer who had been appointed to keep the relief under surveillance recalls, "The camp was to be at Lohri. Everyone was to come there and pick up the stuff. But the night was very dark, as dark as the hair on your head. It was very hot as well. I was sleeping outside. Suddenly, a strange sound! I got up, and saw tiny little people—kids, probably—running away with the sacks" (8). The offenders are mysterious and allegedly cruel creatures who look "not like human children" (9).

During Singh's first night of guard duty at his camp, as it had happened before, two sacks of rice are stolen from the supplies. Compelled to act against the mysterious gang of robbers, the relief officer starts chasing them deep into the jungle. Once he reaches the crowd, they position themselves "in a circle around the sacks, like crouching animals" (M. Devi 1998, 18). At that sight, a terrible fear fills Singh's heart: He has to confront a scene that is both strange and familiar. The indigenous people surrounding him have gray hair and sagging breasts: They are not children, but adults. When one of the old men starts speaking, he finally reveals that they are Agariyas of Kubha. Their tribe was decimated when they had to abandon their hereditary occupations of mining and iron trade because of forceful land expropriation. Only a few of them are alive: "Just 14 of us left, now the rest are dead. Our bodies have shriveled and shrunk from lack of food. The men can only piss, they can't get up anymore. Women can't bear children. So we steal relief. We must eat and grow again, mustn't we?" (20).

With her chilling dialogue and graphic language, Devi shows how "tribal people have been literally and figuratively crippled in post-independence India" (Loomba 2005, 14). But also, by showing that Adivasis' subhuman aspect is not the mark of their association with criminality but the consequence of induced poverty, Devi's narration performatively unsettles the legacy of the CTA. "Shishu" stages a tribal revolt against the nation: The relief officer is hunted down as a representative of democratic India, from which the Agariyas have been marginalized. Exposing their malformed bodies, Adivasis force the middle-class bureaucrat to stare at the ugly and dark side of development: "They circle him, laughing. Their penises rub against him, reminders that they are men, adult Indian males" (M. Devi 1998, 20). The Agariyas' lack of access to substantial citizenship rights, including education and welfare, challenges the common understanding of what it means to be an adult Indian citizen. As Kapur puts it, "The naked, shriveled adults of Devi's story [are] an indictment of the façade of the socialist rhetoric of the development state, or its refusal to live up to the adulthood of a self-reliant nation committed to social justice for its citizens" (J. Kapur 2013, 51). The Adivasis' state of endemic deprivation sets them among those people who, as Devi affirmed in her letter denouncing Bhadra and Budhan's cases, the "state and its machinery have failed to protect" (M. Devi 2011, 53).

As Parama Roy notes, Devi skillfully uses the "enormous allegorical fecundity of famine, and its capacity to stage questions about responsibility, humanness and the character of subaltern being" (P. Roy 2010, 27). Figures of the nonhuman, such as the ghost in the case of "Shishu," become emblematic representations of famine.[11] The extreme level of destitution portrayed, which was forced on indigenous people as a consequence of industrialization and deforestation, justifies their disrespect for national laws. Even the officer Singh "comes to the burning awareness of his own complicity in a system whose 'relief' is better stolen than received gratefully" (J. Kapur 2013, 52).

Agariyas are marginalized and criminalized citizens, but they do not simply claim a liberal extension of rights; instead, they respond to the fundamental injustice instituted by colonial law, and reenacted in the postcolony, claiming the legitimacy of the right to steal. In the preface to the collection *Bitter Soil*, in which "Shishu" is published, Devi says, "The starving Aagariyas are savagely angry at a system under which some people eat three meals a day while they are forced to starve! For I believe in anger, in justified violence, and so peel off the face of the India which is projected by the government, to expose its naked brutality, savagery and caste and class exploitation; and place this India, a hydra-headed monster, before a people's court, the people being the oppressed millions" (M. Devi 1998, 1). Agariyas angrily reveal that India is a hydra-headed monster; and casteism, classism, and the colonial legacies of the legal system are some of its deadly heads. To fight against this giant, Devi envisages a people's court where, in an action of protest, oppressed citizens can put on trial the nation and its colonial heritage. This image is not a mere carnivalesque inversion; it epitomizes the creative overturn of power that Devi's writing performs. In "Shishu" the point of view of the relief officer is progressively pushed to the margin and replaced by the accounts of the village people. Finally, agency is placed in the provocative actions of the abject subjects rubbing their naked skin against the officer's body. In stark contrast to the nakedness of Adivasis, citizenship emerges clothed in an orientalist and colonial heritage and in the othering of native bodies through charges of animality and criminality.

CONCLUSION: REWRITING ORIENTALISM

I began this chapter with the stories of Budhan and Bhadra to provide a sense of Devi's activist commitment in the legal and social field. These personal narratives also tragically show that endemic poverty and the bias of criminality, which are the main themes of "Shishu," still define the lives of denotified tribals.

"Shishu" communicates the anger of Agariyas against a system that has pushed them to the margins, forcing them to starvation, but it does not claim to represent the tribals or to speak on their behalf. The narrative point of view progressively moves from the relief officer to the surviving tribals, but instead of inhabiting Adivasi subjectivity, the story dwells on the friction between the tribal experience and the egalitarian narration of democratic India. Despite its brevity, the short story presents a lucid and accurate critique of a long history of social neglect. Targeting the entanglement of law with the history of colonialism, Devi exposes the legal orientalism that sustained the criminal nature of tribal groups and shows how orientalism rubs against the skin of the independent nation.

In chapters 2 and 3 I focus more closely on the continuity between the language of colonial acts and the contemporary idiom of citizenship. But because Devi's fiction and nonfiction writing is grounded in activist work, we cannot overlook the history of denotified tribes and the roots of the deeply embedded prejudices against indigenous people. Their condition of neglect, for Devi, is paradigmatic of the formal inclusion without substantial rights that characterizes Adivasis' citizenship.

In this light, literature can deorientalize modern history only if it is rooted in the social fabric and material reality of rural India. Indeed, Devi believes that talking and walking with the tribals are necessary practices for taking part in the process of rewriting citizenship. When asked about the inspiration for her writing, Devi recalled her first trips to the villages.

> As I first started writing, I also started going to the people, going to villages, walking miles. . . . This is the only way: to go and see with your own eyes. Now I am running 86 [her age] and cannot go anymore, but I used to go, to reach Purulia and reach my center. Every day I would walk to a different village. I went to them, stayed very close, and with the Lodhas I started my movement first. I walked and walked and talked about their rights, about citizenship, about women going to school, about getting education; about getting everything an ordinary Indian *citizen* gets. . . . That continues, because I wrote to the newspapers, they came to my house.[12]

The struggle that Devi serves through literature, journalism, and legal activism is the struggle for the poor to receive what ordinary citizens get, or should get. With the Kheria Sabars of Purulia, where the center of the association Paschim Banga Kheria Sabar Kalyan Samiti is located, Devi writes petitions, appeals, and letters of protest and tries to concretely bridge the gap between the language of institutions and the people. Creative writing serves as an extension of the legal tools to resist cases and instances of discrimination. By rerouting subjugated subject positions toward visibility in the public sphere, Devi's texts become acts of resistance against legal and cultural orientalism.

2

"HOW DOES A LAW HELP?"

Struggles for Citizenship in the Forests

Mahasweta Devi's literature and activism tackle and sometimes appropriate the language of law. In chapter 1, I discussed how Devi and other scholars' writing on law and orientalism showed that British colonial laws institutionally introduced an orientalist bias against tribal groups. In this chapter I concentrate on Devi's narrations of contemporary, or postcolonial, forms of orientalism. Jawaharlal Nehru's paternalism, for example, saw the tribals as "noble savages" to be assimilated into the linear narrative of progress. Paradoxically, though, his centralized form of government and Indira Gandhi's rule during the Emergency (1975–1977) had the effect of widening the distance between poor citizens and the modern state. A close reading of "Operation? Bashai Tudu," "Draupadi," and the novel *Chotti Munda and His Arrow* as well as extracts from my interview with Devi reveal the limits of the language of law and citizenship for obtaining equality in contemporary India.

Devi often refers to citizenship as an aspiration or an ideal status, but as Gayatri Spivak notes in "Woman in Difference," she does not use the "miraculating name 'citizen'" (Spivak 1990, 112) as an actual attribution for her characters. For the communities of destitute subjects and bond slaves that Devi portrays, poverty, exploitation, and caste discrimination stand in the way of the homogenizing language of the nation. Devi's stories dwell on the fictitious nature of the "race between Empire and Nation" (107) and show that for a section of the Indian population these two political terms are interchangeable. Devi's writing and activism place the ideals of justice and equality of postcolonial citizenship on trial: By writing letters to legal and political authorities, Devi supports Adivasi struggles in the public forums of civil society; also, her stories oppose the erasure of indigenous cultures in the race toward progress.

The identification of tribal groups with the state of nature, which sustained their criminalization during the Raj, survived colonialism in two ways. First, it was culturally integrated into Nehru's discourse of modernization, which reinforced the idea of tribal backwardness; second, the legal act "denotifying" Adivasis could not erase the cultural prejudice instituted by the Criminal Tribes Act (CTA). I deal briefly with the first of these points before looking at how Devi's fiction challenges the equation between national law and the achievement of justice.

At the Scheduled Tribes and Scheduled Areas Conference, held in Delhi in 1952, Nehru gave a speech addressing the role of "the tribal folk" in independent India. Speaking of tribal groups as "the people of the frontiers or those who live away from the interior of this country" (Nehru 1955, 8), Nehru assumed a sympathetic and even paternalistic tone to argue for the protection and safeguarding of tribal territories. He spoke of a common history and his sense of familiarity with "the tribal folk": "The tribal people of India are a virile people who naturally went astray sometimes. They quarreled and occasionally cut off each other's heads. . . . It is often better to cut off a head or a hand than to crush and crumble on a heart. Perhaps I also felt happy with these simple folks because the nomad in me found congenial soil in their company" (Nehru 1955, 3). Behind the declared affinity with indigenous people, the rhetoric used by Nehru reveals the perpetuation of colonial discourse through images that represent tribal groups as trapped in the "state of nature." Historical change did not affect the tribals, who appear fixed in the image of noble savages. Because of their simplicity, even the violence they perpetrate is primitive and irrational.

Nehru's words attempt to account for Adivasi subjectivity by creating a picture that is innocuous enough to promote the incorporation of indigenous people into a socialist and secular India. As David Ludden (1993, 271) remarks in his study of orientalism and Indian nationalism, Nehru was responsible for crafting a charter of the nation that overlooks specific differences in the name of a common cause and sustains the importance of the state as the guarantor of citizens' equality. Nehru's childhood memories of playing with tribal children, which indicate a relation between infancy, tribal freedom, and the state of nature, strikingly contrast with Devi's accounts of Adivasi life.

CAN LAW HELP?

Although the CTA was repealed in 1949 following independence and thus the tribals, once criminals, became members of "denotified tribes" (Sharma 1979, 22), colonial violence remained inscribed in the newly coined term *denotification*. The tribals were marked forever. The negation contained in the prefix *de-* could not conceal the process of notification, or criminalization, which constituted a strategy of colonial management. Ironically, the term had the effect of reiterating the colonial disregard of forms of indigenous knowledge and self-government, instead of rectifying it. In our interview, Devi said, "The Criminal Tribes Act was ultimately abolished. But there is continuity in the way in which people perceive the tribes as criminals. Though the government has declared that there is no criminal tribe, everywhere these people were known to be criminals and in the cities they could be killed. That kind of cruelty was going on."[1] The colonial formation of indigenous subjectivity, with everyday practices sustaining the view that Adivasis are essentially dangerous, could not be undone just by formally revoking the CTA. Once denotification was proclaimed, no plan of action was undertaken to spread awareness of the abolition of the British law, and the absence of state action clashed with the pervasiveness of colonial policies. Instead, the process of notification was enforced through regular fingerprinting, registrations at police stations, and the institution of strict regulations of movement. According to Devi, "They were denotified, of course, but in the area where they lived, there the people did not know . . . and the government did not inform them. Lodhas were among those tribes, and they were illiterate; . . . they did not know their rights."[2] The abandonment of Adivasis in postcolonial India here appears to be caused by the unintelligible curtain of the language of state authority.[3]

If independent policies and legislation were meant to reduce the gap between the citizens and the state machinery, the postcolonial state can be said to have failed in its democratic project. Devi repeatedly asks, "If you pass a law, for whom are you making the law?"[4] The legal reform of a preexisting colonial code, undertaken in the name of minorities and discriminated citizens, did not bring about any significant change for them.

As with her interviews and activist writing, Devi's fiction creatively critiques contemporary forms of Adivasis' marginalization and their estrangement from the language of law. The short story "Operation? Bashai Tudu," for example, brings to the fore the lack of communication between Adivasis and the loci of power. It revolves around the mythical figure of Bashai Tudu, a member of the Santal tribe who fights against the institutional predation of natural resources and supports the rights of agricultural laborers. Disillusioned by party politics, Bashai accuses the Communist Party of abandoning poor villagers to starve and of serving instead the interests of a handful of politicians. Always wanted by the police, Bashai is officially declared dead several times, only to reappear in new raids and armed actions. The cycle of Bashai's death and resurrection epitomizes the spiral of oppression of tribal groups that continues unabated; as Alaknanda Bagchi notes, "This repetitive sign of violence and defiance inscribed in thin air becomes Bashai's/Mahasweta's *writ* of the nation upsetting the linear, holistic narrative of cohesiveness and solidarity" (Bagchi 1996, 47; emphasis in original).

In Bashai's world the police are only another oppressor acting on behalf of an obscure machine called the government, and law is not a guarantee of justice. The paradox of the modern Indian nation is that despite the country being predominantly rural and its economy reliant on cultivation, "the agricultural labourer . . . got bypassed by every organization" (M. Devi 1990, 32). Politicians and parties neglect the centrality of peasants and land workers. For example, the lack of enforcement of the Minimum Wage Act (1948), allegedly passed for the benefit of rural citizens, reveals that tribals and wage-earning agricultural laborers are the forgotten citizens of India.

When Bashai campaigns for a minimum wage, he soon realizes that the existence of a law to safeguard the poor is not enough to bring about real change. Rather, a law can be an empty promise that will not be translated into concrete action. He states, "When I launched the struggle for the minimum wages, I discovered for the first time that the Labour Department had gone on raising the minimum wage every year. The government reports recorded suggestions for new laws and even reported the laws coming into force. But the minimum wage never came to us" (M. Devi 1990, 35). Even after the regulation of a fair minimum wage, the livelihood of millions of citizens did not improve. For this reason Bashai reflects on laws as strategies for governing the poor rather than as instruments of emancipation. When laws are passed without spreading awareness of their existence or without creating the conditions for their enforcement, they appear useless and even harmful. The indirect effect of creating a law that fuels hope and expectations for social change is that it defers and temporarily annuls any resistance. As Bashai puts it, "No administration would ever forgive the crime of resistance. In its reprisal the administration would prove how much more potent the bullet was than the tribal spear or arrow or sickle, how omnipotent the indirect repression of the administration could be, and how effectively it could operate without leaving a bloodstain behind. Pass laws that promise minimum wages for agricultural labourers, and then shelve the laws" (M. Devi 1990, 103). The act of shelving a law epitomizes the indifference of the state system and its administration to the needs of the poor. Despite there being democratic ways of fighting abuses, such as turning to the police and appealing to the courts, tribals and peasants are crushed by the coalition of elitist forces, including landowners and moneylenders, and cannot access the necessary legal routes to obtain justice.[5]

Bashai's political interrogation is a fundamental one: "How does a law help?" (M. Devi 1990, 122). And what is the meaning of democracy if its very system remains inaccessible to the majority of poor citizens? The preservation of feudalist power dynamics empties the nation of its promises of freedom and development for all. Independence is meaningless without the achievement of basic rights for agricultural workers, for whom the new laws and the constitution may prove to be meaningless. The narrator in Bashai Tudu pessimistically observes, "With the omniscience of the ancient sages, they knew that laws are made only because they have to be made, that they need never be enforced, and that those for whom the laws are made need never reap the benefits" (M. Devi 1990, 61). Bashai Tudu sees the legal system as a strategy of government enacted by the elites against the masses. Social change will not be achieved through the constitution, because merely declared rights will not uproot the inequalities of rural India. Even after independence, Bashai's view on the promise of social change represented by the constitution leaves little space to hope: "The Indian constitution respected every citizen's fundamental right to become whatever he could by dint of his guts. The poor therefore had the right to become poorer still" (M. Devi 1990, 87).

Spivak notes that Devi often uses mocking expressions to reference "regulatory metonyms" of the nation, such as the Indian national anthem (Spivak 1987, 352); similarly, the constitution is often the target of her irony. This is clear not only in "Operation? Bashai Tudu" but also in the short story "Draupadi," which is dedicated to the Naxalbari peasant insurgencies of the 1960s. The narrator of "Draupadi" says, "By the Indian constitution, all human beings, regardless of caste or creed, are sacred. Still accidents like this do happen" (M. Devi 1990, 150). This bitter remark introduces the ironic use of the word *accident*, which refers to a police encounter that leads to the killing of the tribal Dulna Majhi. After the murder, Dulna's wife, Draupadi Mehjen, later called by the more colloquial name Dopti, is arrested by the Special Forces for her role in the tribal armed rebellion. After being interrogated, she is then stripped and gang-raped. Assimilating the male power of the police to the patriarchal violence of the nation, Spivak defines the rape as "the culmination of her political punishment by the representatives of the law" (Spivak 1981, 388). When summoned before the military specialist Senanayak, Draupadi confronts him with her exposed, bloodied body. Her naked resistance is enacted against the government's obscure logics that, according to the narrator, are "as incomprehensible as the Male Principle in Sankhya philosophy or Antonioni's early films to *hoi polloi*" (M. Devi 1990, 150). The story reveals how feudal protection and control are gendered and sexualized (McCall 2002, 39), but it also powerfully shows indigenous people in opposition to the government and its military apparatus (Wenzel 1998, 151). As we are warned by Devi, "In the forest belt of Jhadkani, the Operation continues—will continue. It is a carbuncle on the government's backside" (M. Devi 1990, 153).

So, what did independence achieve for the majority of indigenous people? Was the integration of tribal heroes into the anticolonial struggle enough to challenge their alienation from mainstream society? The narrator summarizes the dark picture as follows: "As the *great, great achievement* of Independence, there came to be a couple of names, or maybe four, of tribals, from the Santals or some of the other tribes, in the massive apparatus of administration. . . . They could put on show whatever necessary like the crocodile cubs in the folktale. But all those who were not good enough for such display lived in the worst conditions" (M. Devi 1990, 49; emphasis in original). The tribal groups continue to face the "worst conditions," because "water for the thirsty and food for the hungry remained fairytale dreams" (84).

CHOTTI MUNDA AND OTHER "BACKWARD CITIZENS"

Spivak points out that Devi's works reveal how the word *India* "is sometimes a lid on an immense and equally unacknowledged subaltern heterogeneity" (Spivak 1990, 108). The term *citizen* can have a similar obscuring function, because it conceals the differences of gender, class, and caste that affect people's possibility of enjoying equal rights. The persistence of bonded labor despite its formal abolition and the lack of enforcement of the minimum wage are just two examples of how citizenship did not fulfill its promise of universal equality. As Arya affirms, tribal areas remained "islands of slavery" in the "vast ocean of independence" (Arya 1998, 102), where questions related to land, water, education, and health care continued to go unanswered. Devi's novel *Chotti Munda and His Arrow* echoes Bashai Tudu's rebellion against the persistence of tribal exploitation, enforced through "bad laws and worse implementation" (Arya 1998, 173). Almost a summa of Devi's work, *Chotti Munda* deals with a wide range of themes, from the criminalization of poverty to the contemporary fear of Naxalite uprisings.

Covering a time frame of more than seventy years, from the turn of the twentieth century to Independence and the Emergency, the novel follows Chotti's life and his gradual ascent to tribal leadership. A young and bright Munda boy, Chotti soon becomes "a famous archer in a community of archers" (M. Devi 2003, 46), who wins fair after fair.[6] His talent in archery is such that his bow is considered spellbound and able to reach any target. Stories proliferate about Chotti while he is trained in archery by the old Dhani Munda. Dhani had been banned from archery after participating in the revolt against the British led by the historical leader Birsa Munda. The reference to the series of rebellions led by the freedom fighter Birsa Munda is significant. Between 1895 and 1900, in a period known as the Great Tumult, tribal groups targeted the British system of control and privatization of tribal land. Police stations, officials, and missionaries were equally attacked. Even though the revolts were eventually suppressed and Birsa Munda died under mysterious circumstances at age 25, the memory of this great rebel fills both history and legend.

By taking Mundas as a paradigmatic example of the simultaneous inscription and marginalization of tribal groups in modern India, Devi's novel reveals the national aspiration of transforming Adivasis from rebellious subjects of a foreign rule into good citizens. But even though the story portrays endless social injustice and exploitation during colonialism, independence, and the Emergency, what arises is a sense of suspense for another revolution to come.[7] The next rebellion will be guided by Chotti Munda, who has the authority to challenge government officers and to lead bond slaves and starving Adivasis against the contractors who exploit their work.[8]

If the truest and most brutal aspect of India is visible in its villages, its administration and wealth appear to be elsewhere. In a dialogue between Chotti and the academic Shankar, the latter says, "The law is not bad, Chotti, but nothing works by the law. For the law is never applied" (M. Devi 2003, 238). Just like Bashai Tudu, Chotti exposes the gap between the spaces of decision making and the reality of the poor. Chotti asks Shankar:

> Who makes this law?
> Government.
> Where does this Gormen live?
> In Delhi.
> It's far away, nah?
> Yes.
> Makes t' law, does good, stays afar. But if Adivasi or untouchable dies in t' forest, they don' know. (M. Devi 2003, 239)

Does this statement refer to the law of citizenship as well? Chotti is denouncing formal inclusion without substantial political rights. Because citizenship, a fundamental achievement for the postcolonial nation, has not reduced the gap between the poor and their entitlements, the reverberating question is, "Can this go on in a civilized country?" (M. Devi 2003, 238). The burning realization for the reader is that the ideal of civilization borrowed from the West could not give an account of the complexity of Indian social and political scenes and it could not simply be contrasted with the tribals' allegedly backward or primitive state.

Chotti Munda reveals an orientalist repertoire of representations of indigenous subjects that highlights the trait of Adivasi backwardness and the threat of their rebellion. Devi tackles these features in particular, because they underscored the creation of colonial laws that officially labeled Adivasi territories as backward. India Act XIV of 1874 and a series of British acts instituted tribal areas as scheduled districts and then as "backward tracts." Kept under the domain of direct governance of the governor general on behalf of the British Parliament, these areas were excluded from governance and representation.[9] The Government of India Act of 1919 openly states that these tracts are inhabited by "people [who] are primitive, and there is as yet no material to found political institutions" (quoted in Jayal 2013, 235). In brief, backwardness was the mark of the lack of political subjectivity, which stood for a more general lack of adherence to modern rationality.

The analysis of Devi's language in *Chotti Munda* and "Operation? Bashai Tudu" and her insistence on the trope of backwardness point to the fact that this attribute survived colonialism, permeating the legal language of citizenship. With independence, the Constituent Assembly writing the constitution used the label "backward communities" in the formation of a group-differentiated model of citizenship. According to the constitution, Mundas and Sabars belong to Scheduled Castes and feature within the wider group of "backward communities." Jayal's seminal work *Citizenship and Its Discontents* traces the language of colonial law in India within the philanthropic discourse of citizenship and notes that "in the tribal case, the ascription of backwardness is a *benefaction* of the colonial state persisting into the postcolonial" (Jayal 2013, 230; emphasis in original). In Jayal's words:

> The marginality of the so-called backward tracts in colonial discourse in late colonial India is paralleled by the marginality of the tribal question in mainstream nationalist discourse. The constitutional incorporation of the Scheduled tribes after independence demonstrates some continuity with the colonial discourse of protection, though there was a remarkable ambivalence about how protection should be conceived. Colonial policy had infantilized tribal communities, seeking to isolate them with the stated objective of providing protection from the destructions of "civilization." (Jayal 2013, 236)

Backwardness was framed as an attribute of diverse communities, including untouchables, aboriginal people, criminal tribes, and other castes belonging to the lowest social strata.

One could argue that categories such as backward classes were created as a tool to tackle class disparity through affirmative action. In fact, the specific overlapping of independence, the birth of the Indian nation, and the creation of citizenship emphasized egalitarian freedom and justice for all. Jayal remarks, "The idea of equality was both the premise and the promise of the conception of citizenship. Its embodiment in the form of constitutionally recognized rights carried the unique ethical mandate of the movement for freedom from colonial rule" (Jayal 2013, 12). For this reason, the Constituent Assembly tried to protect civil and political rights of minority groups, opting for a model of group-differentiated citizenship, where citizenship is mediated by the community. Unfortunately, the assumption that the creation of exceptional tags, such as Scheduled Tribes or Denotified and Nomadic Tribes, would be effective in tackling inequality was defied by the social destitution of millions of citizens still living below the poverty line. For Jayal, "The very act of naming these categories for special provisioning ended up entrenching exclusions" (Jayal 2013, 18). She concludes that this group-differentiated strategy of inclusion, which depended on the creation of new categories of exception, caused the failure of the constitutional plan for equality.

Chotti Munda implicitly poses an urgent question: Given that the colonial mark of backwardness remained attached to Adivasis' national status, how could rebellious archers, like the Mundas, become straight-arrow, law-abiding citizens? In a spirit that is similar to Jayal's, Devi rebels against social categories such as Denotified Tribes that retain the prejudices of colonial ideology. She maintains that the existing disregard for tribal communities, still considered backward, and the failure of the implementation of welfare actions in their support, worsened their conditions of social marginalization.

To summarize, the joint reading of Devi and Jayal highlights two issues. First, constitutionally crafted group tags became prescriptive rather than descriptive markers of identity and had the effect of keeping people in separate social groups; second, inequality has to be fought at a formal and material level, because laws are meaningless if they are not implemented. But Devi does not portray Adivasis as passive recipients of the colonial heritage inscribed in the language of law or of the neglect of government actions. Her aim is to collect acts that testify to how tribals fall outside the categories of primitive subjects of the empire, or citizens belonging to constitutionally prescribed groups.

REWRITING CITIZENSHIP RIGHTS

Devi's resignification of the language of citizenship is a recurrent literary strategy. In *Chotti Munda* she targets both backwardness and savagery. When the novel begins, we are introduced to Chotti's character with a caustic sentence: He is "a Munda, a savage, they always shoot arrows. Arrows are their companions" (M. Devi 2003, 25). The book often makes reference to the point of view of the police and government representatives, who maintain that tribals are savage and mysterious creatures and that the forest remains "a savage place even after Independence" (106). On the other hand, Chotti proposes to replace the image of savagery with accounts of actual exploitation. First, he questions how civilization can coexist with bonded labor. Then, referring to the image of savagery, he asks, "We are savage jungle folk, what is our crime that so many police have descended upon our area? So sir, if you say that the state wants the house, who am I to say no?" (226). The interrogative style of Chotti's discourse in relation to authority is far from submissive. It is a prelude to the final scene of revolt, in which Chotti is under the threat of being killed by a subdivisional officer (SDO). Almost representing decades of subjugation, the tribal and the officer stand on opposite grounds. Chotti "on one side. SDO on the other, and in between a thousand bows upraised in space. And a warning announced in many upraised hands" (288). Stubborn bows and raised hands perform a gesture of subaltern solidarity in resistance that contradicts the narrative of Adivasis' helplessness. Through his subversive act, Chotti's performance of savagery in the novel resignifies the attribute of backwardness that defines indigenous citizenship.

Devi's appropriation of the language of norms and rights sheds light on an untold history of inequality and dispossession, but it also supports new claims for social equity and justice. In an interview I recorded with Devi, the author questioned the view that Adivasis are trapped in the state of nature and emphasized the freedom allowed by their social organization. About their alleged lack of culture or civilization, she said:

> I went to the tribals and I thought: they were deprived. The outer world is always writing of the tribals as if they know nothing. They are not civilized; they have to be civilized. . . . I stayed with them. I have been with them so many times, and I have found them as civilized as human beings can be. . . . They understand life, ordinary life. Ordinary life has norms as well as rights: like the right to remarry, the right to have a free sexual life. These rights belong to so many tribes all over India. Wherever the tribes are, you will find these rights.[10]

Provocatively speaking about "tribal civilization," Devi reclaims the richness of indigenous societies by using the vocabulary of norms and rights.

Citizenship rights call on the authority of the state and include the "right to drinking water, right to cultivation. A minimum right as the right of literacy."[11] Despite the fact that these rights are not enjoyed by most of the tribal groups, other rights, such as the one to remarry and have a free sexual life, seem to be a prerogative of Adivasis. Also, indigenous people do not discriminate between sons and daughters in matters of inheritance. For Devi, these cultural characteristics set Adivasis at a degree of civilization higher than mainstream Hindu society.

The idea of civilization appears as a battlefield where indigenous people and colonial and postcolonial authorities occupy opposite sides. In this fight, Chotti Munda, Bashai Tudu, and Draupadi are icons of the tribals' resistance to the government and its military apparatus. Allegations of backwardness and savagery do not represent inherent characteristics of tribal groups, but they express a widespread preconception stemming from colonial discrimination and dispossession. In attacking this persisting prejudice that haunts Adivasis, Devi resignifies the commonly accepted meaning of civilization and reveals the orientalism inherent in the idea of backwardness and the stigma of criminality, which are written into the idiom of citizenship. With these two moves—deorientalizing backwardness and tribal criminality and resignifying civilization—Devi exposes the epistemic violence and cultural oppression imposed on tribal groups.

In all the narrated stories the tribal heroes are criminalized even before taking up violence against injustice. In "Operation? Bashai Tudu" and *Chotti Munda*, Devi shows how, in different moments of recent Indian history, the government has flaunted the specters of Naxalite guerrilla armies to cast indigenous peoples fighting for their rights as anticitizens. But social inequality, widespread prejudice, and the unfair conduct of the police are enough reasons to push some people to take up arms against the authorities. Against the polarization of "good" and "bad" citizens, Devi portrays Draupadi, Bashai, and Chotti Munda's resistance as justified revolts against a colonial and postcolonial history of structural injustice. With a bold move, Devi transforms their acts of resistance into instances of active citizenship, which reinscribe Adivasis as citizens of the nation. Chotti ends with the image of many bows raised against the authorities who have kept the Munda tribe under strict surveillance, limiting people's movements and political agency; Draupadi and Douloti, the heroine of Devi's story "Douloti the Bountiful," discussed in chapter 3, expose their wounded and ill bodies to the representatives of the nation's civil and military spheres in their ultimate encounters with modern India; and Bashai's unverified relationship with the Naxalites exposes doubts about the government's depiction of national enemies. Still today, while the government wages war against the Naxalites through massive military operations, such as Green Hunt, Devi sees Adivasis' violent actions as the desperate struggles of small people motivated by their small dreams of escaping poverty.[12] Legitimizing their right to dream for a better life, and to strive for it, Devi rewrites indigenous people's rights to dream as a fundamental citizenship right. This right underpins the creation of a new form of citizenship that does not rely on identity politics or on the classification of classes and castes: a new, performed citizenship that is free of orientalism.

3

MODERNITY AND MODERNISM

"Real" Political Subjects

Devi's literary and political activism, as demonstrated by her fight to achieve justice for Budhan's brutal killing and her protests against the exploitation of Agariyas, Mundas, and Sabars, opposes the legal tags of "backward classes" and reminds us of the colonial ideology that informed their making. Moreover, Devi's stories mock the egalitarian principle and democratic task of the Indian constitution. They highlight that "the state's coercive shaping of the constitutional subject of the new nation has had a repressive effect on the identities and rights of women, religious minorities and the poor" (Rajan 2003, 29). Against the universality of the legal subject of the constitution, Devi's realist prose draws readers' attention to tribals as political subjects who claim and enact citizenship. In addition, her works reinstate the diversity of the subcontinent through the use of a *bhasha* language in all its varieties, including tribal Bengali.

In this chapter I conclude the discussion on Devi, presenting a reflection on her language and style in relation to modernism and the origin of realist novels. Within the literary and artistic production of the twenty-first century in India, Devi's prose is reminiscent of the kind of social realism and political engagement that was embraced by the writers of the All India Progressive Writers Association beginning in the 1930s. Taking a look at the Indian tradition of anticolonial and socialist art, I highlight that the ethical aspect of Mulk Raj Anand's production is particularly close to Devi's work. Devi's connections and affinities with early socialist Indian writers, who are rarely brought to the fore, are crucial to understanding why her writing has found wide uptake in India, with Devi herself becoming an icon of literary activism.

I propose to look at Devi's writing as rooted in Indian modernism. Scholars have demonstrated that modernism in art and literature coincides with anticolonial resistance and sets the scene for nation building and the legal constitution of citizenship. Focusing on the intersections of modernity, modernism, and modernization, in this chapter I tackle two common assumptions: first, that modernity coincides with the creation of citizenship and access to the democratic idea of equality; and second, that modernism is the language of modernization and anticolonialism. I aim to question this thesis by referring to the previous close readings of "Operation? Bashai Tudu" and *Chotti Munda and His Arrow* and to other stories that rewrite citizenship and social justice. Then, by looking at the relations between modernity, progress, and nationalism, I define Devi's work as a type of "oppositional modernism" that challenges both anticolonial and nationalist ideologies (Chaudhuri 2010, 956).

Finally, after questioning the validity of equating modernity, modernization, and anticolonialism through writing and art, in the last sections of this chapter I propose a critique of Dipesh Chakrabarty's (2000; 2002) view of citizenship as the recognition of the politicality of the subaltern subject. Devi's literary modernism, especially if associated with the political work of the Subaltern Studies Group, calls for an evaluation of both Indian citizenship and modernity in relation to their promises of democracy and egalitarianism.

INDIAN MODERNISMS: MULTIDISCIPLINARY PERSPECTIVES

How is Indian modernism defined? Since the turn of the 21st century, a number of critical works have examined the emergence of modernist art in the subcontinent, looking at the timing of its appearance and the characteristics it presents. Geeta Kapur (2000), Partha Mitter (2007), Rebecca Brown (2009), and Supriya Chaudhuri (2010) have provided valuable contributions that explore modernism in literature, visual arts, and cinema. Their works have prompted debates on the canonization of this trend, on its relations with Western formative influences, and on the different ways that modernism and modernity are related.

The diffusion of artistic modernism in the subcontinent is often attributed to the dialogue initiated by personalities such as Benoy Sarkar (1887–1949) with the European avant-garde.[1] But it was the Bauhaus exhibition of 1922, organized by the Indian Society of Oriental Art in Calcutta under the aegis of Rabindranath Tagore (Mitter 2007, 17), that is generally understood as marking the beginning of modernism in India.[2] This exhibition showcased works by, among others, Wassily Kandinsky and Paul Klee and sparked discussions in India about the languages of Western and Soviet art and the influence that they could have in the subcontinent.

Despite this genealogy, modernism in the subcontinent was far from merely imitative of global trends. It was a complex artistic phenomenon shaped by the specificity of Indian politics. The rise of Gandhian nationalism and modernism was informed by the anticolonial movements that opposed British values, from individualism to urbanism. In this chapter I focus on the intersection between political modernity, which coincided with the creation of the nation-state with new membership regulations, and its aesthetic representations in art and writing. Because "modern notions of citizenship evolved from the ideological, material, and social formations of modernity set in motion by Enlightenment thought" (Anupama Roy 2005, 79), it is important to examine critically how colonial modernity was endorsed and resisted in India. For this purpose I look at how the language of modernism complicates the relationship between progress and nationalism. Then I turn to Devi's aesthetics to analyze how they renew a modernist tradition of primitivist and socialist writing.

Rabindranath Tagore, arguably the most prominent figure in the modern history of Bengali literature and arts and the first non-European to win the Nobel Prize for literature (1913), was inspired by Gandhi's project of noncooperation when, in 1921 (only one year before the exhibition), he founded the University of Santiniketan in a rural area outside Calcutta. The aim was to boycott English education and its urban institutions, declaring the countryside to be a privileged place for the diffusion of anti-imperialist ideas.[3] Mahasweta Devi attended Santiniketan when Tagore was still alive, and Tagore's focus on rural themes and his minimalist aesthetics and anticolonial political messages influenced Devi's artistic sensibility.

Like Tagore's, the anticolonial critiques of the early twentieth century often made use of modernist aesthetics. However, an analysis of a wider artistic repertoire, including literature and architecture, reveals that the relation between colonialism and modernism is not simply complicit or antagonistic. As I illustrate in these first sections, the deployment of a modernist artistic language can be ambivalent about discourses of nationalism and progress and the colonial heritage they retain. Appropriately, Kapur warns us to be cautious in tracing a direct correspondence between modernism and the nationalist struggle: "Modernism has no firm canonical position in India. It has a paradoxical value involving a continual double-take. Sometimes it serves to make indigenist issues and motifs progressive; sometimes it seems to subvert if not nationalism, then that on which it rests and purports to grow, that is, tradition" (G. Kapur 2000, 292). The relation between the language of art and the context of its production cannot be reduced to binary terms where indigenism and progress simply occupy opposite sides; instead, the transition from colonialism to independence reveals a higher degree of complexity.

Although apparently in tune with Western criticisms of industrial capitalism, the primitivist aesthetics of Rabindranath Tagore, Jamini Roy, and Amrita Sher-Gil had their roots in the history of the subcontinent and in Gandhian nationalism. Partha Mitter highlights that "Indian artists used primitivism as an effective weapon against colonial culture" (Mitter 2007, 12). Anticolonial ideology endorsed the foreignness of rural India to British indoctrination and turned images of village life into iconic representations of the authentic nation. Idealized rural India became the essence of the nation and constituted a foundational myth for the nationalist discourse, thus linking modernism to early nationalism. As in modernist visual art, in the field of literature the diffusion of primitivism inspired a wave of realist writers who focused on the mundane reality of village life rather than on "higher" epic themes. Many turned to the genres of novels and short stories, which were considered more appropriate for expressing the reality of the lives of ordinary people.

Intellectuals of the All-India Progressive Writers Association (AIPWA) increasingly voiced their aspiration to direct nationalism toward socialist ideals in the early 1930s. Munshi Premchand and Mulk Raj Anand were among its members. Their novels *Gaban* (1931) and *Untouchable* (1935) inaugurated a turn to realism that established a new mode of social criticism: They "set out to use literature and the arts to reshape society as well as give expression to people's lives" (T. Ahmed 2006, 5). The group was so successful in encouraging the use of new aesthetics that, as Ahmed's study illustrates, "by the mid-1930s a particular brand of realism had come to hegemonize the thinking of the radical intelligentsia" (7). Despite many writers of the AIPWA having a middle-class background, they took up the task of "redirecting the course of independence towards a socialist vision" (7) under the inspiration of ideas of freedom and equality.

Anand, for example, was educated in England, but soon after he completed his studies, he decided to disconnect himself from the work of the Bloomsbury Group in London. In 1927 he traveled back to India and reached Gandhi's Sabarmati Ashram in Ahmedabad (Anand 1999, 19). His *Untouchable* resonates with the Mahatma's belief that art is to be found in the lived experience of the poor rather than in abstract philosophical systems and literary trends. Anand recalls, "As I gave up systems of philosophy and wrote about the human condition, I was unable to sleep easily. I woke up every morning to see how men and women dreaded other men and women, how they were always benthead before the White Sahibs and the Bania moneylenders, landlords and sarkari officers. There were millions of the disinherited who ate only one meal a day" (21). Such a commitment to represent India's forgotten subjects triggered a renewed focus on rurality and its uneven logics.

The emergence of social novels took place under changing economic and political conditions, when the push toward technological modernization also caused a growing gap between the rich and the poor. As Venkata Reddy highlights:

> Inspired by the exigencies of socio-political history of the country, the Indian novelists took upon themselves the responsibility of giving artistic articulation to the problems that beset the common people and their joys and sorrows, the crusade against the tyranny of poverty, illiteracy, suffering, superstition, caste and sex. Resulting, in a number of novels the protagonist is a farmer, a labourer, a factory worker, a patient or a virtuous woman pitted against a *zamindar*, a landlord, a factory owner, or a ruthless, callous hard-hearted man. (Venkata Reddi and Bayapa Reddy 1999, 3)

The choice of primitivism, with its rural settings and modest characters, responded to growing anticolonialist feelings and concerns for social justice. As Chaudhuri affirms, it was not the case that many communist progressive authors were modernists (see Chaudhuri 2010, 948).[4]

These same stylistic innovations also influenced the birth of the novel in Bengali. In his writing on nation and imagination, Dipesh Chakrabarty labels the Bengali novel as a "modern" object. Referring to a number of critical sources, he emphasizes that political and social transformations of nineteenth-century Bengal found an expression in realist prose: "Srikumar Bandhyopadhyay's comprehensive and masterful survey of the history of the Bengali novel, *Bangla shahitye upanasher dhara*—first serialized in a Bengali magazine around 1923/1924—made much the same connection between the realism of prose fiction and the coming of a new, modern politics of democratic sensibility" (Chakrabarty 2000, 154). The novel is the genre where modernist and modern sensibilities overlap most.

Not only does Chakrabarty maintain that the commitment to naturalism transformed literature into a means for interrogating contemporary politics, but he also suggests, citing Bandhyopadhyay, that the modernity of the Bengali novel depends on its connection with the diffusion of democratic ideals. When representations of popular struggles and of the social oppression of the poor became the main subject of fiction, the broader national quest for democracy emerged as the main concern of literary modernism. Chakrabarty then clarifies, "My use of the word 'modernism' follows that of Marshall Berman in designating the aesthetic means by which an urban and literate class subject to the invasive forces of modernization seeks to create, however falteringly, a sense of being at home in the modern city" (Chakrabarty 2000, 156). The language of modernism, taken up by the elite, sustains the values opposing British colonization that are embodied in rural Indian life. Nevertheless, modernism appears to stand in a dual relationship with colonial ideology: On the one hand, it sustains resistance against the British rule, and on the other, it derives from the discourse of Enlightenment that promotes ideals of equality and democracy along with a teleological idea of progress. Modernism seems to be born at this conjunction between the struggle for freedom and the invasion of the forces of modernization.

MODERNIZATION, MODERNITY, AND CITIZENSHIP

It is difficult to establish a neat time frame for Indian modernism because of regional differences and its wide reach. Although scholarship on art and literature has linked the emergence of modernism to Gandhian nationalism, studies in film and architecture date Indian modernism to a couple of decades later, considering it to be coeval with the Nehruvian era (Brown

2009). Colonialism, its aftermath, and the drive toward "the new," however, still remain its main subjects. New representations of Indian identity arise in dialogue with Western artistic avant-garde trends: Italian neorealism influences Satyajit Ray and, in architecture, Le Corbusier starts designing Indian cities.

In 1950, Prime Minister Jawaharlal Nehru commissioned Le Corbusier, who had established his reputation as a modernist city planner with his "Plan for a Contemporary City" (1922), to design Chandigarh, the provincial capital of Punjab.[5] The city, he maintained, was to be the icon of the new, independent India, striking a balance between the international modernist syntax and the Indian idiom (Brown 2009, 109). The fame of Chandigarh rests on its being the first planned city in India, designed to be rich, prosperous, and green.[6] The rhetoric surrounding its conception reveals not only how the modern city came to be seen as a positive representation of the nation but also how modernism and the rhetoric of modernization converged.

Although modernism was the aesthetic language adopted during the transitional stage out of colonialism, its emphasis on technological modernization reflects the persistent presence of colonial ideology during nationalism. From the beginning the British imperial government used the promise of modernization and development through infrastructure as a justification for colonizing. With independence the idea of development became the gateway to a Western idea of modernity. The example of architecture exposes what Brown calls "the paradox of the modern": "the paradox of constructing modernity in the face of both the universalizing modern and the particularity of India" (Brown 2009, 3). Modernism also was caught in this paradox: Although it aimed to resist the universalization of British cultural values, it incorporated a model of development and an idea of modernity that were inspired by Western discourses of conquest.

As a consequence, modernity itself appears as a condition of cultural imperialism. As Das Gupta and Panikkar point out (1995), neither modernity nor modernization in India can be disassociated from the operational logic of colonialism; tracing the relationship between the epistemology of "the modern" and the process of industrialization of the country means reestablishing the centrality of British dominance in the history and culture of the subcontinent. Similarly, for Brown, the modern is "a particular approach to the world embodied in an epistemology of progress, a faith in the universals, the primacy of the subject and a turning away from religion toward reason" (Brown 2009, 4). Secularism, individualism, and the universal values of European Enlightenment remain at the core of modernity.

In colonial discourse, modernity stands for the path toward a higher form of civilization to which colonized subjects should aspire in order to free themselves from the ties of their "primitive" culture. As Chakrabarty stresses in *Habitations of Modernity* (2002), the very creation of modernity as a category contains an impasse: To define what it *is* means to implicitly define what it *is not* and therefore to confine some people to the domain of premodernity and backwardness. Characteristics such as religiosity (equated with a lack of rationality) and traditionalism keep colonized subjects out of the modern state.

Tracing a "small history" of the Subaltern Studies Group, Chakrabarty emphasizes their interest in deconstructing the equation of premodernity and the lack of politicality. The purpose of Ranajit Guha's investigation of peasant insurgencies was precisely to demonstrate how and under what circumstances the often overlooked activity of the masses emerged as essential to the political domain. Outlining the continuity between anticolonial struggles and independence, Chakrabarty states, "The formal granting of the rights of citizenship to the Indian peasant after the achievement of independence from the British simply recognized his already political nature" (Chakrabarty 2002, 19). Chakrabarty thus reiterates a direct link between citizenship, politicality, and modernity. Citizenship acknowledges the political nature of the subject, who acquires modernity by belonging to the new secular nation. Technological modernization starts with colonialism, and the transition from imperial rule to national citizenship forms the main preconditions of modernity. This figure of the citizen as a member of the state is a particularly Western, if not liberal, notion. Yet there is another image of the citizen—as a political subject who exercises the right to have rights—that might pave the way for uncovering other imageries of the citizen that have barely been unearthed.

DEVI'S CRITIQUE OF MODERNITY

Unlike the universalist epistemology of the modern, which marked colonized subjects as backward, modernism is an aesthetic space where more nuanced perspectives arise. Kapur views modernism as an exploration of subjectivity in a moment of turbulence; it "refers to the project of figuring subjectivity as a locus of potential consciousness" (G. Kapur 2000, 300), where the subject acts politically and in unpredictable ways. Modernist art challenges the pristine image of the modern self as inherited from Cartesian thought and filtered through the Enlightenment. In doing so, it also challenges the legal and cultural discourse of the nation that is rooted in that tradition. The ideal of the Indian citizen identifies the modern subject as conscious, rational, and law-abiding.

But the issue of citizenship in modern India is not unproblematic, and the question of which subject position a citizen inhabits cannot be satisfied with a simple answer. Can widows, poor people, and tribal groups who face discrimination and do not benefit from the basic rights of education and welfare be considered citizens in practice?[7] With the transition from colonialism to the postcolonial state, this preoccupation opened up a new field of investigation, and writers of the AIPWA made peasants, the lower castes, and village people the protagonists of their works. Literature addressed issues of hunger and poverty, social backwardness, and political subjection. It also echoed a broader quest for democracy, social justice, and equality.

After independence this tradition inspired new explorations of the limits of the nation and the definition of the citizen. Listing modernist Bengali writers from the 1930s onward, Chaudhuri remarks, "Women poets and novelists such as Devi evolved radically oppositional modernisms rooted in subaltern experience" (Chaudhuri 2010, 956). Although Devi's literary activity started only after independence, the form and the content of her works are in tune with modernist themes; her critique of modernity unveils the injustice hidden behind the flag of progress.

Devi's criticism is finely illustrated in "Douloti" and "Operation? Bashai Tudu," two stories that create a series of short circuits between the foundational values of independent India and its cruel aspect. Questioning who is to be called a citizen today, the stories stress the persistence of precolonial systems of inequality and colonial legal discourses at the heart of the national enterprise.[8] "Douloti" denounces casteism for supporting a system of bonded labor that still survives today, despite the constitutional ban. Bashai Tudu's eponymous story, introduced in chapter 2, unmasks the brutal use of force by police and government officers against tribal members and poor villagers in West Bengal. By focusing on the social marginality of lower castes and Adivasis, Devi's stories reflect on the paradoxical experience of modernity for the citizens who remain marginal to the formation of the new nation.

Devi's writing fosters discussion about different approaches to Indian modernity. A close look at modernism and modernization suggests two definitions of modernity. First, modernity can be considered the introduction of a colonial epistemology that promotes a singular model of the individual on which the state and its laws are based. Second, modernity stands for the institutional proclamation of Indian independence. However, for Devi, the way in which these possibilities merge into each other exposes the continuous oppression of the poor despite the promise of modernity. By drawing attention to this continuing subjugation, Devi maintains that granting citizenship to tribal groups and marginalized subjects did not change their condition of deprivation.

Devi dramatizes this modern paradox by revealing that the concept of independence is still unintelligible for part of the Indian population. "Operation? Bashai Tudu" deals with this peculiar sense of foreignness of tribal members and villagers toward the language of the nation and points out that "ten per cent of the agricultural laborers said they did not know India was independent. They thought that the Englishmen had been given a new name, the Indian government. One hundred per cent of them said that they had never heard of minimum wages for the agricultural laborers" (M. Devi 1990, 63). Tribals' sense of foreignness toward modernity arises from the fact that they cannot experience the difference that independence makes because it has no relation to the people's demands for basic rights. In 1968 the gap between the state and the poor was still too wide.

Bashai supports the ideology of the Naxalite revolutionary movement, but his criticism is equally directed against the government and other forms of local power. He rejects the upper- and middle-class leaders of the Communist Party, whose actions rarely aim to help agricultural laborers. Bashai's dissent, expressed by his refusal to be affiliated with any party, transforms him into a "continent" of his own. Devi makes the rebel an epitome of exclusion from mainstream politics: "No bridge could ever be built over the raging sea of incomprehension that rolled between Bashai and the Party. Bashai was now a strange continent. But a continent that one could not attack, *explore* or *colonize*" (M. Devi 1990, 29; emphasis in original).

Devi refers to colonization to draw attention to a deep-rooted and ongoing history of tribal exploitation. Bashai decides to break free from institutional politics because he is aware that without the promotion of education for poor villagers and Adivasis, oppression and abuse will not end. Bashai is aware of the essential role played by rural workers in the Indian economy and is forced to witness their transformation into a mass of forgotten citizens: "Ours is an agricultural country, isn't it? In this whole music that runs and grows through the sowing, the planting, the weeding, the harvesting and the paddy carried to someone else's granary at the end, the lead singer was the agricultural laborer, who got bypassed by every organization" (M. Devi 1990, 32).

The song created from the sounds of working the land dissolves into the modern and rising national anthem. As a result, the traditional singers become depoliticized, and their exploitation becomes part of the newly established system of managing resources. Bashai Tudu summarizes the chain of exploitation by citing a protest song.

> "Gandhi Raja said, you're all *harijan*s,
> And there're three of us here
> To steal all that you have."
>
> Yes Kali-babu, there were the three of them. Bhuinya the *zamindar*, Sau the moneylender, and Barari the *jotedar*. I don't recollect a single day that I hadn't had a drubbing from all the three devils. (M. Devi 1990, 23)

In the independent nation, the state is the prime owner of the land and stands at the top of a feudal hierarchy allowing proprietors, moneylenders, and bureaucrats to perpetrate abuses.

Devi points out that this current situation of mass exploitation in rural and Adivasi areas is a persisting heritage of the system of land management that was crystallized by the British. As early as 1824, the English Crown began a process of privatization of resources and, with a series of laws (including the Land Acquisition Act), acquired all the lands that were vital resources for grazing and firewood for nomadic tribes, thereby effectively abolishing their customary rights (Singh 1986).[9] The assimilation of the British system and laws in the modern nation granted no freedom to marginalized citizens, establishing a state of paradoxical alienation of the ordinary people from the Indian system.

Like "Operation? Bashai Tudu," "Douloti the Bountiful" exposes the distance between the material subjugation of lower-caste and indigenous people and the democratic principles of nationalism. The story revolves around a bonded laborer living in the village of Seora in Palamu, in modern Jharkhand,

and unveils exploitation in its clear brutality. Douloti is the daughter of "crook Nagesia," who became crippled after being forced by his master to carry an ox yoke on his shoulders. Douloti's fate is to repay her father's debt. Sold to become the wife of a brothel owner disguised as a Brahmin, she is forced into prostitution and dies of venereal disease at the age of 27, on August 15, 1975, which is Independence Day. Her body, tortured by the illness, collapses on the map of India drawn in chalk in the courtyard of a village school: "Filling the entire Indian peninsula from the oceans to the Himalayas, here lies bonded labor spread-eagled, kamiya-whore Douloti Nagesia's tormented corpse, putrefied with venereal disease, having vomited up all the blood in its desiccated lungs. Today, on the fifteenth of August, Douloti has left no room at all in the India of people like Mohan [the schoolmaster] for planting the standard of the Independence flag. What will Mohan do now? Douloti is all over India" (M. Devi 1995, 94). In this tragic ending, the harshness of the story is conveyed by its bare, even stifled, literary language.

Devi rebels against the elitism of literature by adopting a simple and direct style, sometimes even using the variety of Bengali spoken by Adivasis. To write the national abject subjects into official history, Devi provokes an interruption in the cohesive language of national identity. Multiple points of view are conveyed in a range of vernacular languages. Her realist aesthetics fragment the authority of the narrator in favor of a plurality of voices that are not represented in the political realm.

In a dialogue between the washerwoman Rajbi and the Gandhian prophet Sadhuji in "Douloti," we are confronted with the stubborn rejection of the concept of the country as Mother India. When Sadhuji explains that the nation is like a mother taking equal care of all her children, Rajbi responds confused:

> "Oh Sadhuji, my place is Seora village. What do you call a country? I know *tahasil*, I know station, I don't know country, India is not the country."
>
> "Hey you are all independent India's free people, do you understand?"
>
> "No, Sadhuji." (M. Devi 1995, 41)

For Rajbi, as for Bashai, "country" and "independence" are empty signifiers, filled only with the experience of gender, social, and material inequality. As Collu says, the story "establishes a parallel between the exploitation of

Adivasi men who become bonded-laborers ... and the sexual exploitation of Adivasi women who are used and abused because they are poor—they own nothing: not the means of their livelihood, nor their own bodies" (Collu 1999, 49).

Unable to rely on the land to sustain their livelihood, Adivasis started to work as cheap manual laborers. But soon the foreignness of a cash economy and their general lack of education made them easy prey for landowners and moneylenders. With the foreign rule of the Rajput, the peasants became slaves: "Who reckons how long the Crook Nagesias have been their servant-*kamiya-seokia* [bonded laborers]? It's a matter of hundreds of years. When did the Rajput brahman from outside come to this land of jungle and mountain? When did all the land slide into their hands? Then cheap labor became necessary. That was the beginning of making slaves on hire purchase" (M. Devi 1995, 21). This form of slavery still exists. The legal framework against bonded labor consists of the Bonded Labor System (Abolition) Act (1976) and is supported by the Minimum Wage Act (1948);[10] yet this practice continues unabated because of failure in the enforcement of law. What rights can people like Douloti or Rajbi, tribals, and bonded laborers claim when the law in place to protect them remains unimplemented? Devi's answer is bitterly harsh: "The Indian constitution respected every citizen's fundamental right to become whatever he could by dint of his guts. The poor therefore had the right to become poorer still. A peasant today had the right to be a landless agricultural laborer tomorrow. There was no governmental agency or strong organization to stand by these men who made a living by cultivating other people's land" (M. Devi 1990, 87). Asserting that the only right left to the poor is to become poorer, Devi severely questions independence and the meaning of the institution of citizenship: Because it does not grant access to equal rights, citizenship is not a gateway to modernity as prefigured by the Enlightenment discourse. Devi's use of the experience of the poor challenges Chakrabarty for equating modernity, citizenship, and politicality. Not only do modernity and citizenship depart from each other, but also the very characters in Devi's stories, as I explain in more detail in the next section of this chapter, defy the idea of the political subject that such concepts presuppose.

Let me continue with this disruption of the normative idea of the subject. Apart from considering independence as the threshold of modernity, I have suggested that modernity can be defined, as Kapur does, in relation to the colonial introduction of Western categories of the individual that inform hegemonic theories of citizenship. The liberal modern citizen is understood as a self-determined, secular, and rational individual and as an owner of private property. None of these attributes, however, can be applied to indigenous people and poor villagers, who are the "others" against whom the liberal citizen is conceived and conceivable. There is a friction between the model of the national subject and the subjects of Devi's stories.

First, Adivasis did not use enclosures, nor did they have any use for the institution of private property. Second, their stories question the notion of self-determination by dramatizing how economic and social forces inevitably hold people down. Douloti, for example, is not in control of her fate; she is doomed to live and die as a slave. Her death, however, is not apolitical; her tortured body performs an ultimate act of resistance, covering with blood a map of the allegedly free and modern India.

Finally, the conversation between Devi's work and the Subaltern Studies Group leads to the assimilation of religiosity into political actions. Ranajit Guha's studies of the peasant revolts reveal the role of religious elements in organizing resistance against the authorities (Guha and Spivak 1988). Referring to a Naxalite as the epitome of a peasant rebel, Devi echoes Guha's work and disputes the notion that religiosity implies an absence of rationality or politicality. She highlights the incongruence between the ideal, autonomous individual and the millions of subjects whose exercise of political subjectivity exceeds the dominant model of the citizen. Her stories show that approaching Indian modernity as an accomplished project consecrated by independence, or as the triumph of the foundational categories of citizenship, equally reveals the paradox of state inclusion without participation.

AN OPPOSITIONAL MODERNISM?

Devi's writing stems from the socialist trend that emerged during nationalism, but her radical and oppositional modernism, as Chaudhuri notes, is different. Her perspective cannot be reduced to the view of the urban elite on rural India, because her works reclaim, through realism, the experience of subalternity of indigenous, lower-caste, and village people.

In relation to the performance of realism in contemporary fictions from the subcontinent, Leela Fernandes expresses the need to overcome the "binary opposition between an authentic speaking subaltern or an unrecoverable subject lost in webs of power and domination" (Fernandes 2001, 68). Devi presents a different opportunity: She invokes the authenticity of subaltern experiences to reconstruct the history of tribal marginalization. She does not portray Adivasis' identity as static or fixed. Rather, she uses realism as a tool to explore the possibilities of communicating the trauma of colonialism, its afterlife, and the inadmissible pain of poverty. As Fernandes notes, the use of realism to represent power and subjection is "contingent upon tactics of rhetoricity, form and context" (Fernandes 2001, 68). Devi, one the other hand, uses the canon of social realism and primitivism, recalling the history of the AIPWA, but renovates its political objective of exploring rural India, incorporating tribal language and folk stories.

The political task of Devi's literature is to open up multiple narrations of national modernity and indigenous temporalities. In her investigation of modernity in the Indian novel, Satya P. Mohanty advocates for a creative and reconstructive project of considering multiple modernities and questioning the repetition of the inherited values of European Enlightenment: "'Alternative' or 'indigenous' modernity points to a project of historical retrieval and imaginative philosophical reconstruction. A critique of colonial ideology, the ideology that is a constitutive element of colonial modernity, is meant to clear the ground for such retrieval and reconstruction" (Mohanty 2011, 3). A critique of colonial ideology is essential to the project of retrieving subjugated indigenous knowledge, but it does not exhaust its complexity.

Chakrabarty's analysis rigidly ties the novel to nationalism and modernity. But taking up the task of pluralizing modernity, as Mohanty puts it, also means looking at how different literary genres have been adapted and modified to disavow the monolithism of the national narration. Devi's political aim of creating a heterogeneous archive of struggles of resistance of subaltern subjects is actualized in many forms, including novels, theatrical plays, and short stories. Short stories are part of a militant literature that implicitly reminds us of Premchand's responses to British oppression, as in "Babu" or "The Salt Inspector," and of Manto's representations of the drama of Partition.[11] But also, short stories are a bridge connecting the folktales to the novels.

Folktales and oral accounts collected in rural villages are regularly incorporated into the fabric of Devi's fiction. As seen in the analyses of the narrations of "Operation? Bashai Tudu" and *Chotti Munda*, songs and digressions enrich the prose of and reveal the influence of oral culture on Devi's writing.[12] Devi's endorsement of the modernist motif of primitivism is apparent in the simplicity of her prose, which is intermingled with the use of the variety of

Bengali spoken by the tribal groups in the stories. The choice of this technique is not merely formal. Devi identifies those who inspire her literature as co-authors, including storytellers and unofficial informants; by doing so, she contests the notion of the singular writer as the Cartesian rational, conscious, and self-determined subject (see chapter 10). Her idea that cultural production entails the formation of a collective subject questions the individualism at the core of the epistemology of the modern condition.

The seeds of such a critique can be found in Chakrabarty's analyses of Bengali fiction. In *Habitations of Modernity* and in "The Birth of the Subject" in *Provincializing Europe*, Chakrabarty investigates Kalyani Datta's essay on the condition of widowhood in Bengal (Chakrabarty 2002, 106), starting with some fictional accounts that brought this social problem to the fore. Through Datta's text and her interviews with the widows, Chakrabarty draws attention to the limits of modern rationality. Against the liberal value of individualism, these narratives show a sense of solidarity that shifts the attention of the reader away from the singularity of the spokesperson. In relation to the possibilities of subverting the authority of the writer, Chakrabarty says, "The subject of Bengali modernity who demonstrates a will to witness and document oppression is thus inherently a multiple subject, whose history produces significant points of resistance and intractability when approached with a secular analysis that has its origins in the self-understanding of the subject of European modernity" (Chakrabarty 2002, 147). Chakrabarty states that the writing subject documenting oppression is involved in a movement of transformation: The author is generated out of the making of a multiple subject that resists forms of understanding that are normatively rooted in the axioms of modern epistemology.

Although Chakrabarty's focus on citizenship as a way to access modernity seems to reiterate a discourse that is drenched in colonial ideology, his reference to literature provides a more challenging alternative. Through literature, Chakrabarty stresses the limits of using hegemonic European categories to understand postcolonial processes of subject formation; he also questions the assumptions on which Western social sciences base the notion of citizenship.

So far, the dialogue I have staged between Devi and Chakrabarty in relation to the political subject has revealed the importance of Western liberal ideology and colonial history for the conception of the modern Indian citizen. Against this, popular protests and the acts of writing they trigger favor the emergence of new subject positions, such as the writer-activist (chapter 4), and highlight trajectories of social engagement that, as Bashai's story shows, do not overlap with the agenda of any political party. I have argued that Adivasis' activism is often simplistically reduced by mainstream political discourses to futile remonstrations or violent uprisings. Devi's literature, on the contrary, does not merely claim specific rights but depicts Adivasis as political subjects. Devi looks at tribal struggles as political acts and, with her literature, she builds an archive of their historical rebellions against colonial and postcolonial oppression. These works reveal the existence of a gap between the citizenship rights granted through the affirmative politics of the constitution and a grim reality of enduring exclusion and deprivation.

In relation to Kheria Sabars in West Bengal but also to Mundas and Agariyas, in this part on Mahasweta Devi I have explored the structural difficulty of living in tribal areas, including the scarcity of water and means of livelihood for traditional forest dwellers. In the next part of this book I focus attention on the Bhils of Madhya Pradesh and introduce the issues of forceful land acquisition, dispossession, and colonial land management policies. The analysis of these topics, which Devi considers necessary to understand the contemporary marginalization of Adivasis, is intertwined with a discussion on the role of award-winning author Arundhati Roy in the struggle of tribals and farmers against the construction of a series of dams in central India.

2

Arundhati Roy

4

"THE COST OF DAMS"

Writing Collective Resistance

> How can we accept that what the government says in the name of your development is for our development, when our lands have been submerged and we are not even being compensated for that? This is total brutality and injustice, this is not any development. We are more enslaved than we were with the British. We are left out in every part of the action of the state. If we ask for rehabilitation, we get jails and *lathi*s. What kind of state and what kind of rule of law is this? They don't see that we are equal citizens in this country.
>
> Surbhan from Kakrana[1]

Surbhan lives in the village of Kakrana in Madhya Pradesh, India. He is one of the Adivasis displaced by the construction of the Sardar Sarovar project, the largest of a set of dams built along the Narmada River in central India since the 1980s. By recalling his personal story of forced eviction and struggle to obtain fair compensation, Surbhan contests the view that the benevolent Indian state takes equal care of all its citizens. He stresses that a combination of force and law carries out injustices against Adivasis. Like Surbhan, hundreds of people lost their houses and lands when this huge development project was implemented, and they have yet to be recompensed. People of the Baiga, Gond, Korku, Bhil, and Bhilala tribes and villagers of the plains

Jobat Dam in the Alirajpur District, Madhya Pradesh.

of Nimad have articulated their grievances against the state by appealing to their rights as citizens: What rights of citizenship do they really have? What does it mean to belong to a state, or to a free country, when the right to land and livelihood of hundreds of citizens in the Narmada Valley, most of whom are Adivasis, has been ignored for almost thirty years?

Adivasis in India are supposedly "equal citizens," as Surbhan puts it, with constitutionally protected minority rights, but the large-scale dispossession without rehabilitation in the Narmada Valley shows an altogether different reality of inequalities and neglect, compelling us to question what citizenship really means. Much has been written on the struggle of the Narmada Bachao Andolan (NBA), the movement that has been fighting resiliently against the construction of the dam and for fair rehabilitation (Sangvai 2002; Baviskar 2004; Klingensmith 2007; Nilsen 2010). A less studied side of the story, though, is how several factors have coalesced to contribute to the dispossession and marginalization of indigenous people: Not only was land acquisition enforced in rural areas predominantly inhabited by Adivasis, but also court judgments and action plans aimed at providing adequate compensation to the displaced remain unimplemented.

The Narmada River in the submerged valley. Photo taken from the hilly village of Bhadal, Madhya Pradesh.

I suggest that the discrimination against Adivasis, leading to their being dispossessed of their resources, perpetuates colonial legacies and is enacted through the legal institution of the independent nation. A form of orientalism against tribals, which has its roots in colonial times, is also actively sustained by the economic rationale of modernity. What are the justifications that write the Adivasis out of the narratives of development? How is the race toward development run at the expense of the poor, ethnically different subjects of the state? These questions are fundamental to understanding Arundhati Roy's account of the Narmada Valley project in her essay "The Greater Common Good," reprinted in *The Cost of Living* (A. Roy 1999). Her narrative, which contributed to the struggle of the NBA at the end of the 1990s, offers a point of entry into the debate over the Sardar Sarovar and other Indian dams. After exploring Roy's use of the vocabulary of citizenship, I consider whether and how her act of writing on the Narmada controversy has generated deorientalizing effects on this well-known struggle of the poor. The context of the struggle in the Narmada Valley is at the forefront of this chapter, but Roy's act of writing within this context triggers my investigation into the emerging language of opposition to the imperatives of neoliberalism, which occupies a great part of chapters 5 and 6. By casting herself as a storyteller who is addressing an international public, Roy supports an assault on global power, which is conceived along the same lines as Hardt and Negri's empire (see chapter 5). She also reclaims the importance of enjoying common goods and collective action, placing emphasis on the creative power and the imagination of the poor.

DID THE VALLEY NEED A WRITER?

Planning for the Narmada Valley project dates back to the end of the 1970s and was quickly opposed by the NBA resistance movement. As Sanjay Sangvai recalls in *The River and Life*, a detailed diary of the history of the conflict in the Narmada Valley, "By 1989, opposition to the dam had crystallized into a two-point programme: first, non-cooperation with all dam related work in the villages; second, the determination not to move out of their land and villages, symbolized by the popular slogan 'doobenge par nahin hatenge' (we will drown but won't move out)" (Sangvai 2002, 51). Since its early days, the struggle has been resilient and nonviolent. The activists have creatively resorted to different means of protest, including satyagrahas, sit-ins, boycotts of dam-related works, long marches, and rallies.

As a consequence of popular unrest and after the release of a critical independent report by Bradford Morse in 1992, the World Bank, which was one of the main funders of the Sardar Sarovar project, withdrew its support. The construction of the dam was suspended between 1995 and 1999, fueling hope for a decisive halt. The sustained fight of villagers against the state, the World Bank, and multinational corporations was regarded with interest and puzzlement, and in Hardt and Negri's *Multitude* (Hardt and Negri 2006, 283), it became an icon of resistance against agents of the modern empire. The present situation, though, represents a different scenario.

On October 18, 2000, a judgment of the Supreme Court of India unexpectedly gave permission for the completion of the dam in accordance with the original plan. After this significant setback, the NBA had to abandon the prospect of stopping the construction but did not end the fight. Its new objectives became the rehabilitation and relocation of the "oustees" (a legal term common in India used to describe the displaced people), opposition to the spread of corruption connected to these activities, and a cap on the height of the dam.

Rather than attempting to draw a coherent history or comprehensive account of the movement's actions of resistance, I want to pay attention here to an act of writing stimulated by the NBA's fight that contributed to the "Free the Narmada" campaign. Arundhati Roy's essay "The Greater Common Good," published in the widely circulating magazines *Frontline* and *Outlook* in June 1999, called for participation in the eight-day "Rally for the Valley," which was to take place in July in the territories scheduled for flooding. In her essay Roy echoes the demands and doubts about the nature of development and raises questions about the common people's belonging and participation in a democratic state. The essay's highly critical content, especially in light of the international fame that came to Roy as a result of being awarded the Booker Prize in 1997, attracted international attention and gathered support for the rally, at which the writer, together with the activist Medha Patkar and other well-known public figures, marched barefoot, in Gandhian style, to express solidarity with the Adivasis.

By reflecting on the language of struggle transmitted through Roy's essay and her active role in the protest demonstrations at the end of the 1990s, I would like to temporarily shift attention away from the traditional spaces of production and contestation of politics in order to examine how noninstitutional forces bring about, stimulate, or transmit sociopolitical change. To do so, I refer to the category of the "act of writing," stressing the creative break that narrations can produce in a given political field. I interpret writing as an act when it asserts the contextual presence of the author in the singularity of an event that intervenes in a given "location of culture." An act of writing can disrupt the iteration of norms that sustain the formation of a national subject or unsettle historical and geographic accounts.[2]

A contextual analysis of "The Greater Common Good" and the Narmada struggle reveals the importance of considering all these elements. Through the specific nature of this struggle, I trace the emergence of the writer's subjectivity as a civic and social actor. It is in no way my intention to favor the construction of an ideal interpretative model that would codify the formation of the figure of the citizen-writer—or the citizen who feels compelled to write—which can be manifested differently in different places. In her essay Roy eloquently speaks out against the label of writer-activist (like "sofa-bed," Roy sarcastically remarks), which in her view is dismissive both of the political capacity of literary work and of the complexity of the activists' thought (A. Roy 2002, 196). I agree with Roy about the inherently political nature of writing social phenomena and, in talking about citizen-writers, I do not mean to replicate the same apparently dismissive attitude that she rejected. To the contrary, I believe it is important to highlight the conditions in which a specific writer feels compelled to act through her works.

Roy often makes reference to the responsibility of writing in contemporary India, and in *The Algebra of Infinite Justice* she states, "To be a writer—a supposedly 'famous' writer—in a country where millions of people are illiterate is a dubious honour. To be a writer in a country that gave the world Mahatma Gandhi, that invented the concept of non-violent resistance, and then, half a century later, followed that up with nuclear tests is a ferocious burden. . . . To be a writer in a country where something akin to an undeclared civil war is being waged on its citizens in the name of 'development' is an onerous responsibility" (A. Roy 2002, 169). In this light, "The Greater Common Good" can be read as a critical interrogation of the notion of development in an incandescent climate of war against its citizens, especially the poor.

In the essay Roy accuses regional and central governments of dispossessing marginalized people in the name of the common good of the nation. Drawing together evidence from surveys, available technical data, and experts' opinions, Roy points out the ineffectiveness of dam technologies.[3] She also exposes the process of recolonization of rural areas by national and global agents, outlining the connection between the central and local governments and the World Bank (for a long time the main funder of the dam industry).

Roy entered the debate over the dam relatively late, when the NBA movement had already achieved significant results by mobilizing local activists and seeking institutional responses. Yet Roy's narrative sums up the ideological foundations of the NBA, the experience of loss shared among the affected people, and their recent history of protest. The vibrant picture of the struggle emerging from Roy's writing is inspired by the various trips she took across the Narmada Valley in 1998. They had the effect of redirecting public attention to the anti-dam campaign when general interest seemed to be fading. Her main contribution was to shape a distinct language of struggle when the movement was looking for more international visibility. Amita Baviskar notes that "just when the [Sardar Sarovar] Project seemed to be a lost cause, the intelligentsia's interest in the issue was revived by Arundhati Roy's eloquent essay" (Baviskar 2004, 240).[4]

Rather than a conscious choice, though, Roy's trip to the valley and her engagement with the NBA appear in the essay as reactions to an instinctive ethical call. Roy sensed that the struggle had entered a "newer, sadder phase" (A. Roy 1999, 12), and she could no longer remain silent: "I felt compelled to set aside Joyce and Nabokov, to postpone reading Don DeLillo's big book and substitute for it reports on drainage and irrigation, with journals and books and documentary films about dams and why they're built and what they do" (9). Roy articulates this same inescapable impulse: "I felt that the valley needed a writer," a feeling that piqued her own sense of responsibility for the role, the scope, and the aim of literature.

Roy's writing carries the burden of recreating her presence in the villages of the valley and the encounters that motivated the essay. "The Greater Common Good" starts with the image of the author sitting on top of a hill overlooking the Narmada Valley and laughing at the undelivered promise of integration and development of indigenous populations made with Indian independence in 1947.

The image of the valley about to be vacated and submerged is physically overlaid by the actual occupation of the site orchestrated during the rally. Through the act of marching, evocative of topical protests in Indian history, Roy implicitly takes a position in the debate over alternative forms of government, which she refers to as the "Nehru vs. Gandhi contest" (A. Roy 1999, 10). By interrogating the unilateral logic of development that imposes an idea of progress on the population as a whole, she shows how the dam construction interestingly revives the opposition between the centralized control of the state and a more dispersed local rule. By showing solidarity with Adivasis and Dalits (untouchables), Roy performs her closeness to the Gandhian tradition of nonviolent expression of dissent and to the struggle against caste discrimination that formed an important part of the Mahatma's political agenda. The acts of writing and marching, laughing at the state's promise, and rewriting its history mutually sustain each other and reverberate both within and without the boundaries of the text.

DISPLACING THE NATIONALIST NARRATION

"The Greater Common Good" starts with an epigraph taken from Nehru's 1948 speech to the people who were to be displaced by the Hirakud Dam: "If you are to suffer, you should suffer in the interest of the country" (A. Roy 1999, 7). Nehru's speech, famously declaring dams to be "Temples of Modern

India," was the starting point for seeing dams as the visible manifestation of the benevolent, democratic process of modernizing the nation. The 1950s, then, saw the start of a dam age, a new era of national history based on the ideology of the development of the wild: of India's 3,600 big dams, Roy notes, 3,300 were built after 1947.

Dams inscribe independent India into the history of Western progress; at the same time, the controversies they raise mark an increased resistance to the acquisition of modernity through technology. McCully reminds us that the Hirakud Dam became an object of fierce dispute as early as 1946, when the police dispersed 30,000 people marching against it and arrested the organizers of the demonstration (see McCully 2001, 302). The reconfiguration of the Hirakud Dam as a protest site marks the dawn of a history of postcolonial mass demonstrations, which continues with the rallies against the Pong Dam and the Chandil Dam in Bihar in the 1970s, the Tehri Dam in the Himalayas in the 1980s, and the Silent Valley Dam in Kerala. Prime Minister Indira Gandhi's dismissal of this last enterprise in 1983 boosted further resistance to dam-related displacement projects and still stands as a victory for national and international protest movements.

These struggles, notable both for their bravery and for the violence with which they were suppressed, provide the background for Roy's entry into the public debate on the contested logistics of large infrastructure projects. Her core argument opposes the nationalist myth initiated by Nehru, which equated individual sacrifice with a valuable contribution to the health of the country. At the same time, she calls into question the construction of the nationalist imagination, referring to its various aspects.

As Daniel Klingensmith (2007) reports, the role that dams play in post-independence India surfaces in the narratives and autobiographical accounts of several personalities who have influenced its history. One of these is A. N. Khosla (1882–1984), the governor of Orissa in the 1960s. He had been a Punjabi irrigation engineer involved in supervising the Bhakra Dam Project and in planning the Hirakud Dam, which was constructed to the detriment of 110,000–160,000 displaced people, mainly Adivasis (Klingensmith 2007, 221). Interestingly, Khosla headed the committee in charge of drawing up the master plan for developing the Narmada water resources in 1961. In analyzing Khosla's scattered writings and *Reminiscences of an Engineer* (1978), written by his colleague Kanwar Sain (who also contributed to revising the early plan of the Narmada dam), Klingensmith traces the emergence of an iconic nationalist figure: the engineer as a modern hero. In significant passages of his autobiography, Sain declares that his job is to serve his country as he would if he were a politician (Klingensmith 2007, 230). Sain not only equates nation building with dam building but also stresses how the engineer contributes to constructing the wealth and the good of the nation.

In her essay Roy intervenes in this narrative, questioning the nationalist assumptions passed on in a period "when dams moved men to poetry" (A. Roy 1999, 14). What is actually gained through the dam and the displacement of millions? What narrations report the voice of the affected? Roy severely questions the validity of the Narmada project through the use of statistics that show the relation between the expected revenues and the long-term sustainability of the financial outlay required by the Sardar Sarovar project and trace the failure of previous dam enterprises. In her account dams appear as an old technology: They age; they are inefficient; they are "uncool" (14); they cannot be considered driving forces toward future economic and sustainable growth. Roy bases her judgment on a wide range of official and third-party reports, including Kothari's (1996) seminal analysis and McCully's (2001) valuable contribution.

These same doubts about the efficacy of contemporary dam projects were later confirmed by a more general report funded by the World Bank titled *Dam and Development: A New Framework for Decision-Making* (World Commission on Dams 2000), which was completed by a committee of representatives of the dam industry and the anti-dam groups. The aim of the report was to respond to the pressing demands of associations like the NBA and the International River Organization and their call for the appointment of a world commission on dams to conduct a comparative review of current projects all over the world. According to the findings of this analysis, the weaknesses of the building plans are considerable: The construction of large dams involves high cost overruns and considerable delays in their completion; 55 percent of dams generate less power than predicted, and they are often counterproductive in relation to flood control (see McCully 2001). Moreover, dams may cause a deterioration in water quality because of the retention of water in the reservoir. Dams alter migratory routes of fish and threaten the survival of some species, as McCully highlights in the case of the Hilsa fishery in the Narmada Valley (McCully 2001, 43). Their social impact is particularly harsh on indigenous and peasant communities.

The first edition of McCully's book was a valuable source of technical data for Roy, but the power of "The Greater Common Good" is that it combines the seemingly self-evident truth of numbers with sharp, persuasive prose that cuts through the abstract ideal of the "common good of the nation."[5]

CITIZENSHIP IN (CON)TEXTUAL ALLIANCES

Roy's essay continued to provoke controversy long after its publication.[6] She was blamed for having moved on to different causes after 1999, leaving the valley for good; and the criticism of her "fleeting" association with the struggle continues. Rather than taking a moralizing position, I look at how Roy's narrative enables the articulation of a version of the story of the Narmada Valley that focuses on people's loss and relocation, on their epic resistance, and on the undemocratic premises of the legal framework of the independent state. As a reaction to the threat of the Adivasis' disappearance from history, Roy's narration has the potential to produce transformative political actions. Such potential becomes visible in her use of the concepts of citizen and citizenship.

In Amita Baviskar's reflection on Adivasis' claim to minority rights, citizenship is portrayed as an ineffective category and indigeneity, though essentialist, appears as a more powerful weapon to deploy: "The language of citizenship rights submerges Adivasi difference into a more generalized subaltern position" (Baviskar 2007, 291). On the other hand, Roy attempts to intervene in the struggle against Adivasis' subalternity without abandoning the vocabulary of citizenship. By using the term outside the legal context, she fills it with new connotations. In this context "citizens" are not only the Adivasis and non-Adivasis doomed to be submerged but also those who witness the valley's drama in India and in different parts of the world and cannot simply ignore it: "The millions of displaced people in India are nothing but refugees of an unacknowledged war. And we, like the *citizens* of white America and French Canada and Hitler's Germany, are condoning it by looking away. Why? Because we're told that it's being done for the sake of 'The Greater Common Good.' That it's being done in the name of the Progress, in the name of the National Interest. Therefore gladly, unquestioningly, almost gratefully, we believe what we are told. We believe what benefits us to believe" (A. Roy 1999, 21; emphasis mine). Being a citizen means being accountable for the actions of the state and for its exercise of violence through coercion and persuasion. The concept of citizenship as used here includes an ethical responsibility toward the environment as well as toward other people.

Roy's act of writing, inspired by her experience in the Narmada Valley, responds to this call, formulating a new demand for public attention and further action. "The Greater Common Good" entails an act of reading, motivating the audience to join the protesters in the "Rally for the Valley," which was scheduled to be held a month after the publication of the essay. Roy's essay, with its provocative and dialogic style, directly interpellates a wide set of readers, ranging from people in the institutions supporting this massively destructive project to Indian and international citizens. To those who supposedly believe in the national narrative that equates progress with technological development, Roy proposes alternative perspectives and urges them to take her story into account: "Allow me to shake your faith. Put your hand in mine and let me lead you through the maze . . . don't look away. It isn't an easy tale to tell" (A. Roy 1999, 21). Here the choice of style is revealing. Roy walks with the readers through the ruins of a "developing" world and into the valley, anticipating the march she was to undertake during the mass demonstration (see chapter 6).

Writing and activism are guided by the same sense of commonality with the struggles against the domination and exploitation of the poor, and equally aim to mobilize a wider audience to support this cause. Creating a strong coalition that would transcend classes and castes was one of the main concerns and objectives of the rally. It was the transformative action to pursue. In a state of crisis the strategy of coalition building challenges the institutionally manufactured image of a common good to promote, alternatively, a shared sense of common belonging to the population of the dominated: "The whole point of the Rally for [the] Valley was to make alliances—urban-rural, writer-farmer, musician-fisherman—the idea was that we were all *citizens of the earth* making a common cause of the struggle in the Narmada Valley" (A. Roy, quoted in Bavadam 1999; emphasis mine).

Instead of "citizens of the world" or "inhabitants of the earth," Roy appeals to the "citizens of the earth" and twists the ordinary language, widening the scope and scale of the struggle in the Narmada Valley. Citizens of the earth, undivided by national boundaries, have a double responsibility to fight against abuse and discrimination and to take care of the earth as a lived and living space. But it is only through the rally that such responsibility is claimed as a right. With their bodily presence, the participants declare their entitlement to express not only their dissent against the government but also their solidarity across caste and class.[7]

Roy is among those citizens. She takes her position in the crowd of the governed and aims to inspire ethically driven political subjects to act along with the local protesters and activists. Lyla Bavadam's article "A Flood of Support," which appeared in *Frontline* on August 14, 1999, acknowledges the boost that "The Greater Common Good" and the "Rally for the Valley" campaign have given to the NBA by inspiring people to action. The journal gathered testimonies and letters affirming people's will to engage in the demonstrations after reading Roy's essay.[8] The leader of the NBA, Medha Patkar, wrote a message to the same magazine thanking the publishers and the writer for their commitment to the Narmada Valley and for helping to mobilize a wider audience: "All of us in the Narmada Valley feel obliged to Arundhati Roy and your esteemed publication for the unique essay 'The Greater Common Good.' The author's rational analysis and emotional appeal have helped us reach out to the hearts of the unaware and the unconvinced" (Patkar 1999). Patkar's comment underlines the active influence of Roy's writing, producing an emotional appeal to the readers' sense of civic duty.[9]

Although it is generally agreed that the solidarity achieved through addressing a large audience brought new life to the NBA's long struggle, it would betray the purpose and spirit of Roy's essay to depict Roy as the conscious director of the movement's policy at the turn of the millennium. Her writing supports people's grievances, stressing their claims to the right to land and to a livable life articulated in a long history of mass demonstrations.

Roy's intellectual commitment is combined with material support, but neither one nor the other is simply the product of her conscious and sovereign will. The story of the Narmada Valley reaches Arundhati Roy, who "feels compelled" to take action. Her writing meets the Adivasis, and her encounters in the valley shape the narrative style of "The Greater Common Good," which she defines as "storytelling." The people's stories "insist on being told" and the writer is commissioned to divulge them.[10] Through Roy's version of the story of the Narmada Valley, a much larger narrative is already being passed on orally, through songs and stories of collective actions.

This participative process, ignited by the people and their struggle, has to go back to them. On June 27, 1999, shortly after the publication of Roy's essay, the writer poignantly donated the income of her Booker Prize, gained two years before, to the NBA. In an interview I recorded in December 2011 with Adivasis occupying government land in an NBA action, Ratan from the village of Sugat interestingly described the boomerang effect of Roy's act, emphasizing how it concretely helped the people: "We later came to know, after some time that Arundhati visited our villages and after two months the book had come out . . . we got to know that she wrote many, many things about our life, about our submergence, about the whole thing. She filled an entire book with our story that was read by many people and that fetched a lot of money. But then we also knew about Arundhati's decision that she wouldn't use any of that money and she *gave it back* to us in the form of the boat and jeep that the Andolan has now. So the proceeds of that book came back to the Andolan and the people who are fighting" (emphasis mine). For the Andolan, the boat and the jeep are essential instruments for crossing the valley and reaching the hilly villages where Ratan and more than 150 families of oustees of Madhya Pradesh are still fighting to obtain land and hold the state to its word.

5

PRIVATIZING THE COMMONS, ORIENTALIZING ADIVASIS

In chapter 4 I highlighted the way in which Roy's essay "The Greater Common Good" challenges the nationalist narration that sees dams as icons of the modern nation. Roy's title openly questions the concept of the nation as an undifferentiated whole and asks which subjects will be forced to sacrifice their land and village life for the benefit of the rich. The answer to this question casts a dark shadow over the entire project; in the case of the Sardar Sarovar project, the main victims of the politics of relocation are Adivasis and Dalits. In Roy's words:

> A huge percentage of the displaced are Adivasis (57.6 percent in the case of the Sardar Sarovar dam). Include Dalits and the figure becomes obscene. According to the Commissioner for Scheduled Castes and Tribes it's about 60 percent. If you consider that Adivasis account for only 8 percent of India's population, it opens up a whole other dimension to the story. The ethnic otherness of their victims takes some of the pressure off the nation builders. It's like having an expense account. Someone else pays the bills. People from another country. Another world. India's poorest people are subsidizing the lifestyle of the richest. Did I hear someone say something about the world's biggest democracy? (A. Roy 1999, 19)

When millions of people from lower classes and castes are dispossessed in the name of modernization, their lives become expendable for the common good of the nation. It does not matter that studies and reports pose serious doubts on the supposed benefits to be reaped; the victims' voices do not reach a wide public and seem doomed to remain concealed.

In this chapter I look at how Roy counteracts the silence over Adivasis' suffering through narratives that reveal how India's neoliberal imperative to achieve quicker economic growth has widened the gap between rich and poor citizens. The stories of dispossession and dislocation of tribals and untouchables in the Narmada Valley stand as testimonials of the social and ecological consequences of India's race toward progress. Roy contributes to the debate over the meaning of development by collecting these accounts and echoing people's dissent. Also, she reflects on the history of the marginalization of these communities through the enforcement of colonial laws, such as the Forest Acts and the Land Acquisition Act, to which I dedicate the first sections of this chapter. Then, I read Roy's use of the concepts of the common and empire in conjunction with Hardt and Negri's studies of the emerging resistance to neoliberal globalization. In this analysis Roy does not simply appear to claim citizenship to highlight existing inequality; she plays with the language of law and with political rhetoric to give flesh to the world that marginalized subjects inhabit and to their portrayals of territorial belonging. The environmental concerns of marginalized subjects and the solidarity created across castes during civil rights struggles emerge as constructing more equitable modes of sociality and imaginaries of the future that oppose the determinism of neoliberal economy.

VIEWS AND WALLS

In their account of the early years of the protest in the Narmada Valley, Gadgil and Guha highlight that the rise of the movement was harshly counteracted by growing state repression (Gadgil and Guha 1995, 75). The violent and authoritarian repression of resistance, which included episodes of unjustified violence perpetrated by police forces against peaceful demonstrators, aimed to silence other visions of development and the voice of conservationist leaders such as Baba Amte, one of the most eminent Gandhian social workers in India's history. Despite his precarious health, Baba Amte actively joined the struggle in the Narmada Valley in 1990 (see Sangvai 2002, 158).

He was among the activists accused in media reports of being an obstacle to the economic growth of the tribal groups and even a contributor to their endemic poverty.

In this battle of worldviews, literature resonated with people's acts aimed at gaining visibility in the public sphere. The regulation of what is visible and audible has the effect of ratifying state-inflicted violence against marginalized subjects. Rallies, demonstrations, and everyday expressions of resilience inspired Roy's politically driven literary account, which helped to bring to the fore in mainstream media and politics the violence that tribal people face. As Butler (2006) observes in her work on mourning and vulnerability, public grieving can be a powerful strategy of governance when it creates interplay between the prominence of certain funeral rites and the exclusion of other subjects from the visual field. Similarly, although there was no public funeral connected to the dam construction, the celebration of the dam itself as an insignia of the state and of its promise of economic growth served to push the oustees further out of the frame.

Nehru considered dams as temples, and in recent times they have not lost their role as visible signifiers of state sovereignty. Manifesting themselves in their monstrous form, dams architecturally revive an archaic strategy of state regulation based on visibility. As Wendy Brown suggests, the massive appearance of dams replicates the intimidating character of the old walled borders (2010, 103). Dams have a theatrical function; by projecting an image of state sovereignty, they perform an ultimate resistance to the global crisis of the nation-states.

But the political function of dams is not limited to the performativity of their architecture. They also present an intimate relation with human life and its management. Although commonly regarded as enterprises destined to improve the basic living conditions for large masses, dams inevitably cause displacement and relocation. The submergence zone has been interestingly described by Trivedi (2006), who applies Agamben's idea of the "state of exception." According to this interpretation, affected people are subjected to the law that dispossesses them and, at the same time, are disconnected from their rights to counteract this process. It is in the creation of these territorial enclaves where rights are suspended, comparable to refugee camps, that modern sovereignty reveals its iron fist. Dams thus appear as biopolitical apparatuses that show how contemporary democratic states have assimilated the use of totalitarian policies. Like walls in the case of migration, they endorse power over people's lives and enact it on targeted groups of the population, supporting the "democratic-capitalist project of eliminat[ing] the poor classes through development" (Agamben 1998, 180). I use the term *apparatus* in its Foucauldian connotation to underline the conjunction of heterogeneous elements that sustain the active power of dams, ranging from architectural forms to legal and administrative measures, from scientific statements to moral propositions.

COMMON GOOD AND PRIVATE PROPERTY

In the context of the Sardar Sarovar project, the construction of the dam, with its brutal evictions and repression of resistance, is inextricable from the forcible implementation of colonial laws. I argue that the use of the Land Acquisition Act (1894) and the Forest Acts (1927–) by the postcolonial nation-state reiterates the othering of indigenous people in disputes over property and land use.

The struggle over the Sardar Sarovar project is a battle over the right to land spread over three states. In Madhya Pradesh the struggle is harsher, because the government has still not offered cultivable or irrigable land to more than 150 affected families. This right, reiterated over the years by Supreme Court judgments, was repeated as a promise by evaluating committees and was included as a fundamental principle in the action plans of the Narmada Valley Development Authority and the Narmada Control Authority, but it still exists on paper only. The Narmada Bachao Andolan (NBA) and the people who have still not been rehabilitated after fifteen years of displacement say that the authorities have conveniently forgotten them after the land acquisition. The fact that the process is justified on the grounds of "public purpose," in accordance with the Land Acquisition Act, exposes the unresolved conflict of interest implicit in this law: The state, being the ultimate judge of what is considered the common good, decides what the benefits are and who should pay the cost of the enterprise it promotes.

Roy's essay stresses how the contest over land between Adivasis and the state highlights a clash of conflicting notions—about who is included in the term *common*, the long history of which refers to imperialism.[1] In a groundbreaking work, Chhatrapati Singh (1986) shows how the confiscation of land initiated by the crown coincided with the introduction of enclosures and legislation regarding private property. As early as 1824, the British started a process of privatization of resources. In that year the Bengal Regulation

Sustainable methods of cultivation of common land. Photo taken in Jobat, Alirajpur District, Madhya Pradesh.

Kamla Yadav, prominent activist of the Narmada Bachao Andolan. She has been involved with the struggle against dams and canals for more than twenty-five years.

allowed the acquisition of land, and the amendments to this law, made in 1870 and in 1894, shaped the Land Acquisition Act, which went through significant changes only in 2013.

The language of law recognizes property as the cardinal principle regulating land use, betraying the customary rights of indigenous cultures. Moreover, the performative impact of this action disproportionately affects the Adivasi economy, which relies on the use of common lands for open pasture, shared agriculture, and other activities. The lands catalogued by the British as "waste lands" and declared property of the crown, for example, were vital grazing and firewood resources for nomadic tribes. In the first version of the Land Acquisition Act, these lands were not even differentiated from those devoted to common cultivation, which still constitutes the principal farming method among Adivasis.[2]

The usurpation of land that followed colonization dramatically impoverished the indigenous people, whose claims over their habitats had never been stated in the language of property: "In the strict sense forest dwellers have not cognized traditionally their habitat as their property, common or private, since such a legal title did not exist in their worldview. . . . The British made use of this fact of monarchical claim over land to introduce the institution of common property over which the sovereign has absolute rights" (Singh 1986, 9). Although the Land Acquisition Act deals with private property, the commons are managed through forest laws. Even these laws fail to include any protection for forest dwellers. Instead, the safeguarding of the environment is the objective to be pursued, in spite of or even against the interests of the inhabitants of these areas.

One of the revealing examples of the new logic of governance, still in use today, is the introduction of a different criminal code for punishing forest-related offenses. Singh analyzes at length how these rules construct a double standard, shaping ranks of citizens ruled by separate codes: "The gradual usurpation of common property resources by the colonizers made it necessary to have two different criminal codes, one for those living on privately owned land, and an additional but different type for those living or dependent for their livelihood on common land, such as forests" (Singh 1986, 13). Among the different criminal procedures prescribed in the Forest Acts, Section 64 is a significant example. It gives full power to forest officers to arrest anyone without a warrant if that person is deemed to be committing an offense pertaining to the forest. The power conceded to forest officers suggests the need for urgent action against possible criminal offenses and reveals the imperial anxiety over controlling Adivasi territories, which remained extremely difficult to colonize during British rule. In establishing special measures of surveillance and punishment for forest dwellers, the Forest Acts have the effect of othering indigenous populations who do not rely on the modern idea of legal property. The acts subject them to different criminal norms. Colonial law thus contributed to the production of an other, which appears backward because it does not comply with the economic and legal parameters of an instituted Western norm and is therefore potentially dangerous.

The enactment of this legal action relied on a traveling evolutionary discourse that relegated indigenous people to premodernity. Anthropological studies of tribal institutions and social organization proliferated in the Victorian age in response to and as a consequence of imperialist attempts to find allies and tame potential threats; on the other hand, they also contributed to "a part of Europeans' attempts to describe their own history and evolutionary origin" (Bates 1995b, 251). As nomadic jungle dwellers, Adivasis were perceived not only as difficult to manage but also as representatives of a state of nature. In accordance with a view that gained momentum after John Locke's *Second Treatise of Civil Government* (1690), in which the title to property is said to originate from human labor applied to a specific piece of land, the absence of private property in indigenous societies was regarded as evidence of their lack of social maturity. One of the most influential Victorian accounts of colonial India, Sir Henry Maine's *Ancient Law* (1861), relates the roots of liberty, freedom, and social progress to the establishment of private property rights, which are a key element to ending feudalism (see Bates 1995b, 252).

The foreignness to Adivasis of such a logic, which was instituted as the only path to progress and modernity, lies at the heart of a process of othering. Bates describes this mechanism of othering created by evolutionist texts as the "principal function of 'orientalist' writing of this period, orientalism being a mode of reasoning and a means of situating contemporary understanding of British and more broadly Western society in a global historical and evolutionary context" (Bates 1995b, 251). Although I agree with Bates's claim that orientalism informs this kind of colonial writing, I want to stress that its outcomes exceed the domain of representation and that it forms part of the basic assumptions underpinning British legal and economic actions. The orientalization of Adivasis takes place at the conjunction of anthropological accounts and law, which misrepresented them as backward and, in cases like the Criminal Tribes Act (1871), criminalized them (see chapter 1).[3]

Both culturally instituted discrimination and inflicted poverty stem from British land policies and still afflict forest dwellers. Singh summarizes the situation with a lapidary statement: "The forest dwellers of India became poor in the first place because the British destroyed their claims to customary occupancy rights and took away their resources, and because the Indian state has continued to do so" (Singh 1986, 46). In the independent nation, questions of occupancy rights have been pushed aside, and the state is the prime owner of the land. British laws such as the Land Acquisition Act, though, remain in use, and the reality of expropriation is still all too familiar to many Adivasis who have lost their land to massive infrastructure projects.

DEVELOPMENT AS "CAPITALOCENTRIC ORIENTALISM"

The evolutionary logic of progress rooted in colonial ideology informs the contemporary economic framework of development, which underpins the thinking behind displacement plans. Equating modernity and industrialization creates a linear representation of the ladder of progress, where the West occupies the higher level. The consequential hegemonic depiction of Southern, indigenous, and marginal economies as backward or lacking the fundamental premises leading to a fully developed economic market has been called capitalocentric orientalism by Chakrabarti and Dhar (2010). In their book *Dislocation and Resettlement in Development* they take a Marxist perspective on the primitive accumulation of common resources as the basis of capitalist economies. They claim that the establishment of private property as the rationale for acknowledging the modernity of economic structures actually marginalizes alternative systems and institutes a form of orientalism.

By virtue of their incorporation into developmental schemes, Adivasis are the targets of both aggressive land acquisition and benevolent activities aimed at managing poverty. Their subjectivity, though, remains effaced from the realm of sociopolitical production: "The 'Adivasis' appear everywhere in the development register, in the thousand models drawn up in their name, but they are only present as a lacking other, as lifeless figures of pathology out of sync with the modern capitalist economy that the discourse of development has established as the norm(al)" (Chakrabarti and Dhar 2010, 44). The stigmatization of this economic backwardness relies on a previously instituted inferiorization that operates within "the political-cultural matrix of

Indian society" (33). Economic and social aspects of Adivasi life are rewritten into contemporary orientalist narratives of development, which are rooted in colonialist norms on land use.

In the case of the Narmada Valley project, the conjunction between the colonial background and a neoliberal economic regime reveals its harshness. The identification of the land to be sacrificed for the Sardar Sarovar project, the loss of the commons, and the neglect of the affected rural dwellers during the relocation are all crucial issues. With regard to these, the enforcement of colonial laws, as highlighted earlier, plays an important role. Often Adivasis do not hold any certificate of ownership of the land where they have lived for generations and cannot claim any legal right over the acquired lands, or over the commons.[4] The scarcity or complete lack of governmental land surveys in remote areas, where registers have not been updated for more than twenty-five years, effectively excludes some of the oustees from the action plans dedicated to relocation and rehabilitation.

In her essay Roy protests passionately that the logic of displacement causes the "disappearance" of millions of citizens: "The millions of displaced people don't exist anymore. When history is written they won't be in it. Not even as statistics. Some of them have subsequently been displaced three and four times—a dam, an artillery proof range, another dam, a uranium mine, a power project" (A. Roy 1999, 20). Property and land ownership are among the essential values inscribed in modern citizenship and constitute the requirements of modernity that indigenous people implicitly defy. The price for this is the disappearance from the national imagination. In a similar vein, Rob Nixon labels the crowds of the displaced "unimagined communities," written out of history and the national imagination (Nixon 2011, 150).

Whereas Guha uses the label "ecological refugees" to refer to the people who had to be relocated as a consequence of environmental policies, Nixon highlights how the dam in the Narmada Valley created a paradoxical figure that is best described as the "developmental refugee" (Nixon 2011, 152). The project of modernizing the nation through big infrastructure projects is sustained by the rhetoric of development. But instead of uplifting the living conditions of the poor, the construction of the Sardar Sarovar Dam, the submergence of the Narmada Valley, and the subsequent displacement caused by the creation of canals subject people to the "slow violence" of capitalism. As Nixon explains, slow violence is "a violence that occurs gradually and out of sight, a violence of delayed destruction that is dispersed across time and space, an attritional violence that is typically not viewed as violence at all" (2). This form of violence falls out of sight, because it is perpetrated in rural areas at the expense of peripheral subjects and does not have immediate or spectacular consequences.[5]

Roy's writing exposes the "imaginative displacement" of local communities "from the idea of the developing nation-state" (Nixon 2011, 150) and denounces the estrangement of indigenous people through the language of law and official documents. The framework of legality (on which citizens ought to be able to rely to obtain justice) does not seem to guarantee any help to the oustees. On the contrary, by instituting an imposed foreign language on the customary management of land, the law creates a yoke of violence on Adivasis deprived of their livelihood. Roy reflects: "The Fifth Schedule of the Constitution provides protection to Adivasi people and disallows the alienation of their land. But it doesn't seem to matter at all. It looks as though the clause is there only to make the constitution look good—a bit of window-dressing, a slash of make-up. Scores of corporations, from relatively unknown ones to the biggest mining companies and steel manufacturers in the world, are in the fray to appropriate Adivasi homelands—the Mittals, Jindals, Tata, Essar, Posco, Rio Tinto, BHP Billion, and, of course, Vedanta" (A. Roy 2011, 25). The principle of equality and the promise of protection of indigenous minorities written into the constitution do not offer tribal subjects adequate weapons to resist displacement. Roy explicitly points to the depredation of tribal land as one of the ways in which a neoliberal war against the poor takes place: "An undeclared civil war is being waged on its citizens in the name of 'development'" (A. Roy 2005, 169). This war, fought in the name of growth, implies a redefinition of national inclusion and of the image of citizenship.

EMPIRE, MULTITUDE, AND THE COMMON

Reflecting on the rising sectarian violence that has troubled the subcontinent since the pogrom against Muslims in Gujarat in 2002, Roy considers that "the questioning of who is an Indian citizen, and who is not" has become a common practice in political discourses (Arundhati Roy 2005, 79). The author does not refer just to the existing tension between religious minorities; as she demonstrates in *Broken Republic* (A. Roy 2011), she is particularly interested in the analysis of the conditions of exploitation of untouchables and tribals after liberalization.

In the much debated essay "Walking with the Comrades," written over three weeks while Roy lived in the jungle with a Naxalite guerrilla group, the writer challenges the government's description of these Maoists combatants as a threat to national security. The violent rulers of forests are "desperately poor tribal people living in conditions of chronic hunger" (A. Roy 2011, 7). She adds, "They are people who, even after sixty years of India's so-called Independence, have not had access to education, health care or legal redress. They are people who have been mercilessly exploited for decades, consistently cheated by small businessmen and moneylenders, the women raped as a matter of right by police and forest department personnel" (7). Roy is aware of the historical factors that, during and after colonialism, contributed to keeping Adivasis and untouchables in a state of indigent poverty. In "The Greater Common Good" (1999) Roy had already pointed out that the exclusion of tribal voices from the mediascape takes place hand in hand with the displacement from ancestral land, the abuse of their labor force, and the institution of a regime of terror in rural villages, where the police carry out theft and rape.

A look at India's rural villages shows the complex situation of a country stranded between two empires: "India is still struggling with the legacy of the Empire. But something new looms on the horizon. It has to do with boring things like water supply, electricity, irrigation. But it also has to do with a process of barbaric dispossession on a scale that has few parallels in history. You may have guessed by now that I'm talking about the modern vision of corporate globalization" (A. Roy 2002, 71). The exploitation of the poor takes place through the revival of the norms of an old colonial system while something new also appears on the horizon. In the liberalized country, the state, supernational organizations, and multinational corporations all profit from the dispossession of Adivasis and lower castes and the exploitation of their labor. Mining sites paradigmatically present contemporary social conflicts. For example, the state of Chhattisgarh, with a predominant indigenous population, has seen a sharp rise in local struggles against companies such as those in Jindal and Balco as a response to public admonitions of evictions and the rampant exploitation of cheap labor in the area. By emphasizing the way in which the neoliberal economy is reshaping Indian society and its underclasses, Roy affirms that a war is being fought against some of India's poorest citizens for the benefit of what she calls the modern empire.

In *An Ordinary Person's Guide to the Empire* (2005), Roy embraces the equation between corporate neoliberalism and new imperialism. The dispossession of land, undertaken in favor of the construction of new plants or for mining activities, and the changes in the job market are two sides of the same coin. National policies related to land acquisition are strategically enforced to support and accommodate the needs of multinational companies, whereas the power of negotiation of citizens and workers in the global sphere has been dramatically reduced. Roy calls empire the joint exercise of the power of capitalism and national governments that helps to subsidize the lifestyle of the rich: "While the project of corporate globalization rips through people's lives in India, massive privatization and labour 'reforms' are pushing people off their land and out of their jobs" (A. Roy 2002, 177). Roy is disturbed by how the rhetoric of greater freedom for all that accompanies global and technological development masks the progressive impoverishment of entitlements and rights enjoyed de facto by the poorest citizens.

Roy's references to concepts such as empire and the common resonate closely with the language and ideas of Michael Hardt and Antonio Negri's trilogy *Empire*, *Multitude*, and *Commonwealth*. In turn, Hardt and Negri paid attention to the protests in the Narmada Valley, in which Roy was involved, and pointed out that the activists' grievances against environmental degradation, impoverishment of the population, and lack of responsiveness on the part of the government emblematically highlighted the state crisis of representative democracy (Hardt and Negri 2006, 283). There is an implicit synergy between the works of Roy and Hardt and Negri, because they express a similar dissatisfaction with the actualization of the idea of democracy in a neoliberal world. Roy summarizes her skeptical view of democracy as the government guaranteeing equal participation to all the people by saying, "Democracy has become Empire's euphemism for neoliberal capitalism" (Arundhati Roy 2005, 155).

To better understand Roy's statement, it is useful to look at Hardt and Negri's conception of capitalist power. In their first book, *Empire*, the authors analyze the segmented and complex composition of global power, which is deterritorialized and does not act within the traditionally bounded jurisdiction of the nation-state. Hardt and Negri summarize the studies of Saskia Sassen and other eminent scholars on the relation between the globalized market and state powers by saying that there is no opposition between them: "The global is in the national as much as the national is in the global" (Hardt and Negri 2000, 224). The power of the empire is all-encompassing and capillary; it is enacted through the control of the media as much as through the strategic deployment of old national armies.

Hardt and Negri provide a picture of the distribution of power as a "pyramid of global constitution" (Hardt and Negri 2000, 309). In the first tier and on the narrow pinnacle of this pyramid, the authors place the power of the United States, followed by the group of nation-states that control global monetary instruments. Networks of transnational corporations occupy the second tier together with the sovereign nation-states, which act locally to "capture and distribute the flow of wealth to and from the global capital, and they discipline their own populations as much as this is still possible" (310). The third tier is composed of the groups and organizations that represent, and filter, popular interests, including the media and religious institutions. Hardt and Negri's pyramid depicts empire as the political order of globalization constituted by the coalition of corporate interests with the actions of state governments and supernational entities, such as the World Bank. Topography does not define the location of the empire, because its range of action is planetary. It has power over life and death, rules over forms of sociality, and decides on the management of the environment.

Reading Hardt and Negri's definition of empire as a totalizing global power, one immediately wonders if the sort of resistance encouraged by Roy and performed by groups such as the NBA is meaningful or useful. Responding to this question, in his review of *Empire*, Balakrishnan highlights that Hardt and Negri believe in the vulnerability of the empire to riots and rebellions. Not only can the empire be attacked by collective forms of resistance struggles, but also its "existence stands as a resounding, if paradoxical, testimony to the heroic mass struggles that shattered the Eurocentric old regime of national states and colonialism" (Balakrishnan 2000, 144). Empire is, in fact, a configuration of power that emerged out of the change in world order that followed decolonization.

As the old colonial powers, the new global empire is targeted by several forms of opposition. In the second book of their trilogy, *Multitude*, Hardt and Negri expand their discussion on the collective subject of resistance: the multitude. *Multitude* contains a list of instances and examples of how organizations of people that are excluded from the dominant political and economic elites have challenged the empire. In an imaginary map of resistance, the work of the NBA in the Narmada Valley stands side by side with the famous popular rebellion that took place in Cochabamba, Bolivia, against the privatization of water. These two cases, fought on different continents for the same principle of universal access to natural resources, demonstrate that Hardt and Negri direct their attention to the heterogeneous threats posed to capitalist consumption by the poor and by environmental and social activists: "The multitude of the poor emerges at the center of the project for revolutionary transformation" (Hardt and Negri 2009, 55); and then, "The multitude is many-headed hydra that threatens property and order" (44). Its demands are explicitly aimed at ensuring that resources, such as water and gas, will not be privatized; in this sense, the multitude "runs counter to the republic of property" (127).

The multitude creates spaces for social and creative encounters that generate new and multiple visions of the future, challenging capitalist relations and modes of production. The third book of Hardt and Negri's trilogy, *Commonwealth*, explores how the poor can organize themselves and break free from the control of the capital. For Hardt and Negri the reason that Cochabamba and partly the Narmada Valley symbolize an important victory against the empire is because they demonstrate that it is possible to hold onto a vision of the future that opposes the social and economic exclusion created by the "republic of property" (see Hardt and Negri 2009, 107).[6]

In Roy's *Broken Republic* the principle of property figures strongly as one of the reasons for the failure of democratic India to integrate its peripheral citizens. Like Hardt and Negri, Roy points to the reenactment, on a global scale, of the process of primitive accumulation that was initially enforced through colonialism. Roy also believes that resisting this process is not just possible but imperative.

The alternative to the subjection to neoliberal capital lies in the construction of collective struggles that promote forms of ecological and social care that resignify productivity and profit: "A democracy of the multitude is imaginable and possible only because we all share and participate in the common. By 'the common' we mean, first of all, the common wealth of the material world—the air, the water, the fruits of the soil, and all the nature's bounty—which in classical European political texts is often claimed to be the inheritance of humanity as a whole, to be shared together . . . [but also] practices of interaction, care and cohabitation in a common world" (Hardt and Negri 2009, viii). The production of the common takes place within both socioeconomic and ecological frameworks. Environmental struggles, feminist struggles, fights for civil rights, and fights against precariousness are modes of producing the common that contribute to the creation of new global imaginaries and modes of sociality.

CONCLUSION: THE NEED FOR IMAGINATION

When Roy wrote "The End of Imagination," the essay was a response to the nuclear tests carried out by the Indian government in 1998. The revival of the discourse on nuclear proliferation sustained the construction of a masculine image of India as a thriving global power, pushing for growth and modernization. The price for this growth, though, is the annihilation of divergent visions of the future; this is what Roy calls "the end of imagination."

This essay, written in 1998 and reprinted in Roy's *Cost of Living* (1999), has a particularly pessimistic tone that reflects the gravity of the historical moment when tension escalated between India and Pakistan following a renewed interest in nuclear power. Roy's subsequent essays, though, assert more faith in the rising global resistance to nuclear plants, mass displacement, and military actions against tribals, including Operation Green Hunt. In *Public Power in the Age of Empire* (2004), Roy sees the power of imagination as an effective political tool. She affirms that imagination is the instrument used by resistance movements, activists, and public intellectuals to counteract the rhetoric of development. The translation of abstract concepts, such as prospective growth, into the lived experiences of exploitation and loss of the most vulnerable groups of India's population has been a powerful means to strip empire of its benevolent mask: "Mass resistance movements, individual activists journalists, artists and film makers have come together to strip Empire of its sheen. They have connected the dots, turned cash-flow charts and boardroom speeches into real stories about real people and real despair. They have shown how the neoliberal project has cost people their homes, their land, their jobs, their liberty, their dignity" (A. Roy 2004, 29). It is crucial that activists and intellectuals translate flowcharts into real stories, because it is even harder for people to lose their homes "to an invisible force. To someone or something you can't see. You can't hate. You can't even imagine" (Arundhati Roy 2005, 191). This work of imagination concretely supports the activities of people fighting unjust dispossessions and impoverishment. In this light, Roy's literature becomes an important instrument of survival. It helps people articulate their resistance and denounce the rise of poverty that characterizes neoliberal globalization. It voices people's dissent against the continuing privatization of common resources.

Hardt and Negri describe empire as being constantly under attack and trying to subsume emerging forms of resistance. The objective of localized and heterogeneous battles against economic, environmental, and patriarchal exploitation is "to isolate the Empire's working parts and disable them one by one. No victory is too small" (Hardt and Negri 2009, 167). These words, which sound like a heartfelt appeal to continue assaulting empire in different places and in different ways, surprisingly seem to echo Roy's final lines of "The Greater Common Good." In the final paragraph of her essay, Roy urges readers to recognize and "unscramble" the logic predicated by neoliberal capitalists: "They scramble the intelligence that connects eggs to hens, milk to cows, food to forests, water to rivers, air to life and the earth to human existence. Can we unscramble it? Maybe. Inch by inch. Bomb by bomb. Dam by dam. Maybe by fighting specific wars in specific ways" (A. Roy 1999, 81). Roy and Hardt and Negri emphasize that resisting empire is possible through fighting wars at specific times and in specific places and that every struggle, not only every victory, is significant.

Every time a collective cause triggers the mobilization of thousands or millions of people, as happened in the Narmada Valley, a new form of imagination is born and thrives to affirm itself. As Roy admits in *Broken Republic*:

> The first step towards reimagining a world gone terribly wrong would be to stop the annihilation of those who have a different imagination—an imagination that is outside of capitalism as well as Communism. An imagination which has an altogether different understanding of what constitutes happiness and fulfillment. To gain this philosophical space, it is necessary to concede some physical space for the survival of those who may look like the keepers of our past but who may really be the guides to our future. To do this, *we have to ask our rulers: Can you leave the water in the rivers, the trees in the forest? Can you leave the bauxite in the mountains? If they say they cannot then perhaps they should stop preaching morality to the victims of their wars.* (A. Roy 2011, 214; emphasis mine)

The survival of Adivasis and untouchables is under threat, and yet their ways of living, at the edges of neoliberal capitalism, trigger the imagination of a future without systemic natural and human exploitation. The long Indian history of active revolts and civil disobedience, from the mutiny against the

Raj to Gandhi's Salt March, inspires faith in the solid power of a dissenting public. If India's best export is, as Roy powerfully affirms, the "globalization of dissent" (A. Roy 2002, 191), it is the Indian poor who stand as the crucial agent of the opposition against empire. The struggle in the Narmada Valley and in the Indian jungles has reclaimed the legitimacy of imagining the right to commonly enjoy water, communal land, and other resources. The struggle has affirmed the legitimacy of imagining and enacting dissent.

6

STORYTELLING AND THE METAMORPHOSIS OF LITERATURE

In the previous two chapters I have explored the sociopolitical context in which Roy wrote "The Greater Common Good," the essay published only one year after she won the Booker Prize for her novel *The God of Small Things*. In this chapter I argue that, despite the fact that these texts are often looked at separately, because they belong to different genres, they are closely related in their expressed commitment to environmental and social justice. They deal with life in remote rural settings, reveal environmental concerns following the liberalization of India, and denounce the deadly consequences of caste and class discrimination. *The God of Small Things* is set in Aymanam in Kerala, where Ammu lives with her twins Rahel and Estha. Because of the violence inflicted on her by her drunkard husband, Ammu returns to her parents' house, where she becomes the victim of her relatives' vexations. She finds relief from the bitterness of life in the relationship with Velutha, a Dalit and a communist. Their scandalous intercaste love will be the reason for the man's brutal murder, a supreme punishment for having "made the unthinkable thinkable and the impossible really happen" (A. Roy 1997, 256).

The last chapter of the novel is a flashback of the love scene that constitutes the scandal of the book; interestingly, it is titled "The Cost of Living," as is the collection of essays in which "The Greater Common Good" was published. The chapter opens with the image of Ammu alone in the house turning on the radio and hearing "Ruby Tuesday" by the Rolling Stones. The lyrics of the song remind her that there is no time left to lose and that she has to pursue happiness in such an unkind life. The chapter continuously emphasizes the conflict between the character's urge for an act of love and the lack of time. The narrator notes, "They looked at each other. They weren't thinking anymore. The time for that had come and gone" (A. Roy 1997, 334). The English song prophetically introduces the idea that Ammu's freedom is a threat to the established order of things, for its lyrics recite, "She just can't be chained / To a life where nothing is gained / And nothing is lost / At such a cost." But there will be a dear price to pay for their pleasure, because the sex scene makes "the cost of living climb to unaffordable heights" (336).

In Roy's narrative the need for love is comparable only with the urgency of social anger. Ammu, filled with rage against her unjust life, falls in love with Velutha's hidden anger: "Under his careful cloak of cheerfulness, he housed a living, breathing anger against the smug, ordered world that she so raged against" (A. Roy 1997, 176). Their sexual encounter thus becomes an act of social and political transgression whose time to perform has finally come.[1] Similarly stressing the importance of expressing the urgency of anger, Roy considers her literary activism an act of protest against inequality and dispossession. In "The Greater Common Good," the writer's anger at injustice appears as an urge to write.

In the following sections I explore the relationship between Roy's novel and essays, considering storytelling as an inspiration and a method for all her acts of writing. Without denying the difference between writing genres, I look at how the aesthetics of storytelling influenced Roy's language and how the embodied act of narrating social protests shaped the prose of "The Greater Common Good."

"THE STORYTELLER IS ROOTED IN THE PEOPLE"

Julie Mullaney highlights that the structure of *The God of Small Things*—with its characteristic open ending, blurred gender identities, and codified images and tropes defining the characters and their roles—is influenced by a specific art of storytelling that is rooted in the dance form of Kathakali (see Mullaney 2002, 56). In a topical scene of the novel, the twins assist with a Kathakali performance. The description of the performance becomes the occasion for Roy to reflect on which stories should be told and how.

> Kathakali discovered long ago that the secret of the Great Stories is that they *have* no secrets. The Great Stories are the ones you have heard and want to hear again. The ones you can enter anywhere and inhabit comfortably. They don't deceive you with thrills and trick endings. They don't surprise you with the unforeseen. They are as familiar as the house you live in. Or the smell of your lover's skin. You know how they end, yet you listen as though you don't. In the way that although you know that one day you will die, you live as though you won't. In the Great Stories you know who lives, who dies, who finds love, who doesn't. And yet you want to know again. *That* is their mystery and their magic. (A. Roy 1997, 229)

The God of Small Things ends with a flashback. This scene of love that closes the book reminds us of the future death of Velutha, an episode that has already been disclosed. As in a Kathakali story, the reader is aware that the promise of happiness, inherent in the romance of Ammu and Velutha, will be broken by a succession of tragic events, but the narrative remains gripping.

Several commentators have highlighted the importance of Kathakali as a source of inspiration and a formal model for the novel. Deepika Bahri notes that the discussion of the dance form contained in Roy's text exposes two contrasting affects. On the one hand, Roy celebrates the great stories told; on the other, she mourns the death of the figure of the storyteller in a way that is reminiscent of Walter Benjamin and his writing on Nikolai Leskov.

In "The Storyteller" Benjamin maintains that the rise of the novel coincides with the decline of storytelling (Benjamin 1970). Novels represent bourgeois ideals, including individualism, whereas storytelling is nourished by shared experiences and requires collective performances. Yet, instead of a neat opposition, Benjamin draws the continuity between novels and oral performances, maintaining that the novel is born out of the epic's womb. Referring to the Kathakali scene in *The God of Small Things*, Alex Tickell notes that the performances of the *Mahabharata* reveal this continuity, because "in her fiction, Roy goes beyond a simple relationship of stylistic inheritance or remaking and maintains the oral past of the novel as an enclosed epic sub-drama (the epic as the ancestral past of the novel)" (Tickell 2007, 157). *The God of Small Things* encompasses the dimensions of storytelling and epics, with its celebrations of local heroes and unofficial pantheons of gods, and shows the interrelation between these genres.

Roy's incorporation of scenes and techniques of storytelling has been noted particularly in relation to her fiction writing, but little attention has been paid to how oral styles and forms permeate her essays, such as "The Greater Common Good" or "The End of Imagination." On the contrary, I argue that Roy's nonfiction works often expose the permeability of the border between storytelling, oral history, and the contemporary novel. Sometimes they explicitly debate the issue of literary genres and their function; other times they present a prose that recalls the conventions of oral language.

The lack of interest in the influence of storytelling on Roy's nonfiction writing can be seen, in part, as the result of the relative scarcity of critical works focusing on the writer's political writing. Only one collection of essays, edited by Ranjan Ghosh and Antonia Navarro-Tejero (2009), has so far been dedicated to Roy's nonfiction, whereas her award-winning novel has been the subject of numerous analytical studies. But also, Roy's nonfiction has often been looked at separately from her literary masterpiece, even though the writer herself has questioned the way in which critics have received "The Greater Common Good" as a desertion of fiction writing:[2] "Now, I've been wondering why it should be that the person who wrote *The God of Small Things* is called a writer, and the person who wrote the political essays is called an activist? True, *The God of Small Things* is a work of fiction, but it's no less political than any of my essays. True the essays are works of non-fiction, but since when did writers forgo the right to write non-fiction?" (A. Roy 2002, 196). The exercise of splitting one's identity into a political side and a nonpolitical side has the effect of creating fictitious and compartmentalized areas of competence.

Following on from Roy, Upamanyu Pablo Mukherjee resists Aijaz Ahmad's claim that *The God of Small Things* sacrifices historicopolitical analyses in favor of privatizing love and pleasure (Ahmad 1992, 104); he argues that the novel should be read in light of Roy's more explicit activist essays (U. P. Mukherjee 2010, 82–83).[3] Mukherjee's study shows that the story can be read, not as a "tale of tragic cross-caste romance and loss of childhood innocence" (103) but as a tale of dispossession. The institutional marginalization of Velutha is related to the unequal distribution of resources that survived colonialism and remained part of the national history.

In a parallel move to Mukherjee's, I claim that the element of storytelling is as significant for the writing of the novel as for the aesthetics of Roy's essays. Roy's arguments about the task of public intellectuals and the traces of her metanarrative reflections, scattered in several works, shed light on the specificity of her writing process and the continuity between fiction and nonfiction texts. For example, in one of her most powerful talks, "Come September," Roy describes her motivation for writing, referring to the importance of telling people's stories: "Stories reveal themselves to us. The public narrative, the private narrative—they colonize us. They commission us. They insist on being told. Fiction and nonfiction are only different techniques of story telling. For reasons that I don't fully understand, fiction dances out of me, and nonfiction is wrenched out by the aching, broken world I wake up to every morning" (Arundhati Roy 2005, 11). Without emphasizing the will of the writer as a public intellectual, Roy describes a process of interpellation through which people's stories call for being shared. Writing allows private narratives to become public testimonies of exemplary experiences. The tragic lives of Velutha and Ammu and the dramatic stories of dispossessed Adivasis in the Narmada Valley epitomize the everyday suffering and broken dreams of discriminated people. Even though the processes that underscore the creation of fiction and nonfiction writing are different, storytelling becomes a platform to share human experiences in both cases. Storytelling both participates in the literary invention and blurs the boundaries between writing genres.

For Roy, as much as for Benjamin, the idea of communicating personal and collective experience is fundamental to the act of storytelling. When Benjamin laments the disappearance of storytelling, he comments, "One reason for this phenomenon is obvious: experience has fallen in value" (Benjamin 1970, 83). Then he reflects, "All great storytellers have in common the freedom with which they move up and down the rungs of their experience as on a ladder. A ladder extending downward to the interior of the earth and disappearing into the clouds is the image for a collective experience to which even the deepest shock of every individual experience, death, constitutes no impediment or barrier" (100–101). The image of the ladder, connecting different dimensions, introduces the idea that stories can be the material fabric connecting the lived experience of an individual to a collective memory. The philosopher highlights that when one listens to storytelling, a sense of human commonality emerges and becomes the basis for a feeling of companionship, which is opposed to the isolation imposed by reading. As Benjamin reminds us, "A great storyteller will always be rooted in the people, primarily in a milieu of craftsmen" (100).

In chapters 4 and 5 I showed how, in "The Greater Common Good," Roy collects and collates the stories of the indigenous people she met on her travels across the Narmada Valley. When Roy writes about their experiences of loss and struggle, she considers her encounters with the characters of her stories as the roots of her act of storytelling. In her narratives the memories of a single person highlight the conditions of the poor's discrimination and dispossession shared across the nation. In doing so, Roy transforms individual instances in exemplary cases and exposes the permeable border between reality and fiction.

In introducing the aims of "The Greater Common Good," Roy exhorts her audience to support the specific causes of small heroes and to resist the violence imposed on marginalized castes and classes: "We have to support our small heroes. (Of these we have many. Many.) We have to fight specific wars in specific ways. Who knows, perhaps that's what the twenty-first century has in store for us. The dismantling of the Big. Big bombs, big dams, big ideologies, big contradictions, big wars, big heroes, big mistakes. Perhaps it will be the century of the Small. Perhaps right now, this very minute, there's a small god up in heaven readying herself for us. Could it be? Could it *possibly* be? It sounds finger-licking good to me" (A. Roy 1999, 12). Using her famous image of small gods, Roy suggests that the suffering and actions of the people fighting against big dams directly remind us of the character of Velutha. The author appeals to a "we," to a community of readers able to share her joy in the perspective that small gods and goddesses, forgotten during nationalism, could be the heroes of the twenty-first century.

As is clear in this fragment, the aesthetics of Roy's nonfiction writing make ample use of a direct style of communication that includes exhortations and questions. Roy juxtaposes descriptive sections with technical content, including explanations of statistics and official reports on dams and irrigation. The narration uses a writing style that creates a performance of orality. The style of speech directly calls on the audience and establishes a fictional synchronic dimension approximating the writer to the reader.

In her analysis of Roy's role in the Narmada contest, Jane Chapman suggests that the successful reception of Roy's essay was due precisely to its fiction of orality (Chapman 2007). "The Greater Common Good" consecrated Roy as the symbol of the Narmada Bachao Andolan (NBA) in the international public sphere because it circulated through widely published magazines. As a piece of journalism, it deployed a remarkably personal style:

"Roy's skills as a fictional author have enabled her to produce a reflexive, personalized style of journalistic writing which invites the reader to share her process of discovery: an approach that encourages support for activism" (Chapman 2007, 21). Persuaded that the story encouraged more activism, Chapman implicitly suggests that a simple division between fiction and nonfiction fails to give an account of Roy's successful, hybrid style.

As opposed to Chapman, who analyzes Roy's work as reflexive journalism, I look at Roy's nonfiction as a strategy of storytelling carried out through a journalistic platform. Even when her writing is clearly political, Roy does not affirm that she will "uncover" the only existing truth or give a factual account of what is happening in the Narmada Valley.[4] Rather, she endorses an idea of narrative as storytelling, the aim of which is to multiply available views of the world. As Roy affirms elsewhere, "There can never be a single story. There are only ways of seeing. So when I tell a story, I tell it not as an ideologue who wants to pit one absolutist ideology against another, but as a story-teller who wants to share her way of seeing" (Arundhati Roy 2005, 14). By sharing the stories of the poor, Roy counteracts the hegemonic narrative of news reports and political discourses, which are drenched in nationalist ideology. By paying attention to her acts of divulging stories, I emphasize the close relation between Roy's fiction and activist prose.

SPEECH ACTS

In her mission of narrating multiple visions of the world, Roy emerges as a "word warrior," to borrow the label created for her by Naomi Klein (2004, vi). The language crafted in "The Greater Common Good" and in more recent essays conveys the urgency of the political messages they carry: Local and sustainable development is to be supported against the master narrative of industrialization. Roy denounces the way in which capitalist ideology and consumerism have appropriated language at the expense of those who do not benefit from rampant privatization and financialization of capital.

> Today, words like "progress" and "development" have become interchangeable with economic "reforms," deregulation and privatization. "Freedom" has come to mean "choice." It has less to do with the human spirit than with different brands of deodorant. "Market" no longer means a place where you go to buy provisions. The market is a deterritorialized space where faceless corporations do

> business, including buying and selling "futures." "Justice" has come to mean "human rights" (and of those, as they say, "a few will do"). This theft of language, this technique of usurping the words and deploying them like weapons, of using them to mask intent and to mean exactly the opposite of what they have traditionally meant, has been one of the most strategic victories of the Tsars of the new dispensation. (A. Roy 2009, xiv)

With the tools available to a literary writer, Roy engages in a war of words. The sensibility of the writer toward the transformative power of language leads her to point a finger at the negative effects of the rhetoric of development promoted by the state.

In "The Greater Common Good" Roy maintains that the linear narrative of progress, on which the idea of development relies, posits Adivasis as expendable subjects (see chapter 4). The title of the essay is clearly sarcastic, questioning what it means to pursue the good of a whole nation. The main point that Roy makes is that the language of national interest, like the language of global markets or human rights, has colonized people's minds, inhibiting their ability to imagine a world devoid of the structures of state power. Even though the voices cheering for the rise of "India Shining" are clearly heard, the tragedy of the displaced and landless tribals remains unspoken or unaccounted for in the public domain: "The millions of displaced people in India are nothing but refugees of an unacknowledged war. And we, like the citizens of white America and French Canada and Hitler's Germany, are condoning it by looking away. Why? Because we're told that it's being done for the sake of 'The Greater Common Good.' That's being done in the name of the Progress, in the name of the National Interest. Therefore gladly, unquestioningly, almost gratefully, we believe what we are told. We believe what benefits us to believe" (A. Roy 1999, 21). In the war of words, Roy states that silences have a crucial function: The tribals' demands for land rehabilitation remain unanswered, and the violent policies against them go unacknowledged. Once marginalized in public discourses, these people's disputes also disappear from the public consciousness. If silences are a strategy of government aimed at averting other citizens' gaze, Roy's essays are a manifesto against the theft of language carried out by nationalism and capitalism.

As Mukherjee highlights, in *The Algebra of Infinite Justice* Roy notes that there is no language in which one successfully connects the several spaces and times of contemporary India (U. P. Mukherjee 2010, 88). There is no language to describe India as a whole because of its linguistic and cultural diversity. But also, there is no language that does not retain the mainstream meanings imposed by global politics, so the task of the writer is to create one. The performative power of Roy's acts of writing accomplishes at least three effects. First, it denounces the ideologies hidden in political discourses and silences. Second, it resignifies that language, deploying it in new and creative ways. And third, it exhorts people to concretely join the struggles of activists in rural and urban India. The objective to incite a general public to get involved in the struggle in the Narmada Valley overdetermines the language that Roy uses and her interpellation of the reader: "Allow me to shake your faith. Put your hand in mine and let me lead you through the maze. Do this, because it is important to understand. If you find reason to disagree, by all means take the other side. But please don't ignore it, don't look away. It isn't an easy tale to tell. It's full of numbers and explanations. Numbers used to make my eyes glaze over. Not anymore. Not since I began to follow the direction in which they point. Trust me. There's a story here" (A. Roy 1999, 21). Before starting to tell a story of the Narmada Valley, Roy appeals to the audience. As a "storyteller in the age of globalization" (Bahri 2003, 200), she tries to gather a public scattered around the world by explicitly producing a synchronous form of communication. Roy uses language made up of incitements, advice, direct questions, and appeals. In her texts she wisely uses the performative quality of speech acts.

Speech acts were first theorized by John L. Austin in his series of William James Lectures held at Harvard University in 1955, published as *How to Do Things with Words* in 1962. In this work, Austin distinguishes between three different functions of language: locutionary, illocutionary, and perlocutionary. To summarize his argument, a locutionary act consists in the use of language for the production of meaning; it "is roughly equivalent to uttering a certain sentence with a certain sense and reference, which again is roughly equivalent to 'meaning' in the traditional sense" (Austin 1975, 108). Illocutionary acts, instead, have to do with the force of the utterance, what it does, and how it performs a convention (100–101). These include actions "such as informing, ordering, warning, undertaking, etc., i.e. utterances which have a certain (conventional) force" (108). Finally, Austin calls perlocutionary acts the ones that produce an effect on the interlocutor (101).[5] These are "what we bring about or achieve by saying something, such as convincing, persuading, deterring, and even, say, surprising or misleading" (108).

Among the illocutionary verbs, which are widely used by Roy, Austin distinguishes five classes: verdictives, which are exercises of judgment (Austin 1975, 152); exercitives or imperatives, which are exercises of power (154); commissives, which are acts of promising (156); behavitives, which perform rites of social ritual and politeness (159); and expositives, which carry out exposition and argumentation (161). Thinking about the illocutionary quality of language is helpful for understanding how the force of language can have an effect on the addressee and what kind of language appears in activist writings and why.

In "The Greater Common Good" Roy consistently uses explicit performatives uttered in the first person (such as those starting with "I bet" or "I declare"; see Austin 1975, 32), including imperative and commissive verbs. She appeals to the audience and asks all kinds of readers, including doctors, teachers, painters, actors, singers, and lovers, to follow her and see the Narmada Valley for themselves:[6] "The war for the Narmada Valley is not just some exotic tribal war, or a remote rural war or even an exclusively Indian war. It's a war for all the rivers and mountains and forests of the world. All sorts of warriors from all over the world, anyone who wishes to enlist, will be honored and welcomed. Every kind of warrior will be needed. Doctors, lawyers, teachers, judges, journalists, students, sportsmen, painters, actors, singers, lovers. . . . The borders are open, folks! Come on in" (A. Roy 1999, 43). Roy's language not only makes use of expositive verbs to describe or explain her vision of the story but also resorts to exercitives to dramatically urge, advise, and warn her audience. Sentences such as "Come on in" or "Go and see by yourselves" are illocutionary speech acts insofar as they convey the force of a passionate invitation. The aim is to mobilize people and to fill the gap between the local instance of protest and wider global exploitation. How to resist? Roy has the answer: "Maybe by fighting specific wars in specific ways. We could begin in the Narmada Valley" (A. Roy 1999, 80–81).

The war of words is just as real as any other conflict, and Roy invites fellow warriors to join in. In the valley the ragged army of tribals, as Roy emphasizes in the short essay "Ahimsa," "is demanding more modernity, not less. It is demanding more democracy, not less" (Arundhati Roy 2005, 6). After listening to her tale, she suggests that the next step is to assess the environmental and human cost of the dam construction. The essay ends with the following statement: "Whether you love the dam or hate it, whether you want it or you don't, it is in the fitness of things that you understand the price that's being paid for it. That you have the courage to watch while the dues are cleared and the books are squared. Our dues. Our books. Not theirs. Be there" (A. Roy 1999, 81). The essay proposes a gradual passage from the plea to listen to the request of engaging in a dialogue with the fighters. Eventually it urges the audience to reach the Narmada Valley. Once there, readers will become a community of activists. Then the illocutionary, or performative, quality of language will have led people to act politically, allowing the emergence of new political subjects.

ENACTING LITERARY GENRES

The task of the storyteller as an activist in the age of globalization, as Bahri puts it, is to contribute to real social change. As suggested before, Roy's citations, word games, and creative uses of language are not only a formal characteristic of her work but also a substantial one. Questioning the discourses of development, national pride, and capitalist and consumerist propaganda, Roy engenders resistance against what she calls the empire of hegemonic forces. She clearly asserted this point in her closing speech at the World Social Forum in Porto Alegre (Brazil) in 2003: "Our strategy should be not only to confront empire, but to lay siege to it. To deprive it of oxygen. To shame it. To mock it. With our art, our music, our literature, our stubbornness, our joy, our brilliance, our sheer relentlessness—and our ability to tell our own stories. Stories that are different from the ones we're being brainwashed to believe" (Arundhati Roy 2005, 86). Her statement of intent, aimed at laying siege to empire, is also an injunction to shame and mock history as the only national narrative. Literature can respond to the discourse on the inevitability of war by multiplying available stories and points of view. This political objective, inherent in the act of telling stories, influences the way in which stories are told. Speech acts have a crucial role in Roy's nonfiction writing because they carry the force to reach out and touch the audience. In this case the relationship between the content of the essay and its form appears to be mutually constitutive: It is not dictated by the normative function of the genre.

In analyzing the influence of Austin's reflections on speech acts on recent literary criticism, Peter J. Rabinowitz (1955) notes that, as Frederic Jameson theorized, literary genres are performative: They require the use of certain tones, conventions, and particular styles. Jameson affirms, "Genres are essentially literary *institutions*, or social contracts between a writer and a specific public, whose function is to specify the proper use of a particular cultural artifact. The speech acts of daily life are themselves marked with indications and signals (intonation, gesturality, contextual deictics and pragmatics) which ensure their appropriate reception" (Jameson 1981, 106). Jameson highlights that in the case of texts, genres have the function of defining their function in the absence of the context. But then he concedes that whether they are articulated as *modes*, brand names, or fixed forms (108), genres are performative conventions that artistic creativity will struggle against.

In the case of Roy, instead of conceiving her nonfiction writing as opposed to traditions of political essays and pamphletism, I want to argue that her style is organically produced as a consequence of her acts of writing and protesting in particular sites. The numerous speech acts contained in "The Greater Common Good," which result in an illusion of orality, reveal that Roy embodies the position of a storyteller; although her feet are rooted in the Narmada Valley, her words reach out for support.

Here, Bahri's analysis of Kathakali storytelling in *The God of Small Things* can be useful to understanding how this performing art challenges the conception of the literary genres as normative. About the specific figure of the Kathakali dancer, his conventional gestures, and bodily expressions, Bahri says, "The complex codes of *abhinaya* imply the act of carrying the spectator toward the meaning through the immersion of the body itself in the communicative performance. The complete identification of the dancer with the character and of the storyteller with the story seeks to collapse the boundaries between tale and teller, form and content" (Bahri 2003, 206–7). This image is important for understanding both the structure of the novel and the writer's conception of storytelling as an embodied practice, where the relation between the speaking subject and the words uttered is not representable as derived from the authority of the writer.

In *The God of Small Things* Roy portrays a relation of symbiosis between the Kathakali Man and his stories: "To the Kathakali Man these stories are his children and his childhood. He has grown up with them. They are the house he was raised in, the meadows he played in. They are his windows and his ways of seeing" (A. Roy 1997, 219). Stories appear as the form and the content of the storyteller's life; they are both the house and the children playing in it. Stories are the windows that allow looking out onto the external world and, at the same time, impose a particular perspective on that outlook. Numerous critics have read this passage of *The God of Small Things* as Roy's metanarrative reflection on her writing process. By reflecting on the technique of storytelling, Bahri looks at the author as a Kathakali dancer, whose narrative voice encompasses multiple characters without subsuming them into a single choir: "It is not the character, or character alone, that is necessarily transformed into narrator through multiple focalizations, but the narrator who is obliged to carry the memory load of multiple characters" (Bahri 2003, 241).

Mukherjee also considers the many ways in which this scene of storytelling can be seen as an interpretative key to the novel: "At the level of the theme, the dance performance names a protest against the blind neo-colonial forces of globalization that ruthlessly commodify all forces of life in contemporary Kerala and India. In respect to the plot, it is the occasion of the twins coming face to face. . . . At the level of the form, Kathakali is the archaic form that fuses with that of the contemporary" (U. P. Mukherjee 2010, 106). In accordance with the conflation of form and content that Bahri sees as characteristic of Kathakali, Mukherjee notes that the quoted scene thematically resists the commodification of ethnic diversity and formally stages a performance that enacts a nonidealized vision of postcolonial reality. The hybrid form incorporating the dance in the novel seems appropriate to register the complexities of the material conditions of life in Kerala, including the historical trajectories of rural exploitation and the modernizing drives of industrialization.[7]

Benjamin's essay on storytelling brings to the fore the importance of understanding the complex relation between the storyteller and his or her community or audience in order to gain an insight into the role of this public art. In this vein, Bahri and Mukherjee highlight how the aesthetics of storytelling, which are inherently part of Roy's language in fiction and nonfiction works, do not reproduce bourgeois and individualistic ideals; rather, they are nourished by shared experiences and collective political acts. In an argument that echoes Benjamin's concept of storytelling as opposing the individualism of novels, though resisting the neat separation of these art forms, I have closely examined the context of Roy's activism to demonstrate how her literary work is influenced by the language of collective action that was generated in the Narmada Valley and how, in turn, her texts inspire other contemporary protest actions against the neoliberal empire. Roy's act of storytelling in "The Greater Common Good," which casts Adivasis and untouchables as coauthors, is not simply a representation of the struggle of marginalized subjects against the regime of private property pervading modern citizenship, which survived colonialism. Roy's act of storytelling creatively challenges private ownership, stressing the collective nature of telling stories; it opposes individual authorship as a form of property.

In other words, if storytelling is the medium chosen to convey the contradictory features of postcolonial subjectivity, then it is not merely because of its representative power. The immersion of the storyteller in a particular site—the Narmada Valley struggle in the case of "The Greater Common Good"—is a fundamental condition for speaking out against the forms of global exploitation. The embodied act of storytelling that derives from the practice of activism has a double objective: First, the text incorporates Adivasis' perspectives, giving them a stage to speak; second, it calls for more action. Its imperative tone is a direct reaction to the experience of listening to the stories of the people who were concretely affected by the dam.

My interpretation of Roy's language highlights how the form of her nonfiction writing was spontaneously carved out of the Narmada experience. Roy suggests that, once in the valley, she felt drawn to technical language and reports and was pushed to leave aside her literary works. On the other hand, the question of which literary form is most appropriate for discussing social matters and inducing real change haunts several of her essays. In the preface to *Field Notes on Democracy: Listening to Grasshoppers* (2009), Roy challenges the common assumption that nonfiction, being devoid of inventions and literary abstractions, is generally the privileged tool to represent the real and act on it. Instead, poetry could be the means of real transformative politics: "As a writer, a fiction writer, I have often wondered whether the attempt to always be precise, to try and get it all factually right somehow reduces the epic scale of what is really going on. Does it eventually mask a larger truth? I worry that I am allowing myself to be railroaded into offering prosaic, factual precision when maybe what we need is a feral howl, or the transformative power and real precision of poetry" (A. Roy 2009, xii–xiii). This passage may be counterintuitive, because Roy here dismantles the basic assumption that the precision of statistics and reports, which she so carefully incorporates into her essay, is vital for persuading the audience to support the anti-dam campaign and determines the successful reception of her work.

However, in this excerpt Roy reveals that she lent herself to the struggle without predetermining the form of her activist contribution: She was "railroaded" into writing nonfiction. "The Greater Common Good" is powerful in its writing precisely because it was organic to the activism of the NBA; its specific prose and style were induced by the material conditions of living, traveling, and meeting people in the valley. From this perspective the "feral howl" of the essay derives from its refusal to give in to a single ideology, be it nationalism or developmentalism, and from the use of persuasive language tools such as speech acts: "The struggle in the Narmada valley lives, *despite* the State" (A. Roy 1999, 40). On the other hand, Roy's doubts on the form of writing to choose reveal the awareness that what she is offering is not factual accuracy. By contrast, her exercise of storytelling aspires to change the language of politics, and the popular reception of infrastructure projects, by multiplying the available versions of truth.

In using this conception of storytelling, I want to conclude with an image inspired by one of the revisions of Austin's work on speech acts. In light of Shoshana Felman's reading of speech acts in Molière's *Don Juan*, I want to consider Roy as a modern version of the character of Don Juan. In her revision of Austin's work on speech acts, Felman (2003) highlights that, in his lessons, the philosopher quickly turns away from the language of truth and truthfulness and embraces a theory of happiness. Austin defines successful speech acts, the ones whose effects comply with the intentionality of the speaker, as "felicitous" (Austin 1975, 41); they are happy, not precise or true. By substituting satisfaction for truth, Austin introduces pleasure in thinking about language. For this emphasis on satisfaction, Felman assimilates Austin to a modern Don Juan: "Modern Don Juans, they know that truth is only an act. That is why they subvert truth and do not promise it, but *promise themselves to it*" (Felman 2003, 121). Roy does not promise truth; she promises a story and says, "Trust me. There's a story here" (A. Roy 1999, 21). In light of Felman's work and the proposed argument on the centrality of storytelling in Roy's fiction and nonfiction writing, Roy emerges as a modern Don Juan who does not promise the excavation of the only possible truth. Instead, Roy's act of telling stories promises itself to multiplying truths.

3

Sampat Pal

7

WARRIOR IN A PINK SARI

A Subaltern Autobiography

In the first two parts of this book I have analyzed the production of two postcolonial canonical writers, Mahasweta Devi and Arundhati Roy, as examples of literary activism. I now turn to a different case of collective struggle that has received substantial media coverage in the last years but little attention from the academic community. This chapter is dedicated to the movement known as the Gulabi Gang, based in Uttar Pradesh, and to its leader, Sampat Pal.[1] Unlike the activist groups I have considered so far, the Gulabi Gang is not predominantly composed of tribals but of poor, lower-caste rural villagers who have turned to Pal for the resolution of disputes related to caste and gender discrimination. Pal usually intervenes personally, like a judge or a mediator, to solve family and community affairs. When she cannot get an apology from the wrongdoers, the gang intervenes and can resort to violence to punish the perpetrators of abuses.

Warrior in a Pink Sari (2010) is Sampat Pal's autobiography. Her story is the tale of the daughter of a shepherd from Kairi, a small village in Bundelkhand, who rebelled against the social customs of her rural community and started a local revolution. Since 2006, Sampat has been the leader of the Gulabi Gang, which took its name from the pink (*gulab* in Hindi) saris that were chosen as the gang's uniform. Being the autobiography of an illiterate woman, the book promises to report faithfully on Pal's life "as told to Anne Berthod." The volume of Pal's personal memories claims to be a translation from Hindi into French and from oral speech into writing. *Moi, Sampat Pal, Chef de gang en sari rose*, translated into English as *Warrior in a Pink Sari*,[2] covers the whole span of Pal's life. Starting with her early memories and her marriage as a child bride, the narrative then deals with Pal's numerous struggles against casteism and violence against women in the villages of Bundelkhand until the founding of the Gulabi Gang. By merging the form of the memoir with the ethnographic account, the book challenges the established autobiographical genre. I propose to examine its particular form as an example of subaltern autobiography.

The extraordinary circumstances that transformed Pal into a popular heroine have also been explored by Amana Fontanella-Khan in *Pink Sari Revolution*, a dense journalistic account of the work of the Gulabi Gang. Fontanella-Khan follows the case of the alleged rape of a village girl by a politician and highlights the efforts made by the gang to support the woman in her attempt to obtain justice in court. During her two-year-long ethnographic research on the movement, Fontanella-Khan collected evidence and witness statements in relation to this and other cases to explain the gang's involvement in local disputes. What appears crucial is the formation of a network of people, predominantly women, mobilized by the idea of social justice, who make themselves available with determination to the project of constructing a fairer society. Even though the effectiveness of the gang's mission is open to debate and although its contradictions form part of my analysis, its mobilization takes place under the banner of equality and justice. The gang maintains that it is possible to construct a new civil society only if one envisages a world where men and women, high castes and lower castes, count as equal citizens. This is a common aspiration but a form of citizenship yet to come.

In this chapter, referring to both *Warrior in a Pink Sari* and Fontanella-Khan's work, I examine the circumstances of the emergence and subsequent popularity of Pal's tale in the postcolonial and international literary scene. I concentrate on the story, its context of gender inequality, and the chosen genre. In chapter 8 I consider the autobiography of another famous rebel, the Bandit Queen, as Pal's literary antecedent. Then I ask whether or not Pal's acts, collected in her autobiographical novel, can be considered acts of citizenship and why.

"FROM ZERO TO HERO"

Warrior in a Pink Sari is the story of Pal's personal growth "from zero to hero" (Fontanella-Khan 2013b, 9). A clever and lively little girl, Pal remembers having a happy childhood. Her only disappointment was not being allowed to attend school regularly, because she had to help with the family's finances by taking care of the cattle. Despite not being formally enrolled in school, she remembers hiding from the teachers and other students and listening to the lessons taught outdoors. The fact of not having achieved the desired level of education had a profound and lasting effect on Pal's self-esteem and constitutes, by her own admission, her weakness. As was customary in her village, Pal was married off at age 12. By the age of 15, she had her first child and, soon, another four followed.

The traumatic experience of being a child bride and the memories of sexual violence inflicted on her immature body motivated Pal to support other women who were suffering from domestic abuse and similar circumstances of poverty and oppression. Having learned how to sew, Pal obtained economic independence and increasingly demanded more freedom from family affairs. Today, she does not live with her husband and spends most of her days traveling across Bundelkhand to help resolve other people's family quarrels and problems with the police and government officials.

For more than ten years, Pal has been involved in establishing support groups for tribal and lower-caste women. She started by organizing self-help groups aimed at obtaining small loans, and in 2003 she founded a nongovernmental organization (NGO) (Fontanella-Khan 2013b, 11). The self-help groups also aimed to disseminate new skills, such as sewing, to enable women who so wished to support themselves and achieve financial freedom. This community work was the basis for the founding of the Gulabi Gang. Pal proudly remembers, "March 2006. The Gulabi Gang was born. I was forty-five years old and I was its leader" (Pal and Berthod 2010, 107). In the same year, Pal also set up a formal trust in the Banda District called Adivasi Mahila Utthan Gramudyog Seva Sansthan (AMUGSS). The aim was to gradually create an infrastructure with a paid staff to manage the operations and various programs of the Gulabi Gang.

Today, the Gulabi Gang's headquarters is located in an office, *karyalay*, in Atarra. It consists of a single room where Pal lives and works with her right-hand man, Jai Prakash Shivhare (commonly known as Babuji), a former schoolteacher turned social activist. Every day they meet numerous women asking for help and attend to their cases. In the space of a few years, the Gulabi Gang has spread across Chitrakoot, Fatehpur, and Banda, three districts of the Bundelkhand region with respective populations of 600,000, 1.9 million, and 1.85 million. According to Pal, the gang has so far recruited nearly 100,000 women.

The Gulabi Gang was founded in reaction to a specific episode of violence witnessed by Pal: a man ferociously beating his wife. Pal intervened and demanded that he stop, but the man turned on her and hit her as well. The next day, she returned with a bamboo stick and five other women to beat him up. Pal then realized that a woman alone is powerless against a culture that victimizes her but that the union of several women can trigger a change. The Gulabi Gang is committed to achieving social change and justice for the poor by addressing the struggles these women face every day. Its main aims are to fight corruption, to ensure the enjoyment of basic rights, and to discourage traditions such as child marriages. "Mind you," Pal says, "we are not a gang in the usual sense of the term. We are a gang for justice" (Biswas 2007).

In the rural villages of Uttar Pradesh, child marriage, dowries, and domestic abuse, including marital rape and female infanticide, are the main issues affecting women's lives (Srivastava 2002). Although specific laws prohibit all these things, Pal protests that the protection promised by emancipatory laws does not reach the people at the grassroots level who need it most: "Theoretically, women are equal to men. We live in a free country, with modern laws, and the constitution gives us the same rights. In recent years the government has bombarded us with slogans asserting women's rights to education, job opportunities and divorce. But the laws that are supposed to protect women cannot be implemented" (Pal and Berthod 2010, 81). For this reason the Gulabi Gang exercises its social authority to put pressure on the police in an attempt to ensure that laws are fairly applied. Fairness and justice consistently feature among the ideals that drive the protest actions of the gang.

However, legal sanctions against the perpetrators of unlawful acts, such as child marriage, have so far proved ineffective, because the legal system in place to protect women relies, for the enforcement of laws, on the same patriarchal structures that oppress them. Policemen are often part of this discriminatory and violent social system. During one of the operations of the Gulabi Gang, Pal tried to register a complaint at a police station, and she was greeted with both physical and verbal abuse. Instead of leaving, she responded by attacking the offending policeman with her bamboo stick. Pal was charged and then arrested, but she does not regret her action. She believes that the use of violence is justified if it helps in the pursuit of justice. In an interview with Amos Roberts, Pal highlighted that when police officers or politicians, who should be the guarantors of the law, do not obey the legal system, they deserve severe punishment: "Why do I have to take the law into my hands? The government does not obey its laws."[3] The collapse of law and order, then, starts with the government's betrayal of the very regulations that were passed for the betterment of the poor. Referring to her refusal to commit to non-violence, Pal added, "I salute Gandhi, the father of the nation, but my style is different. I am Sampat Pal. I do what I think is right."[4]

The *lathi*, or bamboo stick, is only one of the instruments used by gang members to achieve justice. To punish corrupt police officers, public figures, and abusive husbands for their wrongdoing, the gang publicly names and shames the perpetrators of offenses. Pal says, "We have social power, not legal power" (Fontanella-Khan 2013b, 126). But the social pressure the Gulabi Gang exerts on the police and community leaders is often enough to get the wheels of legal justice moving. Pal's charismatic rhetoric is another of her weapons; her loud voice is as powerful as her big stick. As Fontanella-Khan notes, "Sampat's expansive body language is matched by an equally loud, attention grabbing voice and *force of speech*—one almost feels that the power at which her words catapult towards you could, hypothetically, be measured with the Beaufort wind scale" (14). It is the force of Pal's speech, motivating women to rebel against patriarchal rules and social injustice, that the autobiography attempts to capture. The transcriptions of Pal's authoritarian language and effective slogans imbue the text with the feeling of a manifesto against the exploitation of women in rural societies.

The image of Pal presented in her autobiography is that of a strong-willed woman with uncompromising faith in the possibility of achieving fairer living conditions for social outcasts. In the book she repeatedly insists that she will never compromise with political authorities and will continue to fight against the subjugation of women to the power of patriarchal males and mothers-in-law. Her heroic self-representation leaves little room for ambiguities and doubts over the correctness of her actions. Interestingly, however, Kim Longinotto's documentary *Pink Saris* (2010) presents a more nuanced representation of Pal and her activist enterprise.

In the documentary the audience follows Pal as she resolves a number of conflicts, but the director does not refrain from showing her making decisions that have a potentially dangerous outcome for the victims. In *Pink Saris* Pal ends up bringing back to her family a woman who had run away after repeated beatings. The woman is a relative of Pal's and had been married into the same joint household where Pal used to live with her husband. After arguing with him about the girl's fate, Pal takes the woman back to the relatives they have in common, encouraging her to work harder to avoid the physical punishments. This deeply contestable act represents an instance in which Pal is obedient to the patriarchal system at the expense of a vulnerable woman. Being subjected to the same authority she is attempting to challenge, Pal cannot in fact free herself completely, as the autobiography seems to suggest, from the power of her husband and his family.

In the last part of this chapter, in which I analyze the aesthetics of Pal's autobiography, I argue that, unlike the documentary, the book is unambiguous about Pal's value and creates a fictitious character aimed at pleasing the taste of middle-class and Western consumers.

ANGRY ABOUT OPPRESSION

Pal's tale, told in first person, represents a widespread reality of exploitation and rebellion. It does not simply portray women as passive victims of a patriarchal culture but speaks about the emergence of a common urge to act against discriminatory social practices that endanger women's lives. In this section I revisit Pal's descriptions of women's oppression. Then, looking at Pal's and Fontanella-Khan's books, I examine the descriptions of the affective labor that appears to hold the movement together, triggering new initiatives of activism.

Even though the Gulabi Gang grants support to all citizens alike and although Pal's right-hand helper, Babuji, is a man, the movement is predominantly composed of women and works for women.[5] Pal speaks eloquently about the crucial role of solidarity for the long life of the movement, considering this feeling of commonality to be an essentially feminine feature: "Women have a greater sense of solidarity than men, but you have to keep them motivated" (Pal and Berthod 2010, 141). Both women's solidarity and their political enthusiasm seem to come from the awareness that they are all subjected to the authority of others, both in the private and the public sphere.

Pal does not mince words when speaking about the position of women in the family: "Women are in slavery" (Fontanella-Khan 2013b, 13). It is women's shared anger about their common conditions of exploitation that generates both rebelliousness and a feeling of unity. Pal uses the analogy of slavery to describe women's life in the villages, their duties, their lack of rights, and their husbands' sense of ownership. Her arguments call to mind John Stuart Mill's advocacy of women's emancipation and rights. In his essay "The Subjection of Women" (1869), Mill attacked marriage laws, likening them to slavery: "There remain no legal slaves, save the mistress of every house" (Mill 1955, 296). Mill also remarked that the emancipation of women is a direct consequence of women's education: "Literary women are becoming more free spoken, and more willing to express their real sentiments" (243). For Mill, writing represents the possibility of a revolution; not only can the writing subject use writing as a tool to free herself from the requirements of patriarchal customs, but also other women, through reading, will share and be inspired by her achievements.[6]

The same image of slavery appears in Simone de Beauvoir's descriptions of marriage in *The Second Sex*, in which the relationship between men and women is reconsidered in light of Hegel's slave-master dialectic.[7] De Beauvoir agrees that women's economic, social, and legal dependence on men, which is proof that the two sexes have never shared the world in equality, approximates marriage to slavery. De Beauvoir shows that women's legal rights are deficient compared to the status of men as full citizens; and even when their rights are legally recognized in the abstract, long-standing customs prevent their transformation into actual enjoyed entitlements (De Beauvoir 2010, 9–10). Describing the relation between women's subalternity and the problem of inheritance of private property, de Beauvoir's critique becomes increasingly sharp and the metaphor of slavery gains solidity. Patriarchal societies are founded on the abduction of women and the preservation of wealth in the male lineage. A woman "is radically abducted from the group she is born into and annexed to her husband's; he buys her like a head of cattle or a slave, he imposes domestic divinities on her: and the children she conceives belong to the spouse's family" (93). As Carol Pateman's work highlights, a sexual contract is at the basis of the social contract (Pateman 1988).[8]

This passage is illuminating with regard to the destructive consequences of patriarchy inherent in the plight of women like Pal. The Gulabi Gang exposes women's oppression and their shared sorrow through their songs. One of them, translated from Hindi and transcribed in Pal's autobiography, says, "A girl doesn't find happiness in her father's house, or in her husband's" (Pal and Berthod 2010, 145). The act of singing songs of liberation during the movement's protests reinforces the members' sense of collective identity and presents an image of an active feminist politics. In Pal's autobiography and in Longinotto's documentary, Pal tells us that she could not find happiness in her husband's house and decided to live alone. She also refused to be subjected to the authority of her in-laws and, only a few years after the birth of her first child, persuaded her husband to leave the family home, where they were living jointly according to the local customs. She remembers storming out, shouting, "I won't stay here as a slave" (Fontanella-Khan 2013b, 79).

Pal is passionate in her fight against the institutions to which she was subjected, such as dowry and child marriage, protesting that they contribute to preserving women's inferior position in the family and in society. The best antidote to the subjection of women, she argues, is education. Both the movement's songs, which are part of a counterculture promoting cultural disobedience and rebellion, and the sewing courses, held by Pal since the early days of the association as a means to promote women's financial and social independence, are a vital part of the movement's influence. But the movement's main achievement was the setting up of the Gulabi Gang Bal Vidyalaya school for young children in Banda in 2008. The school is run entirely by members of the gang and is an attempt to increase the level and scope of girls' education in an area where government institutions often fail to function.[9]

Pal's autobiography, as I have mentioned, speaks eloquently about Pal's own struggle to get an education, but this personal account is also presented as a paradigmatic example of the experience of other women in the area; the title of the book, *Warrior in a Pink Sari* (in the original version, *Moi, Sampat Pal, Chef de gang en sari rose*), emphasizes the personal experience of the leader of the gang, but the subtitle promises to unveil "the inside story of the Gulabi Gang," opening the scope of the investigation to the rest of the group. From the beginning the book is telling two stories. It is an account of the life of an individual who finds herself compelled to take action against her caste and gender discrimination and, at the same time, the chronicle of the foundation and development of a large movement.

The ethical aspect of Pal's rebellions and her mobilization of other women sheds light on why the vigilante group is an interesting case for investigating citizenship as political subjectivity in rural India. As Engin Isin highlights in his most recent work, *Citizenship Without Frontiers*, political subjectivity can be considered the emergence of moral conduct in social relations. Isin looks at citizenship as "how subjects come into being as ethical or moral subjects":

"I am interested in political subjectivity as creative, inventive and autonomous ways of becoming political through relating to oneself and others" (Isin 2012, 108). Pal's case and the stories of the women involved in her movement, who use sewing, demonstrations, and fights as tools to break free of patriarchy, are examples of creative and inventive ways of relating to others.

In her journalistic account of Pal's life, Fontanella-Khan sets out to explore how Pal succeeded in gathering together such an extended network of women and managed to create an association that has survived for many years: "Why did these women, who had never before rebelled, join Sampat's nascent vigilante gang at this stage of their life? Lungi Dai, one of the elderly women, put it this way: 'Hope is a very big thing. Sampat gave it to us every time she came to the village'" (Fontanella-Khan 2013b, 22). Hope for a better life and anger at recurring violence give rise to an affective contagion that can support new protest actions.

Fontanella-Khan's reports of the Gulabi Gang's actions for social justice are full of descriptions of personal and collective anger. One of these recollections has to do with the first protest Pal led as a child: She persuaded a group of her friends to defecate in the fields of a higher-caste woman who had banned Pal's family from crossing her fields. The leader recalls with some amusement, "I was so angry. I was a child, so doing these things wasn't disgusting to me then" (Fontanella-Khan 2013b, 34). The anecdote is just the first of a series of tales in which the woman's rebellion, her ways of breaking social customs, originated from anger. In other circumstances she remembers feeling "a fit of anger" (Fontanella-Khan 2013b, 174) or recalls situations in which "anger suddenly flared inside me" (Pal and Berthod 2010, 49).

Anger should not simply be considered here as a personal quality defining Pal's self-representation; it surfaces in numerous texts by journalists and commentators. When Fontanella-Khan describes Pal as a public figure, she says, "If you were to watch Sampat at a distance, out of earshot, you might be able to gauge every flickering emotion within her by watching her exaggerated expressions—the red-hot anger in her scowl, the happiness in her child-like grin and the surprise in her leaping eyebrows" (Fontanella-Khan 2013b, 14). Against this image of Pal's charisma and her overflowing emotions, Prasad highlights an irascible vein that is not always positive: "Pal is difficult company. Those not showing her the utmost respect get crude abuse. Yet in a place where expectation of female restraint is so faithfully observed, only someone as irascible as Pal could defy it" (Prasad 2010, 330).

Pal admits this: "I know I fly into a rage easily. When I am angry I become stubborn" (Pal and Berthod 2010, 149). More important, though, her anger is the main mechanism triggering resistance. This becomes evident in Pal's description of her response to the casteism of villagers. After Pal ate at the house of a Charmar, a member of the untouchable community, she was marginalized by her fellow villagers for disregarding the belief that the impurity of untouchables is contaminating. She says, "I had become a pariah. I, on my part, was overcome by a strange feeling. I didn't know what to make of their absurd attitude. In fact, I was stumped by their stupidity. But not for long. Very soon I was overwhelmed with fury. I remembered my uncle's advice: 'If someone hits you, hit them back'" (Pal and Berthod 2010, 59). Pal then provoked the community even more by deliberately eating at the house of another lower-caste individual in front of witnesses. She paid dearly for this provocation: She had to leave the village and uproot her family to escape an assassination attempt.

But the principle of paying back offenses by hitting people harder is still the central tenet of Pal's work. Her rebelliousness, which provoked her estrangement from the community, also helped her become a leader. Pal's anger arouses heated reactions in other people. This mechanism, which could be described as an affective contagion or shared rebelliousness, is clearly portrayed by Fontanella-Khan in her account of Pal's protests against some hospital staff members who refused to treat her because she belonged to a lower caste: "When Sampat arrived at the hospital, other patients who had also been mistreated became angry" (Fontanella-Khan 2013b, 230). Anger, then, is not simply a personal characteristic but a shared emotion; it arises in moments of collective actions and is transmitted to others who also feel that they have been wronged. In the narratives about the Gulabi Gang, anger is constantly present, like a trademark. Gang members are described, even by sympathetic commentators, as "angry, shouting women," "armed with bamboo *lathi*s and dressed in their pink sari uniforms" (Fontanella-Khan 2013b, 220).

In chapter 10 I offer a closer examination of the ethical dimension of anger, but here I want to stress the crucial role of anger as a motor for shared social change. The movement's initiatives are driven by indignation at the constant discrimination against powerless, marginalized citizens, the most vulnerable of whom are village women of lower castes. The Gulabi Gang's actions of vigilantism, recorded by the media and disseminated by word of mouth, constitute a repertoire of acts that can be deployed by other people in their civic struggles. Pal's autobiography, then, presents a particular aesthetic form, shaped by its state between oral and written language, born in translation between different languages (mainly French and Hindi) and between different genres.

In chapter 8 I analyze Pal's autobiography in light of Isin's work on citizenship as political subjectivity, which prompts us to rethink citizenship struggles in their three fundamental aspects: political, ethical, and aesthetic. But first, in the following section, having considered the ethical aspect as a result of an affective contagion, I take a brief look at the aesthetic dimension of Pal's autobiography before asking whether her violent deeds can truly be considered acts of citizenship.

WHO WRITES?

The focus on anger highlights that Pal's autobiography not only reveals the story of one woman but also publicizes the actions of a movement as a living, breathing, and feeling organism. This ambiguity, which politically enables the construction of activism on the basis of solidarity, becomes more problematic when we consider the question of writing and representation. Who wrote the autobiography? Who approved its content? The answer is far from simple. The original title in French, *Moi, Sampat Pal, Chef de gang en sari rose*, clearly suggests that it is Pal herself who wrote it, but the book cover reveals that the story was written by Berthod, after a series of conversations with the gang leader, and that the book was first published in French.

Looking at this text through the lens of Gayatri Spivak's essay "Can the Subaltern Speak?" we are obliged to ask fundamental questions about the politics of representation in the text. In her essay Spivak reflects on the Hindu custom of the sacrifice of the *sati*, the ritual of the self-immolation of widows, and highlights its relation to women's subaltern legal and economic status: "This legally programmed asymmetry in the status of the subject, which effectively defines the woman as object of one husband, obviously operates in the interest of the legally symmetrical subject status of the male" (Spivak 1988, 98). Because the law recognizes private property owners as citizens, the death of a husband determined for women the loss of any legitimate legal status.

Pal's description of women as either daughters or wives recalls the status of subjection that Spivak defined as legal and social annihilation. In the same essay Spivak states, "Within the effaced itinerary of the subaltern subject, the track of sexual difference is doubly effaced. . . . If, in the context of colonial production, the subaltern has no history and cannot speak, the subaltern as female is even more deeply in shadow" (Spivak 1988, 82–83). When colonized or "third world" subjects are women, black, and poor, they are subjected to a triple discrimination and become three times silenced in the public domain.

For Spivak, the information retrieval and recent focus of numerous studies on the subaltern in humanities and social sciences in the West are both welcome and suspect, because they are coupled with a decreasing critical focus on the role of the intellectual. By interpreting subaltern stories, intellectuals implicitly write new narratives. In this sense, Spivak discusses the two senses of the term *representation*: "speaking for," as in politics, and "re-presenting" as in arts and philosophy. In joining these two meanings, Spivak claims that Western intellectuals represent oriental and female others while simultaneously representing themselves as transparent. The attempt to capture the essence of Indian culture as an undifferentiated whole by turning to native elites reveals vestiges of a colonial attitude: "Certain varieties of the Indian elite are at best native informants for first-world intellectuals interested in the voice of the Other. But one must nevertheless insist that the colonized subaltern subject is irretrievably heterogeneous" (Spivak 1988, 79). Referring to Karl Marx's writing and his description of the subject of class-consciousness as dislocated and discontinuous, Spivak reminds us that subaltern subjectivity is not a coherent category. In Spivak's investigation the expression of agency from a position of subalternity cannot take place in the hegemonic language; its form is, by definition, elusive and exceeds the colonial mapping of legal and political subjectivity. It is through acts of disobedience, insubordination, and resignification of customary practices that women rewrite the social text.

Sampat Pal presents us with an example of a rebellious character who disregards religious beliefs, caste hierarchy, and male superiority. She undoubtedly initiated a change in her own community by defending and protecting powerless village people. But the question I want to pose is related to the possibility of her self-representation through her autobiography. Pal is a strong and powerful figure, so much so that in Longinotto's documentary Pal does not hesitate to call herself the "Messiah of women" (*Pink Saris*, 2010), but the authorship of her story is not under her control. Pal's story was written by Berthod. Hers is an instance of subaltern autobiography that presents an irreducible paradox. Berthod's writing encodes Pal's participation into the social and political scene and acts as a guarantee of the truthfulness of the events told.[10] Yet, even though Berthod's intermediation is so important, the book contains no information about her. Pal's story is written in first person, as though Pal is engaged in a direct dialogue with the reader. The writing style therefore succeeds in making Berthod's role completely disappear.

The fame of the book, seen as particularly poignant in the West, where it was translated into several languages, may be partly due to this illusory direct contact between the audience and the heroine, whose life of sorrow is slowly uncovered. The book satisfies the rising global hunger for tear-jerking stories of social depression. As in other famous literary and visual representations of destitute citizens, such as Danny Boyle's film *Slumdog Millionaire*, the harshness of extreme poverty titillates people's morbid curiosity. In this vein, I propose to look at *Warrior in a Pink Sari* as a subaltern autobiography, which promises to unveil the brutal aspect of gender and class discrimination while revealing the resistance of global dynamics that subject the stories of subaltern women to commodification and global consumption. By claiming to represent the real story of the Gulabi Gang standing up to injustice, the book in fact exploits the marketability of "authentic" subaltern narratives. But as Spivak points out in her essay, one can never reach pure subalterns. When a subaltern subject expresses herself in the dominant language, she remains subjected to the control of patriarchal and colonial (or nationalist) culture. A subaltern autobiography is thus a contradiction in terms; it disguises other people's authoring to satisfy the increasing global interest in third world stories of subjection.

The original title of the novel inspired by Pal's life, *Moi, Sampat Pal, Chef de gang en sari rose*, closely recalls the contested autobiography of Phoolan Devi, *I, Phoolan Devi: The Autobiography of India's Bandit Queen*. Phoolan Devi was a well-known bandit who spread terror across Uttar Pradesh in the early 1980s (see chapter 8). Her autobiography, like Pal's, was written on the basis of oral interviews and produced and published in English by a British publishing company in 1994. Leela Fernandes proposes a critical reading of the book and of the transposition of Devi's life on screen in Shekhar Kapur's *Bandit Queen*. Fernandes's consideration that the "collaboration between First and Third World in making *Bandit Queen* signifies the production of and desire for a Third-World authenticity" (Fernandes 2001, 54) is relevant for my analysis of Pal's autobiography. Fernandes denounces the danger inherent in the projects of publishing stories that promote exemplary representations of real life in the developing world.[11] The fact that the writing of Devi's story, like Pal's, takes place through an international coproduction does not seem to challenge the hegemonic power of the West in the creation and consumption of the story. Fernandes says, "The translation and writing of Phoolan Devi's life story occur through a form of collaboration that defies a clear-cut classification of the book as either 'Western' or 'Indian.' I want to suggest, following the work of Trinh T. Minh-ha, that this very mark of collaboration, which appears initially to interrupt the First World/Third World binary, is a central means for the production and the consumption of modernist Third-World authenticity (Fernandes 2001, 53). In *When the Moon Waxes Red* (1991), Vietnamese scholar and filmmaker Trinh T. Minh-ha notes that the authentication of works written by and dealing with former colonized subjects often takes place by claiming coproduction. Fernandes finds that editorial projects in which Eastern subjects speak only through Western channels present a similar case of disguised hegemony; they foster a desire for consumption of developing world authentic stories and, through an emphasis on realism, sustain an essentialized concept of Indian tradition.

In Pal's case I do not mean to suggest that she is completely silenced by the autobiography. In fact, the publication of the book created the occasion for Pal to give talks and interviews across the world and to appear at the Woman's Forum annual summit in France, and her life inspired a Bollywood movie titled *Gulaab Gang* (2014). All this media exposure increased her local power, enabling her to gain social authority. But the point I want to make is that with its promise of realism, contained in the subtitle, the book subscribes to a particular genre of postcolonial narrative that can be considered the autobiography or even the bildungsroman of the poor.[12] This genre revives the figure of the native informant and transforms personal stories into allegories of "other," backward worlds.

Aijaz Ahmad criticized Frederic Jameson's essay "Third World Literature and the Era of Multinational Capital" for claiming that "all third world texts are necessarily . . . and in a very specific case . . . to be read as national allegories" (Jameson 1986, 69). Ahmad finds Jameson's description of the developing world and his texts to be essentialist and orientalist. Jameson's investigation is mainly concerned with Western readers and their reception of oriental literature as allegories of distant, and more backward, nations (Ahmad 1992, 95–101).[13] A similar critique can be made in relation to numerous recently published subaltern autobiographies that have been written for, and often by, middle-class women and that deal with the lives of lower castes and tribals. Pal's acts of social rebellion, for example, are countersigned by Berthod's piece of writing, but Berthod's disappearance reveals the paradox inscribed in the label "subaltern autobiography."

By way of comparison, let us consider a literary case that is similar to Pal's and analyze the way in which subaltern stories reproduce old cultural stereotypes and prejudices. Shailaja Kalelkar Parikh's *And Still My River Flows: Story of a Tribal Woman from the Hinterlands of Gujarat*, published in 2010, also focuses on the geography of Indian gender oppression. Even in its title, the woman who is the main character of the book is absent. Her name, Hiru, does not figure until the introduction, whereas the place she comes from and her belonging to an indigenous community are in full focus from the start. In the book Parikh, the landlady who employs Hiru, reconstructs the tragic life of a woman in tribal society, suffering the hardship of having a drunken and abusive husband, and her struggles to feed her children before and after her husband's death.

The similarities in the topic of *And Still My River Flows* and Pal's autobiography are striking. Hiru, an Adivasi woman from the Panchmahals District of Gujarat, could be one of the women who regularly visit Sampat Pal asking for help. As in Pal's case, it is another woman, living in a position of comparative privilege, who writes Hiru's story. In her preface to the book, Parikh explains that Hiru's story was told to her "bit by bit, as Hiru swept the floors of my house, washed our utensils and hung bucket-loads of clothes on the clothesline. It took almost a year before I got the whole story out of her" (Parikh 2010, x). The social asymmetry between the two is clear, and the benevolent attitude of the house owner betrays her curiosity in reconstructing Hiru's life and recounting her suffering.[14]

Unlike Pal's autobiography, which is written as a first-person narrative, in *And Still My River Flows* an omniscient narrator tells the story in third person and warns the reader that the book is "a heart-breaking story of unimaginable physical and mental torture, sexual abuse and physical degradation" (Parikh 2010, x). Great emphasis is again placed on the truthful reconstruction of all the events. For the sake of retelling the story faithfully, the narrator admits visiting Hiru's remote village and attempting to learn about tribal customs in order to better explain the events of her life: "I have tried to portray as accurate a picture of tribal life and customs as possible by personally visiting the Panchmahals and talking to as many members of Hiru's extended family and neighbours as I could, in the effort to gain a better understanding of this culture. Nevertheless the reflections and perceptions of life expressed in this book remain those of Hiru" (xi). To prove the accuracy of her account, Parikh refers to the legal complaints filed by the abused wife against her husband and to the battle with her in-laws for the custody of the children.

Parikh's narrative, though, is informed by an orientalist attitude toward tribals, which frequently emerges as a kind of generalized exoticism or as a reference to their backwardness. When Parikh praises Hiru for her good character, despite such a difficult life, she says, "She still had an innocence and softness and sweetness about her, which I learnt later, most of the tribal people who live in the forests and hills still possess" (Parikh 2010, 4). Later in the text, Parikh considers that "tribals in general have lagged behind in progress due to the relative remoteness and inaccessibility of the tribal-belt, the poor quality of arable land, the scarcity of water and a strong adherence to centuries-old blind beliefs and taboos" (16). The fact that no mention is made of the exploitation of tribals and lower castes during and after colonialism sustains orientalist beliefs in the primitiveness of tribal culture.

Ultimately, one can say that Hiru's story shows the brave struggle but inevitable defeat of the individual and her limited power against an oppressive culture. Parikh reiterates a paternalistic attitude toward tribals and lower castes, overshadowing the heroine she means to praise. The main difference with Pal's story is that *Warrior in a Pink Sari* deals with collective actions and hope for change, whereas the disappearance of the author in Hiru's story raises significant questions about the political effect of rendering the writer an invisible translator of a different world. Can this act of translation really bear no trace of the translator's subjectivity? Following Spivak, I do not think this is possible. In her book Pal says, "Until you speak to the oppressed, you will never hear them" (Pal and Berthod 2010, 104); yet one cannot help wondering just who is writing this woman's oppression in her own autobiography.

On the question of agency and the relation between the oppressed citizens and writers or public intellectuals, it is important to highlight the difference between Parikh's or Berthod's writing and Mahasweta Devi's works, to which I have dedicated the first part of this book. A novel such as *Chotti Munda and His Arrow*, which could be considered a bildungsroman dealing with the life of a tribal subject, reveals that Devi is capable of striking a fine balance: Her art relies on collective knowledge and stories, but she does not refuse the burden of authorship. The presence of autobiographical elements is a fundamental component of Devi's works, in which the author proposes that a form of politics based on solidarity is possible in contexts of subaltern oppression. On the one hand, the language of struggle influences Devi's aesthetics. On the other, the writer never hides behind the objectivity of her ethnographic work. Devi's texts reveal that ethnographies are also inherently autobiographical accounts: The author comes into being through the response to the social and ethical call of writing (see chapter 10). Her frequent oscillation between singular and collective actors shows that organic intellectuals can be born out of the process of taking up responsibility for social justice and constructing alliances with other groups. The subjectivity of writers is unavoidably present, whether in their portrayal of characters or in their praise of heroic and collective subjects.

8

ACTS OF VIOLENCE OR ACTS OF CITIZENSHIP?

Amana Fontanella-Khan spent two years researching the Gulabi Gang and its leader, Sampat Pal, before writing *Pink Sari Revolution*. When asked about why she decided to write an ethnographic novel and what her ultimate goal was, Fontanella-Khan explained that *Pink Sari Revolution* could be considered a valuable repertoire of women's acts of bravery: "I wanted to write a book on these women because they teach us an important lesson about power, which in times of extreme inequality is easy to forget: even the absolute weakest members of society can manage by extraordinary *acts of will*, luck and some recklessness to fight back" (Fontanella-Khan 2013a; emphasis mine). Pal's personal story is interesting because, instead of being an isolated instance of rebelliousness, it prompted the emergence of a network of women's deeds that contested patriarchal authority and traditions, such as child marriage. The book constitutes an archive of the Gulabi Gang's demonstrations against institutionalized forms of female exploitation. Their joint actions, expressing collective agency, transformed social relations in their communities and showed women freeing themselves, maybe temporarily but often unexpectedly, from socially prescribed subaltern positions. *Pink Sari Revolution* focuses on the circumstances that enabled the activities of Pal's gang to be reproduced and recognized worldwide as acts, sometimes violent, of cultural deviance. But can these acts that rewrite women's widely accepted social roles in the nation also be considered acts of citizenship?

With the expression "acts of citizenship" I refer to Engin Isin and Greg Nielsen's theorization of acts as ways to approach the concept of citizenship not purely as status or practice. Encouraging scholars to think of citizenship in new ways, Isin says, "It is no longer adequate (if it ever was) to think of states as 'containers' of citizens as its members. New actors articulate claims for justice through new sites that involve multiple and overlapping scales of rights and obligations" (Isin 2009, 370). Because different actors claim rights and justice on the global scene, often without appealing to the institutional power of the state, Isin disengages citizenship from the domain of the nation-state and theorizes political subjectivity as emerging from specific acts of bodies moving in particular spaces: "If we approach citizenship as acts, we would be interested not only in what people do but also in how the things they do break away from norms, expectations, routines, rituals, in short, their habitus" (Isin 2012, 110). Instead of embracing customary practices as elements defining one's belonging to a given culture, Isin sees acts of claiming justice that disrupt or redefine the codes of mainstream culture as challenges to common understandings of citizenship.

In the case of Sampat Pal, violations of social and traditional norms are the basis of her campaign for a fairer society. Asking whether her disruptions of social codes can be considered acts of citizenship means exploring if, and how, they can be reread in light of Isin's fundamental coordinates. In this chapter I discuss Isin's writings on acts, and in the final section I ask the sensitive yet necessary question of whether acts of violence that appeal to the ideal of redistributive justice can be considered acts of citizenship. Hence I look at their creative power in inventing a more equal society.

SPEECH, ACTION, AND ACTS

In several works Isin proposes to look at acts of citizenship as fulfilling four fundamental conditions. First, "To recognize certain acts as acts of citizenship requires the demonstration that these acts produce subjects as citizens" (Isin 2009, 371). Isin considers the production of citizens as the coming into being of political subjects who contest, articulate, or resignify their experiences of belonging to a given territory or state. From this perspective the emergence of a political subject is a consequence of, not a prerequisite for, the making of a deed. Second, acts "create new sites of contestation, belonging, identification and struggle" (371), because their unfolding modifies the general perception of specific spaces. Acts remap physical and imaginary places.

The third condition is a corollary of the previous one: "Acts of citizenship stretch across boundaries, frontiers and territories to involve multiple and overlapping scales" (371). The scales of struggles, demonstrations, or specific acts are always multiple and changing, because acts travel across imaginative, cultural, and media landscapes. Finally, for Isin, theorizing acts implies shifting the focus of social research from what people say (opinion, perception, attitudinal surveys) to what people do.

My reading of Isin intends to complicate this last division between the domains of words and acts. Because my framework for investigating acts of writing relies on speech act theory, I do not uphold a theoretical separation between language and deeds (see also chapter 9). I believe that, particularly in the case of the writers I have analyzed so far, the place and time in which their acts of writing took place is as important as the style of their works. Thus, in my reading of Isin's work, a better description of the shift in knowledge that is produced by theorizing acts has to do with the passage from a descriptive idea of social sciences to a performative one. In other words, instead of conceiving social research as a privileged route to describe what happens in the world, researchers who think about politics through acts are encouraged to consider the multiple levels of reverberation of specific events as well as their own involvement as interpretative agents in their field of knowledge. Moreover, Isin's work itself, if considered an intervention in the field of political theory, blurs the boundaries between saying and doing. His notion of acts of citizenship initiates a transformative inquiry that creates and promotes the use of the new vocabulary of sites, scales, and acts. In this section I expand on the definitions of sites and scales as elements constituting a body politic (Isin 2009, 371) to analyze the reach and resonance of Pal's pink activism.

Isin rejects looking at states, or even regional powers, as points of departure for political theory. For example, when non-European citizens claim rights in an international forum, such as the European Court of Justice, they present us with a case for which old and state-centric views of politics fall short of explanations. On the other hand, Isin does not abandon a classical emphasis on rights and rights-claiming subjects, because the deployment of the language of rights and citizenship by marginalized subjects in official and nonofficial contexts can help pave the way for empowering battles.

Pal's language, which highlights that women live in slavery despite their formal equality, is not just an exercise of eloquence; her speech is one of her weapons to exert social power. Pal's speech acts are doubly productive. First, her vigorous rhetoric and her strength of speech give flesh to her opinions. She encourages the women of her gang to speak out and resist abuses: "Make your voices heard. Come with me!" (Fontanella-Khan 2013b, 55). Second, language is important for Pal because it is an instrument of social shaming. Fontanella-Khan tells us, "Sampat used a well-known technique of protest in India called *gherao*, whereby the public, driven by a sense that they have no traditional recourse to justice, and no power on their side except their sheer numbers and anger, surround an offending government establishment . . . to demand justice" (46). Language is an instrument to demand justice, but it also constitutes relations and enhances resistance against widespread abuses. Pal says, "The *lathi* is our last resort and has never killed anyone. It's not like a knife or a gun. Believe me, my unbeatable arguments are my most effective weapon" (Pal and Berthod 2010, 129). Indeed, the way in which Pal challenges common conventions through speaking out against oppression and the way she gathers support through making claims to justice suggest that her speech and acts interrupt the conventional understanding of women's role in society and are the basis for the creation of new and solidaristic relationships.[1]

Acts, speech, and intersubjective relations are at the core of Hannah Arendt's theory of action, which Isin discusses at length in *Citizens Without Frontiers*. I want to examine the ways in which Arendt's work highlights that speech and acts are not separate and together create the possibility of human connectedness. Arendt considers action as the very condition of human togetherness.[2] Acting is inherently political, because it means to disclose oneself to the unexpected and to open oneself to otherness (Arendt 1958, 180). In *The Human Condition* Arendt opens up this notion of disclosure and affirms that the disclosure of a human being, which presupposes "freedom" to do the unforeseen, takes place through words and deeds. Speech is needed to make actions meaningful and to coordinate with others. Action without speech would lose the possibility of connecting subjects. For Arendt, in fact, action and speech are interdependent: "Speechless action would no longer be action because there would no longer be an actor, and the actor, the doer of deeds, is possible only if he is at the same time the speaker of words" (178–79). Not only are relations often negotiated through language, but Arendt also believes that without language there would be no acting subject at all. The birth of the "who," in fact, is a linguistic event: "Without the accompaniment of speech, at any rate, action would not only lose its revelatory character, but, and by the same token, it would lose its subject, as it were; not acting men but performing robots would achieve what, humanly speaking, would remain incomprehensible" (178).

From this perspective speech is life and cannot be disconnected from it. Through speech, individuals can narrate themselves and become aware of their uniqueness. The creation of narratives is a human function that generates knowledge and binds actions to a collective memory that lives on. For Arendt, narratives reveal the meaning of acting in its complex, overlapping levels. For this reason, "Action reveals itself fully only to the storyteller" (Arendt 1958, 192). The storyteller, though, does not have complete freedom in narration but is accountable to the community during the enactment of his or her public performance.[3] The storyteller is imbricated in the web of relations that acts of speech create.

Isin does not uphold the importance of speech in Arendt's theory of action, even though he highlights the crucial role of Arendt's philosophy for understanding social actions, such as civil disobedience, as the beginning of something new (Isin 2012, 113). Three elements of Arendt's theory of action, in particular, influence Isin's formulation of acts of citizenship: the emphasis on disclosure as creation, the idea that actions are dependent on interpretation, and the belief that their full meaning cannot be understood until the action has ended and its effects have become apparent over a period of time. In fact, Isin affirms, Arendt's theory of action, considering acting as beginning something new, "comes close to saying that an act does not require a prior convention or authorization" (Isin and Saward 2013, 24). The fact that acts perform or enact their own demands without authorization and convention is a fundamental element of Isin's theory.

Arendt does not differentiate between acts and actions, whereas Isin distinguishes "between acts as relatively lasting forms, repertoires or descriptions and the relatively short-lived actions that actualize these acts" (Isin 2012, 119). In other words, actions are transitory manifestations of people's performances of claims to rights, whereas acts are the repertoires according to which we are able to interpret those actions as a breach of the norm or the canon. Elsewhere, Isin notes that acts take place "when several actions come together to create a condensed effect" (Isin and Saward 2013, 32). If this effect consists of the extension and assertion of a right, through a claim and its interpretation by a narrating agent, then an act can be interpreted as an act of citizenship.

Going back to the example of Sampat Pal and the Gulabi Gang, the question that arises is, Do her rebellious actions constitute an act? And if so, is it an act of violence, an act of citizenship, or both? Interestingly, when Isin proposes examples of the common use of the word *acts*, he often mentions acts of violence (Isin 2012, 122–32). By doing so, he highlights that acts of citizenship are not necessarily positive means to expand inclusion but that they confront us with paradoxical situations that challenge common understandings of how political subjects conduct themselves. Because one of the main features of acts is the rupture they cause in the habitus, their enactment often calls into question the paradigms of legality and illegality as well as the norms of what is socially acceptable.

I have already highlighted that Pal's autobiography often uses the vocabulary of acts. Gathering her gang members, she exhorts, "We need to act. And fast!" (Pal and Berthod 2010, 55); she also clearly describes herself as "a woman of action" as opposed to a reflective character (102). At the same time, Pal affirms that her most effective weapons are language and rhetoric. This constitutes only an apparent paradox, if we consider, with Arendt, the interdependence of action and speech. Pal's activism is framed in several anthropological works (Sen 2009, 2012; White and Rastogi 2009) as an instance of women's vigilantism in India.[4] In this light, one could argue that in vigilante movements "the organisation's vocal and charismatic leadership" often plays an important part in the success of the organization (Oomen 2004, 158). Pal's case, then, would seem to be no exception.

SITE, SCALE, AND ANSWERABILITY

To understand whether or not Pal's rebellions in Bundelkhand can be considered acts of citizenship and what this theoretical framework reveals about the social commitment of her movement, it is necessary to look at the site and scale of her actions. Acts take place in specific sites of struggle; as Isin highlights, "The 'sites' of citizenship are fields of contestation around which certain issues, interests, stakes as well as themes, concepts and objects assemble" (Isin 2009, 370). Rather than seeing sites as real geographic places, they appear as spaces and fields that through the act become imbued with symbolic meanings. In *Citizens Without Frontiers* Isin says, "Sites are places or locations only insofar as social or political struggles invested in these places or locations with strategic values express them symbolically or materially. . . . What renders a location or place as a site is the strategic value for the struggle for rights that is the basis of enacting citizenship" (Isin 2012, 133). In the case of Sampat Pal, the site of her activism is the geographically delimited region of Bundelkhand, one of the poorest districts of Uttar Pradesh, India's most populous state. Over 20 percent of its 1.6 million people, living in about 600 villages, is of lower caste or an untouchable. As Ravindra K. Jain notes in *Between History and Legend: Status and Power in Bundelkhand* (2002), the dominant economic structure of agrarian villages in the region is heavily influenced by their social fabric, which is mainly patriarchal and dependent on the occupational divisions of the caste system. Partly because of the endemic poverty of the district, an area particularly prone to droughts where agriculture and irrigation are particularly difficult, the history of Bundelkhand is inextricably linked to violence and dacoity (an Anglo-Indian term meaning "banditry").

Dacoits have always terrorized the region, carrying out lootings, robberies, rapes, and murders, usually targeting higher castes and men with property. In tracing the development of brigandage in central India during the Raj and up to the twentieth century, Kasturi (1999) notes that the combination of economic, social, and political elements contributed to the development and the persistence of dacoit activities in Banda. Since the Raj, the dacoit menace has been present in particular in the border territories with the princely states, where the existence of separate authorities rendered the enforcement of law and order particularly difficult. Finally, violence in such areas was fueled by the so-called *bhumeawat*: fights for identity and territory that brought to the fore the existence of conflicting political alliances and ideas of social belonging (see Fischer-Tine and Mann 2004, 121).

As I mentioned in chapter 7, an important part of the history of banditry in Bundelkhand was written by a woman: Phoolan Devi, the Bandit Queen. Devi led her gang of robbers and murderers in treacherous actions, which have become legendary and have inspired numerous representations of her life, including Mala Sen's novel and Shekar Kapur's highly controversial film *Bandit Queen*.[5] Devi's angry and often gruesome reactions against her own subjection to gender and caste exploitation, documented in the autobiography *I, Phoolan Devi: The Autobiography of India's Bandit Queen*, granted her the status of hero. Devi's story is relevant for the analysis of Sampat Pal's actions because these women's violent rebellion took place in the same area of Banda, under the same conditions of poverty and discrimination. Devi's and Pal's narratives created iconic representations of strong leadership and justified violence; their deeds challenged the relation between law and justice, exposing enduring social inequalities. By turning into a bandit, Devi dramatically revealed "wrongful social norms whose persistence into the postcolonial welfare state challenges the liberalism of the rule of law" (B. Ghosh 2009, 26). Pal's attempt to create a female gang similarly vindicates the principle of equality inherent in legal citizenship. In the eyes of wide subaltern audiences, who experienced similar forms of discrimination, these women's offenses are justifiable social crimes.

By registering the popular support granted to Robin Hood–like figures such as Devi, academic discourses in the subcontinent have often interpreted dacoity by turning to Eric Hobsbawm's *Primitive Rebels* (1959), which framed social bandits as "good criminals" (Kasturi 1999, 77). On the other hand, in light of Hobsbawm's understanding of banditry as a primitive form of social movement, nowadays almost extinct, the resistance of dacoits in India appears as an anachronism (Rajan 2003, 218). Modern dacoity, though, cannot be dismissed simply as a residue of the past. As Rajan notes, "The composition of dacoit gangs in recent times—predominantly men belonging to the lower castes, especially significant in Phoolan's and Vikram Mallah's gang—has given dacoit activity a distinct political aspect as underclass and caste resistance" (220). Casting banditry as an uncontrollable illegal activity means depriving it of any political meaning, whereas gangs of lower castes often do more than pose a threat to law and order: They reveal fundamental and systemic failures of the modern state. To recognize that the performance of justice often requires (sometimes violent) breaking of the law is neither to condone or condemn this violence but to understand its place in politics. In this light, anger appears as the affect that brings this realization into being.

In her autobiography Phoolan Devi powerfully affirms, "I was born with my mother's anger" (P. Devi et al. 1996, 11). As Fernandes points out, her words "move the reader away from an individualized vision of her rebellion and compel the reader to view her rebellion in relation to her mother's struggles with and critical consciousness of the socioeconomic hierarchies in her everyday rural life" (Fernandes 2001, 64). The struggle of the Bandit Queen is not merely a reaction to a life of brutal oppression and repeated rapes; rather, it is to be understood as a social protest against the structural injustice of the caste system and the sexual abuse of the poor (see Longfellow 2002, 249). The sexuality of Dalit women, often charged to be promiscuous or deviant, is "overdetermined by their location in caste hierarchies" (B. Ghosh 2009, 28).

Rape thus becomes a proof, impressed on women's bodies, that poor women are the property of upper-caste men.

It is hard not to think of Phoolan Devi when one reads about Pal's contentious methods of securing justice through the use of *lathi*s and her influence on and popularity among lower castes. In both cases, though, defining these women's ferocious doings merely as criminal acts fails to capture the challenge they posed to the social and political structures of the postcolonial nation. On the basis of the work of Rajan, Ghosh, and Kasturi, among others, activities bordering on criminality, such as banditry or vigilantism, can be seen as responses to enduring oppression and widespread mistrust of the police and the court system. The history of informal rebellions in Bundelkhand has to be understood in relation to the institutional and political corruption.

Until 2012 the chief minister of Uttar Pradesh was Mayawati, the first Dalit woman to have attained such a high post in any Indian state. Despite this achievement, Mayawati is not very popular among her electorate, and she is often blamed for not living up to her electoral promises of achieving more equality and social justice. Having appeared at public events with garlands of money around her neck and having spent millions to erect statues of herself across the capital of Lucknow, Mayawati is also known for being corrupt.[6] When the chief minister learned about the rise of the Gulabi Gang, her first concern seemed to be whether it might pose a political threat. After appearing hostile to the group, she finally offered Pal the opportunity to run for local elections under her party's banner. Pal's autobiography, though, clearly expresses dissatisfaction with Mayawati's political work, especially because her campaign to be re-elected for a second mandate was directed mainly toward upper castes. According to Pal, "Mayawati has betrayed the cause she believed in and deceived those she said she would defend. Most importantly, Mayawati of all people should have defended women and encouraged them to express themselves. She never has. . . . What a disappointment from such a fervent activist" (Pal and Berthod 2010, 172). Pal believes that Mayawati exchanged her initial hunger for justice for vanity and popularity.

To summarize, the site of Pal's activism and the growing resonance of her rebellion are constituted by evoking the powerful ghost of Phoolan Devi and her story of violence, in a moment when Uttar Pradesh seems to be sinking under growing corruption. Pal's similarity to the Bandit Queen's personal narrative is reiterated through the title of her autobiography, which closely recalls its antecedent and appeals to an already constituted audience.

The question of the resonance of Pal's actions introduces the second element that is important for this analysis: the scale of her acts. According to Isin's theorization of acts of citizenship, looking at the scale of specific actions means identifying "the reach and scope of various actions assembled and interpreted as acts" (Isin 2012, 134). The duration of the act cannot be reduced to the moment of its performance, but it includes its subsequent interpretation and description. In other words, "Scales are scopes of applicability that are appropriate to these fields of contestation" (Isin 2009, 370). In this light, even though it is crucial to identify the specific site where Pal's actions took place and how the echoes of similar stories vividly impressed in the collective memory legitimized her doing, the scale of Pal's actions goes well beyond the borders of Bundelkhand. Such scale has to take into account the extensive media coverage of her personal and collective work; but it also has to refer to the particular readership of her autobiography.

In chapter 7 I considered how the process of writing the autobiography, which took place in conversation with the French journalist Anne Berthod and led to the publication of the book in French, played a part in the fame that the narrative gained in the West. The publication of the book and the media reports motivated several directors, including Enrico Bisi (*Pink Gang*, 2010) and Kim Longinotto (*Pink Saris*, 2010), to produce documentaries on the Gulabi Gang. Thus, although locally Pal's actions and her plea for more social justice encouraged women, as well as a few men, to join the pink revolution, the global mediascape created a dispersed audience of fans and followers. Local and international audiences alike were interpellated and exercised by the moral dilemma posed by the use of violent forms of resistance in the quest for more justice for poor villagers.

The fact that the subjects caught in violent acts and their followers appear answerable to the idea of justice is one of the main features that suggest looking at Pal's acts as acts of citizenship. Isin considers answerability as the force that mobilizes subjects to act in response to a call that compels them to take an ethical position:[7] "Often what gives direction, guidance or orientation to acts or acting under description are those responsibilities that implicate or interpellate certain bodies" (Isin 2012, 129). Answerability, though, can initiate responses that do not match and can even challenge the responsibilities prescribed by the law. Pal's acts expose the urgency of taking a clear stand against serious cases of oppression and interpellate a wide audience toward achieving more social equality. Answerable subjects are pushed to take risks and often invoke the solidarity of other possible allies. In relation to the necessity of taking risks, Pal's autobiography describes the members of her female gang and her followers as subjects demonstrating the courage to act and defy social conventions: "It takes courage to wear a pink sari, the courage to reject social conventions and to assert one's beliefs" (Pal and Berthod 2010, 152). By displaying this courage and even resorting to violent actions, Pal and her vigilante gang have directed the attention of a global audience to a resistance struggle, which takes place in the poor province of Uttar Pradesh.

As seen so far, Pal is outspoken about her struggle, and she outlines in detail the causes and the aims of her sustained efforts of social engagement. As Isin reminds us, though, the purposiveness of the act is not to be confused with the intentionality of the acting subject. The creativity of acts and their consequences are often surprising and cannot be controlled. In this regard, Fontanella-Khan reports a crucial conversation in which Pal reveals her own doubts on her conduct: "Sampat does not know exactly why she has persistently felt compelled to get involved in other people's business—indeed, it represents one of the greatest mysteries that she has encountered in her life. She once declared that 'not even I understand Sampat Pal'" (Fontanella-Khan 2013b, 28). Pal depicts her life as an inevitable sacrifice to society or a sort of spiritual call (30). Her ways of taking the side of the poor through public and violent protest actions constitute a creative ethical act that questions accepted social norms.

To summarize, when Isin lists the complex qualities that constitute an act, he considers the creation of "paradoxes of legality and illegality, responsibility and answerability, intentionality and purposiveness, acts and actions, and rupture and change" (Isin 2012, 112). After having considered the elements of site, scale, and answerability in Pal's actions of protest, we can affirm that these actions amount to an act that challenges the legal system and the failure in the implementation of modern laws passed for the benefit of the poor. Pal's act of defiance springs out of answerability to justice, and it disrupts the social construction of female subordination through a performance of violence and authority.

VIGILANT(E) CITIZENS: ON SPONTANEOUS VIOLENCE

Having examined Pal's act in its site and scale, I now review current debates on vigilantism in India before asking whether Pal's acts of violence can be considered acts of citizenship. Then I turn to Hannah Arendt's dialogue with

Frantz Fanon on violence to deal with anger and its outbreak as justified reactions against oppression.

The activities of the Gulabi Gang, which range from supporting runaway couples to defending victims of domestic abuse and punishing the perpetrators, have been the object of ethnographic studies that define the movement as a vigilante organization (White and Rastogi 2009; Sundar 2010; Sen 2012). Although it is important to analyze the wider national context in which other groups have taken justice into their own hands, I argue that the social commitment of the Gulabi Gang has been primarily studied as a response, somehow mechanical, to the systemic oppression of Indian patriarchal society. On the other hand, the gang's infrequent use of *lathi*s, which are their main weapon, has not been aptly considered. Pal has often said that her approach to violence is not programmatic but pragmatic: "I don't believe in violence, but one has to be pragmatic. Women don't know how to use their fists, so they are much more vulnerable than men. When they are armed they feel stronger. Fortunately, we have seldom had to use our *lathi*s and we have only ever given one policeman a thrashing" (Pal and Berthod 2010, 129). Pal is interested in the confidence women gain when carrying a *lathi* rather than in its actual use.

Anthropologist Atreyee Sen dismisses the gang's rare use of violence as a strategy of survival of the movement, because it is crucial for the gang to "partially distance itself from violence, use the secular language of human rights, and to accept the support of rural men in order to lend ethical legitimacy to their collective actions" (Sen 2012, 10).[8] Instead, I argue that even though the Gulabi Gang does present some typical features of vigilante movements, its use of violence is neither programmatic nor ritualized. In Pal's autobiography and Fontanella-Khan's ethnographic novel, women's anger is the main element that provides ethical legitimacy to violent acts. The occasional outbreaks of violence in which the gang was involved appear spontaneous and unplanned.

In India vigilantism takes several forms, more or less organized and institutionalized. In some cases major political parties, such as the Bharatiya Janata Party (BJP) and the Congress Party, have supported the formation of vigilante groups, and their activities resulted in large-scale massacres of citizens, in so-called communal riots (Sundar 2010, 115).[9] In other instances the patrolling activities have involved ordinary people lynching suspected thieves or rapists.[10] In relation to women's vigilantism, their violent acts are rarely articulated as the result of a drive to define the boundaries of religious and cultural belonging. Rather, women's use of violence is frequently justified as a response to brutal forms of oppression and mistreatment. In these cases the unfolding of violent acts poses a moral dilemma. As Sen recalls, the outburst of violence against the serial rapist Akku Yadav, who was castrated, blinded, and killed by a group of victimized women outside court, obtained widespread public approval and almost sympathetic media reports (Sen 2012, 4). The expression of popular sympathy toward the treacherous act reveals a growing popular desire for redistributive and reparative justice.

In their discussion of the Gulabi Gang's activities and other women's vigilantism, White and Rastogi highlight the importance of setting justice as the ultimate objective. The authors do not refrain from expressing support for forms of violence that can be considered ethical, that aim to repair the wrongdoing in the face of the victims and the community:[11] "We argue that some forms of women's vigilantism are legitimate acts of violence in specific political contexts where local judiciaries fail to protect women against gross human rights abuses" (White and Rastogi 2009, 316). For example, as Barbara Oomen highlights, the rise of the South African vigilante group Mapogo A Mathamaga coincided with the crisis of law and order that followed the end of apartheid: "The vigilante organisation was a forceful response to rampant crime in the area and the incapacity of existing institutions to deal with it" (Oomen 2004, 155).

White and Rastogi emphasize that vigilante activities surface and develop when the following conditions apply: "(a) overwhelming structural conditions of injustice exist; (b) individual experiences of criminal victimization are experienced collectively; and (c) an atmosphere of everyday violence pervades society" (White and Rastogi 2009, 314). It is true that all these conditions are met in the context where Pal and the Gulabi Gang operate, because the group's members fight everyday against brutal oppression and injustice afflicting the lives of lower-caste women. But considering vigilantism as a form of resistance that arises systematically in similar contexts of structural imbalance can diminish the disruptive potential inherent in the rebellions of Pal's gang.

Through the years the Gulabi Gang has repeatedly challenged the corruption of state representatives who oversee the distribution of provisions to the poor and the handling of government aid. Both Fontanella-Khan (2013b) and Sen (2009) report one of the cases when the gang directly antagonized dishonest officials. Sen writes, "In June 2007, the Gulabis received complaints that a government-run fair-price shop was not giving out grain. Sampat and her gang surreptitiously observed the shop owner. The gang eventually intercepted two truckloads of grain marked Below Poverty Line as they were being shunted off to the open market. Armed with their evidence, the gang members pressured the local administration to seize the grain and hand over the shop owner to the police. But when local authorities refused to register the case, angry gang members assaulted one of the police officers" (Sen 2012, 6). Sen's report depicts an angry and shouting mob of women trying to stop the theft of goods destined for the poorest citizens. These women's anger, though, is far from irrational and has its reasons. As White and Rastogi highlight, "The reasons women cite for engaging in violent activities reveal their decisions to be rational, community-oriented informed choices, despite the media's inclination to portray them as irrational, spontaneous mob violence" (White and Rastogi 2009, 314). I do not agree that the gang's acts of violence are simplistically illogical, but I also do not want to reduce the hazy immediacy of anger to the clarity of a conscious choice. Pal's acts are purposive but not necessarily intentional.

Arendt's famous essay *On Violence* here helps me to disengage the actions springing out of anger from the domain of irrationality or pathology (Arendt 1970, 63). The political theorist sees acts motivated by anger as a consequence of a surfacing sense of justice: "Rage is by no means an automatic reaction to misery and suffering as such. . . . Only when our sense of justice is offended do we react with rage" (63). So when rage against injustice triggers violence, this is "neither beastly nor irrational" (62). Arendt does not sustain the acts by which men take the law into their own hands for justice's sake and considers them to be apolitical and "in conflict with the constitutions of civilized communities" (64). Yet she understands violence as instrumental to the achievement of specific and short-term goals. As in the case of Pal's work, violence "can serve to dramatize grievances and bring them to the public attention" (78). In these cases violence can be justifiable, but it is not legitimate.[12]

As Finlay points out in his discussion of the relationship between Arendt's writing on violence and Frantz Fanon's *Wretched of the Earth*, which is one of the targets of Arendt's criticism, the two texts take strikingly similar positions in relation to violence and anger. Fanon often refers to the natives as carrying a burden of anger, which cannot be freed so long as they are trapped in the tight links of the chains of colonialism (Fanon 1963, 42). To

Fanon, anger is the instrument of a violent type of reparative justice, which "frees the native from his inferiority complex and from his despair and inaction" (74). As such, individualized violence is a cleansing force, and anger provides the energy to act. Finlay describes the use of violence as the instrument to achieve a specific goal and a fairer society: "The participation of empire's victims in counter-violence helps them to claim back their dignity and to heal the psychological wounds inflicted by the settlers" (Finlay 2009, 33). In this sense, Arendt's justification of violence is not opposed to Fanon's belligerent position.

Reading Fanon with Arendt is particularly important for understanding Sampat Pal for more than one reason. First, the authors clarify the idea of legitimate, short-term violent actions in contexts of oppression. Second, they help us to understand anger as a nonirrational force arising from the drive toward justice. Third, Fanon suggests reading anger as the trigger for enacting a fairer society and a more just idea of citizenship. In fact, when Fanon describes the structural oppression of colonialism, he speaks of "two-fold citizenship" (Fanon 1963, 35), through which the settler can set himself apart from the native population. Looking at the split between the urban spaces of the European minority and the Arab quarters, Fanon highlights that this material separation represents the construction of a double citizenship. Against the segregation of the least powerful groups, Fanon sees violence as just.

In the case of Pal's gang, the context in which they act is not binarily divided between natives and settlers, but citizenship and its entitlements are experienced differently in relation to gender, caste, and class. As in Fanon's description, though, lower-caste women carry the burden of a lifelong anger; they stand by the fence, ready to jump at the opportunity of receiving justice. The oppression endured by the pink warriors has taunted their sense of justice long enough. Their acts of violence dramatize their grievances against a patriarchal and authoritarian system and galvanize public attention. Sundar believes that these forms of subaltern insurgencies are aimed less at reorganizing the state and directed more toward obligating it to live up to its promises (Sundar 2010, 116). But I argue that the performative and creative aspect of the gang's acts should not be overwritten by an emphasis on the pitfalls of state. The Gulabi Gang's critical acts are also creative ones. In this regard, Sen highlights an interesting aspect: "Not only do these vigilante groups exist outside the purview of the state, but they further emasculate the malfunctioning state by highlighting its paternal failure to protect vulnerable women" (Sen 2012, 9). Taking the mask off the benevolent rhetoric of the postcolonial nation, women's activist groups perform a type of citizenship that is not yet there.

The Gulabi Gang does not merely carry out operations of surveillance and punishment. It provides social services for poor women, offering accommodation and food to those in need. Its extensive network of relations delivers to women both material and emotional support. The gang teaches self-defense as well as sewing, so that women can become economically self-sufficient. Yet, despite the achievement of public services, these women are "good bad citizens" (Sen 2012, 11) and occupy an uncomfortable position in the public imagination. Standing up to widespread abuse is a risky affair, and Pal has been accused of being a Naxalite (Pal and Berthod 2010, 228). White and Rastogi admit, "These women risk being criminalized and dangerously attacked themselves when violent retributive definitions of justice are carried out" (White and Rastogi 2009, 324). Pal has several charges pending against her and a long list of detractors. The deeds of the Gulabi Gang highlight the connection between the achievement of equality and the danger of criminalization. The movement is dreaded not only for their power of holding the state accountable for its actions but also because their acts initiate something new.

Instead of autonomous or alternative forms of citizenship (Oomen 2004, 168), the Gulabi Gang performs a fairer image of a citizenship to come. It responds to everyday experiences of oppression with anger, to the isolation of the poor with collective acts. The affective work of the group members provides emotional support to people who feel vulnerable and forgotten and is directed at changing the structural conditions of gender and caste discrimination. The gang's endorsement of justice and equality as guiding principles and ultimate objectives motivates their acts of protest. Can these acts of occasional and spontaneous violence be acts of citizenship? As Isin suggests, acts have to be seen as performing their demands. In this light, the violent acts and the threats of violence of the warriors in pink saris (Singha 1998), which spring out of a demand for social justice, also create a network of social relations based on collaboration and mutual support instead of exploitation and marginalization.

4

Between Theory and Practice

9

PERFORMING CITIZENSHIP

Resignifying Literature

Having read Mahasweta Devi, Arundhati Roy, and Sampat Pal's fiction and nonfiction works in their specific contexts, in this final part of *Acts of Angry Writing* I present a more theoretical argument on the relation between law, citizenship, and literature. The acts of writings of these three women present challenges to specific laws, highlighting that the existence of legal provisions does not guarantee the achievement of justice for the poorest Indian citizens. More specifically, Devi's writing contests the legacy of the Criminal Tribes Act and the enduring prejudice that identifies indigenous people as dangerous. Roy criticizes the enforcement of the Land Acquisition Act, claiming that it reiterates a form of economic orientalism against Adivasis. Pal demonstrates the persistence of customs and institutions, such as dowry and child marriage, that discriminate against women despite their official ban. Claiming citizenship as substantial equality, both in society and before the law, these activists oppose these forms of everyday and institutional injustice through their life and writing.

The analysis of the literary texts proposed suggests that it is possible to think about a productive relation between literature and citizenship if we abandon the idea that literature is nothing but a parasitic description of the world. But so far I have not offered a theoretical statement to sustain the legitimacy of framing the specific discussion of law through literature.

Thus in this chapter my aim is to tackle the possible objection that literature is a representative art and, as such, has a different status from law and citizenship, which intervene in the real world through normative statements. To maintain the importance of taking into account the creative potential of literature in contexts of conflict and social change, I present here a review of a philosophical tradition that deconstructs the idea of normativity and frames literature as an arm of politics. In looking at theoretical debates on speech acts and performativity, I suggest that several scholars, from Austin to Butler, Felman, and Sedgwick, have found exciting ways to investigate the relation between literature and law, pointing to the importance of looking at what literature "does" and how it intervenes in social struggles.

In this chapter I reduce law and literature to their common denominator: their performative force. Law gains its normative power from its repetition, which allows the transformation of a statement, a speech act, into a norm or a behavioral code. But the ways in which the repetitions of a norm take place cannot be strictly predicted; as Devi, Roy, and Pal show, the proclamation of a law and constitutional statements do not guarantee material success in ensuring citizens' protection or operating change. The law is vulnerable to failure. Made of language, it is built of the same substance of literature and, being always subjected to interpretation and re-enactment, it can misfire. In the following sections I expand on this theme through a discussion on the materiality of language, the question of intentionality, and how these issues relate to the ideal of the liberal citizen that underpins contemporary citizenship.

The production of speech acts that question and defy established norms and laws is inherently part of the production of writing that constitutes Devi, Roy, and Pal's acts of citizenship. Because one of the questions driving this volume is whether and how literature can create political imaginaries of citizenship, in this chapter I respond to the disciplinary separation of the fields of literature and citizenship by positing them as two sides of the same coin. This move of legitimizing the discussion of law through literature is a necessary prelude to chapter 10, where I move on to expose the primary role of affects and anger in the production of political texts.

"DOING THINGS" WITH AUSTIN

The performative tradition has its roots in John L. Austin's *How to Do Things with Words* (1962), which demonstrates how certain utterances, pronounced by the right people at the right time, can constitute acts. Austin's reflection on speech acts questions the distinction between saying and doing, between language and the world. It demonstrates how language actively affects our networks of relations and modifies our present.

According to Austin, language can be performative. I argue that literature, as the field of knowledge that reflects deeply on language, surely retains some of this performative power. In this chapter I offer a critical review of the literature on speech acts to suggest that the performative character of literature, highlighted by Jacques Derrida in response to Austin and John Searle, can influence and even change our relation with politics, rights, and conceptions of citizenship. How does reflecting on the linguistic subject affect our understanding of the citizen-subject? After considering these issues with reference to the writings of Shoshana Felman, Judith Butler, and Eve Sedgwick, I explore how accepting the performative power of language modifies our conceptions of the practice of reading.

But, first, let me explain why it is important to return to Austin to approach the topic of writing politics. In *Speech Acts in Literature* (2001), Hillis Miller reveals Austin's compliance with an anthropocentric perspective, according to which the world exists "out there" for the subject to get to know through experience. Communication in this schema is mainly a vehicle for knowledge and transfer of information. But Austin's innovative idea of performative utterances highlights not only how language can be a tool for action but also how it can become an act itself, insofar as the subject proffering the speech act complies with defined external conditions of possibility (Austin 1975, 6–7). For Austin, the circumstances under which certain words are uttered have to be appropriate: "There must exist an accepted conventional procedure having a specific conventional effect, the procedure to include the uttering of certain words, by certain persons in certain circumstances" (26). For example, in a scene of marriage the felicity of the statement "I declare you husband and wife" depends on the fact that the speaking subject is a religious leader or an official invested with the authority to celebrate the union between two people. Only in this case does the marriage take place and the speech act can be considered successful (or felicitous).

Speech acts are therefore fundamentally tied to questions of authority, because the felicity or infelicity of a performative utterance depends on the structure of power that supports or denies its validity. Moreover, Austin's theory presupposes total coherence between the intention and the actions of the speaking subjects and that they perform their speech acts by observing the rules and responsibilities prescribed within a modern state. For example, acts such as cheating and lying exceed the domain of verifiable truth and therefore, according to Austin, cannot be classified as felicitous speech acts. Taking into account all these elements, in his critique of Austin's work, Miller says, "Austin reinforces a whole set of presumptions, including the subject/object split and the concept of the democratic nation-state with its free, responsible citizens; the notion that fictions are 'etiolated,' parasitic on representational, verifiable truth-telling; the subordination of women and animals" (Miller 2001, 60).

Austin adhered to a liberal worldview; he believed in the sovereignty of the subject and his or her free will and supported private property and individual rights. These aspects were taken up and further developed in Searle's *Speech Acts* (1969). On the other hand, a number of subsequent critical studies of speech act theory focused on how Austin's work can actually be used to question the very assumptions he aims to uphold. For example, an interpretation of Austin's reflections on performative utterances, first by Jacques Derrida and then by Judith Butler, challenged the idea that subjects are completely in control of their will and their intentions. By focusing on these readings endorsing anti-essentialist notions of identity, Sedgwick points out how Austin's work has been fundamental for the development of the fields of deconstruction and gender theory (Sedgwick 2002, 6). Derrida's references to performatives in "Force of Law" (1990) and "Before the Law" (reprinted in *Acts of Literature*, 1992) are an important contribution to the purpose of challenging classical conceptions of the naturalness of law and its role in the pursuit of justice. Butler frees gender identity from its subordination to the imperative of biology and shows how biology itself is a discourse that creates and normalizes gender difference while describing it (*Gender Trouble*, 1990; *Undoing Gender*, 2004). In this chapter, in referring particularly to Felman and Sedgwick's ways of "queering" Austin's work, I consider three points: (1) how theories of performativity can deconstruct the division between idealism and materialism; (2) that an examination of speech act theory introduces a discussion of the citizen as a nonsovereign subject; and (3) that revisiting Austin can help us appreciate the importance of looking at fictions for the study of law.

THE MATERIALITY OF LANGUAGE

In *The Scandal of the Speaking Body* Shoshana Felman explains that performatives are "expressions whose function is not to inform or describe, but to carry out a 'performance,' to accomplish an act through the very process of their enunciation" (Felman 2003, 6). By establishing a relationship between language and actions, between saying and doing, performatives challenge the idea that language is merely representational. The referent cannot be accessed directly. It can be approached only through language, which is not a neutral tool of representation but a force of transformation. As Derrida puts it, performatives reveal the scandal of knowledge: "The scandal is that the sign, the image or the representer become 'force' that makes the world move" (Derrida 1992, 85). Because the theory of performative utterances maintains that the only possible way to attain the world is through the mediation of signs, it questions the very existence of a world outside the speaking subject that can be known through representation.

Taking her cue from Derrida, Felman uses the image of scandal to stress the creative power of language and its material existence. Language does not substitute for reality but generates a force that acts on it: The referent is "no longer a pre-existing substance but an *act*, that is, a dynamic movement of modification of reality" (Felman 2003, 51). As a consequence, referential knowledge "is not knowledge *about* reality, but knowledge that *has to do with* reality" (51). The effect of certain utterances is to perform an action that exceeds language and modifies the real. Felman suggests that the originality of Austin's theory lies in its potential to undo the traditional separation between materialism and idealism: "It is precisely here that Austin's originality lies, for through the new concept of language act he explodes both the opposition and the separation between matter (or body) and language: matter, like the act, without being reducible to language, is no longer entirely separable from it, either" (108–9). In accordance with Derrida, Felman considers the speech act as the materialization of a communicative force. Speech acts constitute "a relation, precisely between the matter of language (little bits of sentences, phrases, signifiers, atoms of the speaking body) and energy or (illocutionary) force, that space of undecidability between matter and energy, between 'things and events'" (109). For Felman, this emphasis on language as material is the most interesting and threatening feature of the performative, which undermines the humanistic faith in the objective existence of a phenomenological reality.

Detecting this threatening potential, Derrida describes the materiality of signs as dangerous. In "That Dangerous Supplement" (reprinted in Derrida 1992), an essay arising from the analysis of Rousseau, Derrida maintains that, whether oral or written, language implies the production of signs that supplement physical and sensorial experience. Writing, in particular, constitutes an attempt to substitute the absence of speech with a performance of presence. Despite the fact that performance is necessarily bound to fail, since representation is not a simple substitution, writing appears dangerous because it claims to be both a sign and a thing in itself: "The supplement has not only the power of procuring an absent presence through its image; procuring it for us through the proxy [procuration] of the sign, it holds it at a distance and masters it. For this presence is at the same time desired and feared. The supplement transgresses and at the same time respects the interdict. This is what also permits writing as the supplement of speech; but also already spoken word as writing in general" (Derrida 1992, 97). The production of a "dangerous supplement" is the fundamental feature of a communicative situation. But what is the danger? If interpretation is understood as an inextricable part of knowledge and if the world is constituted by and through language, then the objectivity of the descriptive language of the law is brought into question. This means that the textual and narrative aspects of politics acquire a new relevance for the analysis of law.

"BEFORE THE LAW" AND THE PERFORMATIVE FORCE

Following an Austinian scheme, one could think that the performativity of law derives from the authority granted by state power. Austin himself points out that "acts which concern the jurist are or include the utterance of performatives, or at any rate are or include the performance of some conventional procedures" (Austin 1975, 19).

Yet in "Force of Law" Derrida invites us to think about the enforceability of the law not only as its applicability but as the original force, or violence, that underpins its creation. The founding of the law, as the law of a particular state, takes place in a performative moment, in which a body of written rules is instituted as a set of injunctions that citizens are required to comply with. At that moment the law consecrates state power through uttering its sovereign power in the language of the majority: "The very emergence of justice and law, the founding and justifying moment that institutes law implies a performative force, which is always an interpretative force: this time not in the sense of law that would maintain a more internal, more complex relation with what one calls force, power or violence . . . the operation that consists of founding, inaugurating, justifying law (droit), making law, would consist of a *coup de force*, of a performative and therefore interpretative violence that in itself is neither just nor unjust" (Derrida 1990, 941). Rather than addressing the problem of violence and the foundations of the modern state, I want to highlight here that Derrida sees laws primarily as performative utterances. By questioning the apparent eternal and universal character of law, Derrida stresses how its making takes place in a textual network and requires an interpretative effort.

"It seems that law should never give rise to any story" (Derrida 1992, 191), says Derrida, because its categorical authority over and relation to the ideal of justice should transcend any context. On the other hand, stories written about the law reveal that a specific set of rights has developed as a result of a particular history and possesses a textual structure that is open to change. Derrida illustrates how to deconstruct law in his essay "Before the Law," which revolves around Franz Kafka's short story of the same name. The story tells of a poor man who enters the gate of the Law and asks the doorkeeper to appear before it, but his numerous requests are always rejected. His failure is irrefutable, because the law never shows itself. The man ages and eventually dies without achieving his purpose. In Derrida's reading, the countryman's failure is determined by his will to relate to the law by trying to touch it and "enter" into physical contact with it. Law cannot be accessed; but it can be "deciphered" (Derrida 1992, 197).

For Derrida, the possibility of deciphering the law (as *droit*) derives from its foundation in interpretable textual strata. But this possibility for the poor and the marginalized becomes a political imperative to take up deconstruction as a political tool in order to counteract the fictitious universality of law as an arm of justice: "Laws, constitutions, the declaration of the rights of man, grammar or the penal code are not 'natural realities' and they depend upon the same structural power that allows novelesque fictions or mendacious inventions and the like to take place. This is why literature and the study of literature have so much to teach us about right and law" (Derrida 1988, 134). Laws are made of the same textual structure as literature, and they share a performative force that permits the creation of a "dangerous supplement": "Literature itself makes the law, emerging in that place where the law is made" (Derrida 1992, 216).

The danger, or the threat to the authority of the institutions, is determined by the porosity of the border dividing fiction from law: "Literature can *play the law*, repeating it while diverting it or circumventing it"

(Derrida 1992, 216). Making use of the double meaning of the verb *playing*, Derrida highlights two points: First, literature can act like or even impersonate the law by reproducing its formulas and imperative tone; second, in doing so and by revealing their common fabric, literature enters the field of law without prior authorization and subversively mocks its universal and univocal authority.

The subversive potential of speech acts here comes to the fore. According to Miller, Austin's concern was to neutralize the threat to the legal authority that was implicitly inscribed in performative utterances. For this reason Miller tried to confine his theory within the limits of moral acceptability dictated by the liberal nation-state: "The ultimate goal of Austin's work is to secure the conditions whereby law and order may be kept. This explains the urgency and determination with which Austin seeks to establish a sound doctrine of performative utterances. The stability of civil society and the security of the nation depend on it. We must have some justified way to hold people to their promises, to put people in jail for perjury, for breach of the promise, or for bigamy" (Miller 2001, 57–58). In the attempt to draw conceptual boundaries for the applicability of his work, Austin in fact clearly states that cheating and lying are infelicitous acts; they are void or without consequences (Austin 1975, 16). Despite the promise made, if the speaking subject is acting in bad faith, the performatives produce "misfire." Promises, as Austin remarks, should always be uttered by those who intend to keep their word (11). This philosophy of language places a strong emphasis on social values, such as morality and accuracy, according to which the production of speech acts should take place within the terms of their actual verifiability.

According to Austin, because literature falls outside the domain of verifiable speech, it is akin to deceitful communication. Misfire becomes its essence: "A performative utterance will be *hollow* or void if said by an actor on stage, or if introduced in a poem, or spoken in soliloquy" (Austin 1975, 22). From this perspective, Derrida's injunction to look at literature to learn something about rights or citizenship appears not simply unorthodox but almost heretical. Yet the French philosopher's argument on the commonality between the performativity of the narrative structure of law and that of literature is a powerful demonstration of why we should not dismiss literature as unproductive. In Derrida's analysis literature becomes a tool for a philosophical analysis of law. If misfire features as an essential element of literature, it does so because in an Austinian framework either the narrative "I" cannot believe in the truthfulness of what it says, or the relation with reality is weak because it is temporally deferred.

Yet in Derrida's words, "The narrative 'I' frightens the law" (Derrida 1992, 206) because it creates a dangerous supplement that not only modifies reality but also multiplies the dimensions that make up our idea of it. Thus, instead of directly approaching the question of what literature can teach about citizenship, I review the idea of the "I" present in Austin's work. The ideal of the classical Cartesian subject, inhabiting Austin's imaginary, has been challenged in Felman's combined reading of *How to Do Things with Words* and *Don Juan*. Departing from Felman, I ask, Do performatives and the possibility of misfire reveal the existence of a breach in the sovereignty of the citizen-subject?

THE NONINTENTIONAL CITIZEN-SUBJECT

Notions such as law and citizenship call for an analysis of the figure of the citizen who is supposed to enjoy bearing his rights. The citizen-subject, who complies with or defies norms and conventions, is also central to the theory of speech acts. Austin notes that the "I" comes essentially into the picture of explicit performatives, which are carried out in the first-person, deploying verbs such as "I declare," "I apologize," and "I promise." When Austin enunciates the conditions of felicity of a speech act, he is placing the intention of the speaking "I" under scrutiny. The continuity between intention, words uttered, and deed done is necessary to avoid misfire.

Austin imagines a subject that unequivocally says what he means and means what he says. This subject, Miller notes, is an abstraction: If Austin had taken into account Freud's work on the unconscious, his ideal speech act would not be so dependent on the correspondence between prior intention and actual deed.[1] In fact, the dimension of misfire, dismissed by Austin as a parasitic feature that empties language of its meaning, has given rise to numerous studies that attempt to rehabilitate its function in communicative situations.

Felman, through the analysis of *Don Juan*, looks at how a series of promises made without any intention of keeping them, such as promises of enduring love and marriage, eventually lead the subject to succeed in his acts of conquest. Felman maintains that Don Juan's use of the self-referential quality of performatives creates an illusion of reality that supports his aim.

His misfire is not merely an unproductive failure: "Such failing is not simple negation, but the enactment of difference (something else is done)" (Felman 2003, 57). It is precisely Don Juan's systematic breach of his promises of love and of commitment to future actions that constitutes the core of his ability to seduce.

Seduction, then, is here reconducted to its etymological sense of separation: A breach is inherent in the performative because, in Felman's psychoanalytic interpretation, a speech act can never be completely fulfilled. Whether promises are systematically broken, as in *Don Juan*, or subjects cannot be fully in control of what they say, as in a Freudian framework, the act is equally defined by the possibility of being unconsummated or falling short of its accomplishment. A certain rupture in the subjects' coherence and in their perceptions of the self is inherent in the speech acts and constitutes their scandalous secret. Felman's definition of the scandal of the performatives can be summarized as follows: "The act cannot know what it is doing: the act (of language) subverts both consciousness and knowledge (of language)" (Felman 2003, 67).

Felman's interrogation of speech act theory, informed by psychoanalysis and contemporary philosophy, has the effect of depriving Austin's model of its intentional subject. Because performatives are fundamentally characterized by failure, they prompt a redefinition of the ideal of the acting subject as an abstract Cartesian subject. The excess of the sovereign will of individuals, brought to the fore by performatives, can question the individualistic, liberal model that Austin tries to sustain, including citizenship and its ideal free-willing model of subjectivity.

In *Excitable Speech* Judith Butler observes that a number of eminent studies on philosophical conceptions, rights-bearing subjects, and citizenship incorporate this Austinian ideal of subjectivity into their theoretical framework. As an example of this, she refers to Rae Langton and Anne MacKinnon, who, in advocating that hate speech should be punishable by law, maintain that continuity among intention, utterance, and deed is a requirement for both political agency and citizenship (Butler 1997, 85). Butler, however, points out that there is a gap between a speech act and its effects that cannot be completely controlled. She reflects on the connection between supporting the role of the sovereign subject and sustaining the sovereign role of the state power in governing citizens' affairs and disputes: "This idealization of the speech act as sovereign action (whether positive or negative) appears linked with the idealization of sovereign state power or, rather, with the imagined and forceful voice of that power. It is as if the proper power of the state has been expropriated, delegated to its citizens, and the state then re-emerges as a neutral instrument to which we seek recourse to protect us from other citizens, who have become revived emblems of a (lost) sovereign power" (Butler 1997, 82). The Austinian model of sovereign citizens fits well in and even reinforces a liberal image of state benevolence, in which decision making is neutrally and equally directed toward all the citizens. But even the performative language of the state and law is bound to misfire.

By looking at the contemporary scene of political resistance emerging against this idea of a sovereign state, Butler points out that the failure of the language of equality and universal rights spoken by state power gives rise to new forms of political agency: "Contemporary forms of political agency, especially those unauthorized by prior conventions or by reigning prerogatives of citizenship, tend to derive political agency from the failures in the performative apparatus of power, turning the universal against itself, redeploying equality against its existing formulations, retrieving freedom from its contemporary conservative valence" (Butler 1997, 93). The "failures in the performative apparatus of power" open up a space for change. For example, the redeployment of the universalistic language of law and rights to uncover injustice is in itself a form of resistance.

Felman had already noted that one of the effects of repeating speech acts is that they become subverted (Felman 2003, 34). Butler, inspired by Derrida, specifies that the repetition of speech acts, instead of reproducing them in their ipseity, is a form of production of difference. The repetition of hegemonic language creates the possibility of the enactment of its resignification: "The resignification of speech requires opening new contexts, speaking in ways that have never been legitimated, and hence producing legitimation in new and future forms" (Butler 1997, 41). This process, not necessarily driven by a sovereign will or intention, has the effect of revealing the failures in the language of power. Agency is depicted as speaking on the border of the unsayable. In this light, freeing subjects from the "reigning prerogatives of citizenship" (Butler 1997, 93) can take place by exposing the limits of the sovereignty of the subject through speech.

OPENING LAW TO/THROUGH FICTION

As pointed out earlier, in Austin's *How to Do Things with Words* literature is presented as "etiolated" (Austin 1975, 92); the philosopher's analysis deprives fiction of force and life. Together with theater, literature becomes confined to the domain of what is not serious. Despite explicitly excluding literature from his classifications of speech acts, Austin often incorporates literary examples into his own writing. References to *Alice in the Wonderland* (90) and *Don Quixote* (27) become valuable tools to explain different aspects related to performative utterances and their consequences. For example, to demonstrate that not all explicit performatives, as in "I think that," express a fact about the subject, Austin evokes a dialogue between Alice and the caterpillar. When the girl starts her sentence with "I do not think . . . ," she is promptly interrupted by the caterpillar with the admonition, "Then, do not talk!" This vignette implicitly demonstrates how literature can present a deep reflection on the nature of language.

These references show that Austin's relation to literature is more ambiguous than he can possibly admit. On the one hand, fiction is dismissed as an illusion of reality, as a fictitious dimension to which the illocutionary power of literary language remains confined; on the other hand, fiction becomes helpful for analyzing the way in which things are done through language. If one considers Austin's text as a speech act that reinforces the separation between what is real and what is not, then its outcome seems to exceed the author's intention. The reiteration of literary sources and the obsessive return to the issues of etiolation and misfire reveal that the performative quality of Austin's text is not under his sovereign control. Commenting on Felman's reading of Austin, Butler points out that *The Scandal of the Speaking Body* reveals how the work of the philosopher of language is implicated in psychoanalysis (also through its use of the semantics of satisfaction) and literary studies. Instead of treating Austin as a sovereign subject, Felman uses his work to exemplify how writers cannot be fully in control of their acts of speech (Butler 2003, 121).

Butler summarizes the core of Felman's work as follows: "Our acts, precisely when they are made of language, carry the force of more knowledge than we can know" (Butler 2003, 123). This excess of force constitutes the enactment of something new, which was not foreseen by the intentions of the speaking or writing subject. In this way Felman demonstrates that the Austinian feature of misfire lies at the core of the performative function of the speech act. Whereas Austin's speech act theory aims to patrol and control language and its possible effects, Felman and Butler embrace the potential opening of language to new uses and meaning.

In this light, Butler explores in *Excitable Speech* the possibility of resignification of hate speech. Instead of merely censoring racist and misogynist speech, she sees language as the condition of both its fruition and transformation. Language can be an object of legal condemnation insofar as it does something and initiates a harmful act. But also, the legal analysis of injurious language and its incorporation into judgments expose the possibility of reproduction as resignification. Referring to an Austinian framework, Butler says, "As acts, these words become phenomenal; they become a kind of linguistic display that does not overcome their degrading meanings but that reproduces them as public text and that, in being reproduced, displays them as reproducible and resignifiable terms" (Butler 1997, 100). Legal acts, though creating a performance of authority, at the same time show that language cannot be set in stone.

Being constituted of and through language, literature and law emerge as performative in two ways. First, they present a performative function, which consists of reinforcing their own authority through the reproduction and demarcation of a certain field of knowledge and conduct. Second, as Butler explains, their common performative means a fundamental openness to rearticulation and resignification. Literature, in particular, can be configured as the space where a deeper reflection on language and its properties takes place. The authority of the field derives from specifically studying the functions of language.[2] It is not by chance that Austin turns to novels, Derrida to short stories, and Felman to plays in order to analyze the complex relation between speech and its effects. Derrida uses Kafka's fiction to expose how the existence of the law is not questioned but that its need to be interpreted makes its authority vulnerable. For this reason, in Kafka's story law is not seen or accessed, yet its existence seems unquestionable; the ultimate law states the atemporal presence of the law.[3] Within this framework, to take performativity into account means abandoning the idea that literature simply transposes reality to a fictional dimension, which remains confined to the pages of a book. Rather, if we take Felman's work on the intimate relation between the body and the speech act and apply it to writing, then the creation of a written piece appears as an embodied act that bears the traces of the specific site in which it is produced.

Writing is influenced and shaped by the contingency of its production, and, in turn, the material form of a text determines its literary character.[4] I here follow Derrida's idea that the literary character of a text is defined by its material, rhetorical, and noematic structure (Derrida 1992, 44). In *Without Alibi* (2002) Derrida refers to de Man's discussions on Rousseau's *Reveries* and *Confessions* to highlight the interconnection between the formal and the material aspect of his texts. Referring back to de Man's conception of metaphors and rhetorical language as supplements to referential illusion, Derrida claims that the formal and material aspects of a text are inseparable from each other and are dependent on (although irreducible to) the textual event of their production (Derrida 2002, 152).

Hélène Cixous's *Readings* (1991b), which starts with the chapter "Law and Writing," notes that the strength and literary appeal of some texts come from their way of exposing the originary gesture of their creation. In an initial and programmatic statement, Cixous says, "I want to work on texts that are as close as possible to an inscription—conscious or unconscious—of the origin of the gesture of writing and not of writing itself" (1). Instead of concealing the tortuous paths of their production through artistic mastery, as in the case of Flaubert's perfectly researched prose, Cixous wants to devote her exercises of close reading to the obsessive and often enigmatic writing of Clarice Lispector and Franz Kafka, among others. Cixous maintains that Kafka's paradoxes, exemplified by the aporetic position of the poor man in "Before the Law," and Lispector's mappings of the female body in the world operate a desacralization of literature: "Clarice's text comes from within. It is written from an unformulated hypothesis that writing is something living. It is not the book as sacred object" (1). This living force is specifically linked to a certain body that communicates by projecting itself in words beyond the subject.[5]

Cixous and Derrida, who share an interest in Kafka's literary reflections on the law, both point out how, in writing, the materiality of language conveys a creative force that overcomes the contingency of the writing act and makes itself tangible even when the speaker is absent. But far from transferring the intention of the subject, the act of writing necessarily involves frustration and dispossession. As de Man says, "Writing always includes the moment of dispossession in favour of the arbitrary power of the play of the signifier" (quoted in Derrida 2002, 159). Disregarding the intention of the writer, texts obey the unpredictable laws of playfulness and arbitrariness. These terms of Austinian derivation are used here in an anti-Austinian spirit. Rather than rejected as aberrations of communicative language, playfulness and arbitrariness are incorporated as integral features of texts having to do with law. After analyzing Kafka's story, both Derrida and Cixous conclude that its scandalous secret lies in exposing the fact that the law is but a word. This is what literature irreverently teaches us about law.

But why do Derrida, Cixous, Felman, and Sedgwick pay attention to deconstructing the imperative of the law by referring to literary writing? On the one hand, Austin upholds the normative function of law for creating accountable and respectable citizens. On the other hand, critical thinkers from deconstructionists to poststructuralists have uncovered the repetitive character and performative work that grants authority to law. Derrida and Cixous are concerned with questioning the law of phallogocentrism; Felman tries to decenter the linguistic paradigm that has effaced the body from the production of knowledge; Butler exposes the performative openness of the law of gender; and Sedgwick focuses on the law of women's oppression, drawing a connection between homosociality and misogyny. If writing resignifies the law, exploiting the openness of its performativity, then it can provide an insight into other ways of being political subjects before, beyond, and even against the law. From this perspective, the experiential and even visceral dimension that gives birth to writing, as opposed to the intentionality prescribed by the law, may be relevant for rethinking citizenship.

THE POLITICS OF READING: PLEASURE, TEXTURE, AFFECT

Arguably, some of these issues concerning the relation between the utterance and the performative situation had already been anticipated by Roland Barthes when he suggested that "the utterance exposes the subject's place and energy, even its deficiency. . . . Words are cast as projections, explosions, vibrations, devices, flavours. Writing makes knowledge festive" (Barthes 1979, 35). Barthes seems to embrace the material aspect of words, which are vibrations that navigate the body of the writing subject. Even when produced by the deficiency of the subject, by its lack of mastery, words are festive. Like atoms making up an utterance, words carry the force of their production and create a happy explosion that marginalizes meaning.

Sedgwick uses the term *texture* to refer to this evident relation between the substance and the surface of writing. For Sedgwick, the language of texture is central to the notion of performativity, because it raises questions about modes of perception that decenter the primacy of the visual field, about affect and the relation between knowledge and phenomenology. Feeling or touching texture brings about a level of perception that runs across the senses and can give insight into its own making. Textural perception participates in the genealogical and analytical task of cultural theory: It impels us to explore how things took the actual shape in which they present themselves (genealogy), and it provokes the affirmative question, What can be done with it? If experiencing a texture means understanding its sedimentation, this level of analysis also calls for political agency.

An example of literary criticism taking into account Sedgwick's project of textural analysis can be found in Renu Bora's essay "Outing Texture," which deals with the erotic and exciting structure of *The Ambassadors*, by Henry James. Presenting a close reading of the novel, Bora highlights its textural language, which involves tactile metaphors and a "liminal, erotic play between shiny/matte and smooth/rough distinctions" (Bora 1997, 95). Bora presents James's textual references to anal, tactile, and visual desire as homosexual "pleasurable topographies and topologies" (95): "Texture can be used as a synonym of materiality itself, inasmuch as I am arguing that a kind of inevitable tactility or human agency, in performance or in labor, is crucial to any definition of what it means to occupy a physical space" (101). James's bodily drive and his unconscious desires shape a particular form of writing that, drawing from Bora, Sedgwick defines as "fisting as écriture" (Sedgwick 1990, 208; 2002, 48). Bora's analysis maps the relation between body, desire, and the materiality of writing, fixing the spotlight on the political significance of queer language and literature, because they question the repression of plural forms of desire and pleasure.

Sedgwick's question on the possibility of converting into action an analysis of the origin and making of writing is fundamental here. For feminist and queer thinkers this analytical work of recovery of the creative process underpinning literature involves paying attention to the body as the primary organ of communication and as the repository of pleasure. In a passage that similarly refers to the importance of writing, Cixous connects the task of writing the female body to the pleasure of orality: "Of importance for a reading concerning our *questions-femmes*, or woman's questions, is the place of origin and the object. What is a writer looking for? What are the stakes in the text? How does one search for something? The movements of the body are determined by what one is looking for and the object one seeks depends on the kind of body one has. We have to work on the first and most primitive pleasure, that is to say, on orality" (Cixous 1991b, 2–3). Despite the differences in their political projects, understandings of sexual and gender identity, and forms of literary criticism, I read Cixous together with Felman, Sedgwick, and Bora to highlight their concern with the materiality of writing. This material aspect has both rhetorical and noematic qualities that are dependent on the event of its inception. They agree that the bodily dimension of desire participates in the shaping of writing.

The dimension of pleasure is inherent in the speech act from the moment of its inception (Felman 2003, 76). By using the semantics of felicity and satisfaction to describe the success of an act of speech, Austin reminds us that pleasure is a fundamental aspect of language. To capture this fundamental orientation toward the constitution of a libidinal economy, Felman uses the phrase "Austin's Donjuanism" (Felman 2003, 41). Like the character of Don Juan, whose use of performative language contributes to an act of persuasion, Austin projects the scene of speech as one of seduction and search for fulfillment. Felman affirms that the semantic field to which Austin refers is filled with an erotic drive: "The question of man's eroticism is raised as the question of the relation of the erotic and the linguistic on the stage of the speaking body" (15). Holding body, desire, and language in a tight triangulation, Felman explicitly shows how the speech act itself is a nexus of bodily and psychic forces (see Butler 1997, 141). Revisiting Austin, Felman concludes that the human sexual act always connotes the speech act (Felman 2003, 79) and that the pleasure inherent in speech depends on the oral act of seduction.

Not by chance, in the case of Don Juan, seduction is carried out through poetry. For Felman, literature is linked to pleasure because, first and foremost, we are being invited to *enjoy* it. In her words, literature "is an interminable dialogue between the voice of the dead master and the voice of the servant who lacks a master, answering each other across the abyss, still prolonging their feast of pleasure—and of stone" (Felman 2003, 47). Barthes's reference to festive writing is here transfigured in the image of a feast of pleasure. Writing is a bodily act: My mouth pronouncing the words I think, and my fingers moving on a keyboard are all involved, as much as my brain and sex, in the production of writing. Desire is a motor triggering and fueling this writing process. Here it is not my intention to endorse a psychoanalytic view of writing as *jouissance* (Cixous) or a call for full enjoyment (Felman). Rather, I want to highlight that there is a social dimension of desire that is inscribed in political and writing activities alike. Desire, for Sedgwick, is an affective or social force, the glue that shapes relationships (Sedgwick 2002, 18), and it influences the way in which these relationships are written.

Sedgwick's and Bora's works on texture show that the act of writing can materialize as an affective transmission that is linked to the body and the desires of the writer. But in addition to this, textural analysis enhances our perception by revealing the triangular relation between the writer, the text, and the reader. Sedgwick notes, "What binds affect and texture together is that they are both 'irreducibly phenomenological'" (Sedgwick 2002, 21); thus, if we consider texture, its historical sedimentation, and its affective quality, then it becomes clear that we need to rethink fiction, and especially political fiction, through a reference to the body. The body is in fact deeply implicated both in the act of writing a text and in its possible acts of reading at different times and in different contexts.

By supplementing the reading of Austin with Charles Sanders Peirce's work, one can notice that Peirce disconnects representation from the dependence on a univocal origin. According to Peirce, the interpretation of a sign is not a meaning but another sign (Peirce 1991, 7). In this light, reading becomes not a process of decoding but one of the production of new signs. Reading does not deterministically trigger a reaction to performatives uttered outside a synchronous communicative situation; rather, it entails the production of new ones. In *Literature as Conduct* (2005), Miller opens the question of reading to the unpredictability of subjectivation as a result of performatives. Miller complicates the relation between literature and acts by referring to conduct: "'Literature as conduct' can refer to the way writing literature is a form of conduct, or to the representation of conduct within literary fictions, or, using *conduct* as a verb, to the way literature may conduct its readers to believe or to behave in new ways" (Miller 2005, 2). The last reference to conduct, as a verb, raises the question of the performative dimension of literature: Writing can propose, guide, or alter forms of political subjectivity. Miller summarizes that writing is related to the emergence of the writer as the subject lacking intentionality; but also, reading brings about another form of subjectivity. In the encounter with the texture of a literary work, even though the subject is not deterministically bound to a certain experience, literature and its affective texture can trigger or inspire political action and participation in a collective form of politics.

In the chapters on Arundhati Roy's writing on the Narmada Valley and Mahasweta Devi's journalistic commitment, I addressed the importance of looking at literary works in relation to the sites that fostered their production. I also followed how specific acts of reading political literature fueled resistance against unjust laws and social discrimination at large. What I have demonstrated in this chapter is that whether literature is seen as an act or as conduct, borrowing Miller's expression, its way of doing things with words involves an affective grip on the body. Through Felman, Sedgwick, and Bora, writing and reading, not just speaking, emerge as a bodily act produced at the limit between the body and the external world.

In this light, it is important to accept that the texture of writing is shaped by the event of its creation, because this thesis bears significant consequences for the creation of new literary criticism. Analytic projects that investigate political writing cannot just focus on the study of the context and structures of power that influenced the subject of a work of art, although these appear as fundamental elements. Looking at the interdependence of the aesthetics and the ethical aspects of writing, giving specific attention to the affective condition of the production of literature, paves the way to investigate the effects of making art. One is compelled to ask, What does this specific piece of literature do? Furthering this discussion on the role of affects for acts of writing, in the next chapter I deal with anger as a fundamental condition for political literature. I also advance the debates introduced here on the issue of the speaker and the writer's intentionality, providing references to Devi's and Roy's passionate reflections on the responsibility and risks embedded in taking up the role of public intellectuals.

10

ACTS OF ANGRY WRITING

....

Ethics, Subjectivity, and Agency

Postcolonial writing is animated by a paradox: The need to remember unspoken chapters of history, collecting and collating archives of personal stories, coexists with the impossibility of narrating the collective trauma of colonialism. Toni Morrison's *Beloved*, the most famous ghost story about slavery, expresses this paradox in its final lines: "This is not a story to pass on" (Morrison 1987, 323–24). The tragedy of Beloved, killed by her mother, Sethe, in a desperate attempt to save her from living as a slave, cannot be truly communicated, and yet it must not be forgotten. *Beloved* conveys the unspeakable horror of slavery through flashes that record the partial emergence of psychic traumas of its African American characters. Morrison's aesthetics refer to the use of fragments of memory and narrative suspense to reveal that writing cannot extensively recover a forgotten past or restore the truthfulness of historical accounts.

The impossible task of transmitting or translating the past constitutes the aporia of the novel, which is epitomized by Beloved's absurd birth and death, or "birth in death." In this light, Gayatri Spivak's reading of *Beloved* emphasizes the significance of Sethe's acts of withholding, underscoring the limits of communication. In the scene in which the mother shows her daughter the scars from the physical branding imposed on her as a condition of slavery, she simultaneously reveals the scars while concealing their meaning. Performing a paradox, she withholds the perpetration of the same fate on her children but transforms them into agents of rememoration (Spivak 2012, 170–72). Similarly, Morrison points to the scar of colonialism but also embraces the limits of translation and representation. Emphasizing that the narrating subject is split by an inevitable contradiction, she embodies a figure of the author who appears to be substantially different from the one discussed by Michel Foucault in "What Is an Author?" where the author is the grantor of "the principle of a certain unity in writing" (Foucault 1984, 97).

In this well-known text Foucault describes the individualization of the author as a historically specific process that sweeps away the centrality of artworks. His discussion on the ownership of literature takes place in the context of a postmodern wave of reflections on the death of the author (Barthes 1977). Instead of professing faith in the prospect of a historical liberation of the audience from the idea of authorship, Foucault calls "author function" the persisting classifying principle that bounds an artwork to a single origin. Foucault claims that, although in ancient oral traditions anonymity was the norm, as in the case of epic poems, the modern concept of the author implies an individualization of the act of creation. The author becomes the keeper of authentic and original forms: "We are accustomed to saying that the author is the genial creator of a work in which he deposits, with infinite wealth and generosity, an inexhaustible world of significations. . . . The truth is quite the contrary: the author is not an indefinite source of significations that fill a work; the author does not precede the works; he is a certain functional principle by which, in our culture, one limits, excludes and chooses" (Foucault 1984, 118). The author here appears as a function that legitimizes the attribution of authority to the writing subject. It limits the circulation of discourses through a claim of ownership over discourse.

Reacting against this property claim, Foucault proposes looking at writing not as the exaltation of the author but as its disappearance: "In writing, the point is not to manifest or exalt the act of writing, nor is it to pin a subject within language; it is, rather, a question of creating a space into which the writing subject constantly disappears" (Foucault 1984, 102). Foucault's essay ends with the thought-provoking question, What does it matter who writes?

This question provokes a strong response from such postcolonial critics as Gayatri Spivak. In "Can the Subaltern Speak?" Spivak exposes the danger inherent in glorifying the dislocation of the author's role; she claims that Foucault's emphasis on discourse diminishes the relevance of properly positioning the speaking or writing subject and eventually authorizes the concealment of power relations that concur in the creation of a literary work. For Spivak, asking who writes is crucial to determining who has the power to speak and be listened to. She warns us that decontextualizing literary works may deprive writers of their political voice. In other words, Spivak highlights that a critique of the author function and capitalist regimes of ownership cannot overshadow discussions on the position and the constitution of the writing subject. My research develops a reflection on this latter point. By analyzing the specific conditions that lead women to write in contexts of social struggles in postcolonial India, I reclaim the importance of looking at their literary works as situated political acts.

Following Hélène Cixous's reflections on the practice of writing, without endorsing her position on how sexual difference generates a particular *écriture feminine*, I claim that looking at who writes not only helps the analysis of global power inequalities but also permits focusing on the stimuli and foundational conditions for the creation of a text. For Cixous, writing is an embodied process, informed and shaped by the location of the body in time, space, and the web of social relations. Its affective states condition the way in which the subject acts and writes, sometimes exceeding its sovereign will.

Looking at the emergence of Mahasweta Devi and Arundhati Roy's commitment to specific struggles of Adivasis, in this chapter I also ask whether acts of writing shed light on the limits of the notion of the political subject, as male, autonomous, and sovereign, inherited by the Renaissance, when theories of citizenship were founded. Devi and Roy's references to anger as a foundational condition for their textual production reveal how the context of the social struggles in which they were involved called for their acts of literary resistance. These writers often stress that the contingency of their acts of writing engendered them as authors. Instead of claiming authenticity and originality, they highlight the importance of shared experiences and common knowledge in their formation as authors.[1]

Taking a cue from these works and referring to feminist criticism, I ask how the emphasis on the element of corporeality helps to reject the singularization of the author and the trascendentalization of its sovereign reason. Although Foucault's famous essay focuses specifically on the author function as a product of the capitalist regime of property, recent readings and critiques of it prompt the formulation of questions on the emergence of writers: how and when someone's act of talking against the grain of mainstream culture and politics is taken up and acknowledged as an artistic intervention. Reading Roy, Devi, and Foucault contrapuntally, the surfacing questions are, Can writing be considered not as the space where the writer disappears but as a situated act through which the writing subject takes up the author function? And is the contingency of the act at least as relevant for critics as the author's role? In the following sections I propose positive answers to these questions, analyzing in detail Roy and Devi's considerations on the birth and life of a literary work.

ANGER-BUILDING COALITIONS

Mahasweta Devi, as I explored in the first part of this book, is both a Bengali writer and an activist for tribal rights. As president of the Paschim Banga Kheria Sabar Kalyan Samiti association for Kheria Sabars in West Bengal and a prolific author of short stories, novels, and plays, Devi is widely recognized for her political commitment both in academia and civil society. Her literature and journalism oppose mainstream political discourses that bear the heritage of colonial racism and Nehruvian paternalism (Kelly 2012), which perpetrate the prejudice confining Adivasis to naivete, primitiveness, and animality. Her aesthetics, including the use of a local dialect of Bengali and the incorporation of popular tales and folktales, subvert the common conventions that define "high" forms of literature and open a space for the emergence of tribal subjectivity. For the active political intervention that Devi's writing performs in support of denotified tribes in Bengal, in the first part of this book I considered her acts of writing as challenging the divisive constitutional nomenclature and the ideal of equality.

In the preface to one of her collections of short stories, Devi indicates that her intellectual task is to further social and political change, and she powerfully invokes the centrality of anger as a force leading to writing: "Forty-one years after Independence I see my countrymen without food, water and land, and reeling under debts and bonded labour. An *anger*, luminous and burning like the sun, directed against a system that cannot free my people from these inhuman constraints is the only source of inspiration for all my writing" (M. Devi 1990, xx; emphasis mine). In both Devi's denunciation of the lack of substantive citizenship rights for tribal members and Arundhati

Roy's engagement in water struggles in the Narmada Valley, anger appears as a foundational condition for political writing. Roy and Devi's public expression of anger relies on the hope that such externalization will be taken up by others, who will formulate contextual responses to their political statements that reflect and support their views. Writing anger implicitly aims at (re) creating a community that shares a similar understanding of the significance of this affect in a particular situation (see Campbell 1997, 136). Instead of focusing only on the reasons or intentions for political action, I here highlight the role of affects in inspiring acts of writing and focus on writing as a collective practice that destabilizes the image of the author as a Cartesian subject (rational and consciously aware of the self, with the mind elevated over the body).

Anger is a much debated affect. In her study of Indian nationalism and the role of women as symbols of domesticity against foreign rule, Anupama Roy highlights that in texts prepared for the education of modern women, anger is expelled by the repertoire of emotions available to respectable ladies (Anupama Roy 2005, 105–10). The ideal Indian woman, representing the values of the free country, has to be able to give up anger and vanity and dedicate herself to the family and wider community. This masculinist rejection of anger promotes women's subjection to a model of rationality based on the dismissal of passions. Such a model underpins the conception of citizenship and places women in an ancillary role in the making of the new Indian identity.

This rationalist conceptual framework that links political subjectivity to the control of the body, though, has been powerfully questioned by foundational texts of feminist theory. Marilyn Frye (1983) looks at anger as a reaction to being wronged and as a tool through which an individual can claim her personhood in a particular social context; Alison Jaggar (1989) includes anger among the "outlaw emotions" expressed by oppositional subcultures to challenge dominant structures; Elizabeth Spelman (1989) focuses on anger as a form of insubordination of marginalized subjects or groups. Audre Lorde, in her famous essay "The Uses of Anger," considers anger as the force leading to actions of protest and dissent: Being "loaded with information and energy," it is productive for antiracist and feminist struggles (Lorde 1984, 127). For Lorde, the process of translation of anger into a communicative form is crucial for building collective reactions against abuses. She affirms that "anger expressed and transformed into action in the service of our vision and our future is a liberating and strengthening *act of clarification*, for it is in the painful process of this translation that we identify who are our allies with whom we have great differences, and who are our genuine enemies" (Lorde 1984, 127; emphasis mine). Lorde proposes to look at expressed anger as an act that promotes connections to antihegemonic and feminist practices.

As Campbell (1997) reminds us in her work on the relationship between the formation and the expression of feelings, the way in which emotions are externalized in a given context has an effect on their interpretation. It eventually contributes to the endorsement of anger as legitimate or to its complete dismissal. For this reason, Campbell highlights the importance of paying attention to the idiom of anger and the way in which it encourages collective uptake. Devi's reference to her fellow "countrymen" barely surviving against a system of exploitation evokes the solidarity of other Indian citizens, who are urged not to dismiss the reasons for her expressed anger. In the context of asymmetric power relations, the role of language becomes crucial for the creation of a shared public ground for political struggles. As Lorde explains in relation to antisexism and antiracism, communicating anger often entails a defense against the accusation of irrationality.

In *The Cultural Politics of Emotion* (2004) Sara Ahmed refers to Lorde to challenge the prejudice that dismisses feminist claims as emotive outbursts of angry subjects (or killjoy feminists) and describes anger as a reaction to a particular reading of the world and power relations from a subaltern position (Ahmed 2004, 172). She explicitly affirms that that there is reason in anger, or anger has its reasons. Its material life, its way of warming up the skin—of burning it, as Devi says—pushes us to think beyond the dualism between body and reason. Anger involves a reading of the world and, as a consequence, an inscription of the aching and burning body within specific configurations of power. In Lorde's words, anger entails an act of naming what it is against. Poetry and creative writing come from anger, which surfaces more strongly when it is shared in women's alliances. In "How I Became a Poet," Lorde affirms, "I am a reflection of my mother's secret poetry as well as of her hidden angers" (Lorde 1982, 32).

Undeniably, Devi directs her rage against the modern state that has failed to deliver human living conditions to its citizens. But her anger does not merely ignite a reactive assessment; it is the source of inspiration for a creative act.[2] Anger and the writing it generates become inextricably linked to poverty, dispossession, and oppression. They highlight the orientalization of Adivasis, who were pushed out of the forests as a result of the land expropriation started by the British during colonization and continued by the independent government. Similar to Lorde, Devi looks at anger not as the affirmation of a form of morality but as a strategy of survival (Lorde 1984, 132) that allows the claim for rights of marginalized subjects to reach the public domain.

Expressing anger blurs the divide between private and public, personal and societal. This is particularly poignant in relation to acts of writing that transmit collective anger, because the relation between the writer and the collectivity she narrates is not easy to trace. Devi's writing, by her own admission, follows from the proximity to Adivasis in the context of struggles against discrimination and from the emotional disposition created by these encounters (see the introduction to Devi's *Imaginary Maps* [1995]). The content and form of Devi's novellas are influenced by her travels in Adivasi villages; the stories emerge from the collection of popular tales, songs, and oral accounts and often incorporate the local dialect of Bengali spoken by the people. Claiming that she only writes about the people she knows, Devi stresses the participation of tribal groups in her creative literary process.

In one of my meetings with Devi, during a trip to Kolkata in 2012, I told her about my interest in the struggles taking place in the Narmada Valley, where the construction of a megadam has caused the displacement of hundreds of thousands of Adivasis. After listening briefly to my experience with activists and villagers and the prospect of a second trip, Devi almost jumped on her chair and exclaimed, "This is the only way: Go there!" She made it clear that encounters and conversations are determinant factors for the birth of a creative text, whether literature or criticism. Rather than sources of information, as in ethnographic accounts, dialogues and exchanges activate a transformation of the writing subject that is central to ethical and political acts. Anger is the epidermic materialization of a feeling of empathy that alters the subject, for whom bodily experiences of encounters constitute a possible method for the production of writing.

In contexts of exploitation, writers become witnesses and inventors of emerging practices of resistance and disseminate them beyond territorial constraints. Devi's writing sheds light on the legacy of colonialism that influences common perceptions of Adivasis as criminals and challenges their categorization in law. Similarly, "The Greater Common Good," written by

Arundhati Roy to protest the construction of a megadam on the Narmada River, contributes to the exposure of the power dynamics pushing the poor to a future of inevitable starvation. This case, which illustrates a local instance at a global level, is equally useful to explore this idea of acts of writing and their political impact. Roy's contestation of the alliance between the government and big corporations to deprive Adivasis of their land excites strong debates. Against rising antagonism, Roy's commitment to organize massive demonstrations and her use of literature to mobilize a wider resistance engender her act of writing.

Anger inhabits every page of "The Greater Common Good" and it is explicitly invoked in some of the passages of the narration. Describing in detail her meeting with Bhaiji Bhai, one of the Adivasis who lost his land with the submergence of the valley, Roy appeals to anger as a motivation for more forceful actions of resistance: "I'd seen him in an old documentary film, shot more than ten years ago, in the valley. He was frailer now, his beard softened with age. But his story hadn't aged. It was still young and full of passion. It broke my heart, the patience with which he told it. . . . Bhaiji Bhai, Bhaiji Bhai, when will you get angry? When will you stop waiting? When will you say 'That's enough!' and reach for your weapons, whatever they may be?" (A. Roy 1999, 77–79). Roy's solidarity with Bhaiji Bhai is intimately dependent on the anger ignited by the stories of dispossession and stark poverty that the writer collected across the valley during her trips.

As Roy outlines in the interview "Scimitars in the Sun?" which is centered on the conception of her essay, her action was ignited by a sense of empathy with the people she interviewed. Empathy led "to passion, to incandescent *anger*, to wild indignation" (A. Roy 2008, 7; emphasis mine). Roy presents here an argument that opposes empathy to concern. Whereas empathy implies an emotional proximity that stimulates actions of solidarity, concern appears to be the motivation for producing scholarly works that do not engage with the brutal reality of people's suffering. For Roy, empathy is one of the elements that help to construct a politics of solidarity, and it should not be dismissed as a "merely emotional" engagement.

Roy's conception of empathy does not stand for compassion. It is not a form of benevolence that replicates the victimization of marginalized groups.[3] Rather, it recalls the "emotional grappling" against common causes of oppression that the Chicana writer Cherrie Moraga considers fundamental for the creation of alliances in the fight against gender and class exploitation.

In *This Bridge Called My Back* Moraga says, "Without an emotional, heartfelt grappling with the source of our own oppression, without naming the enemy within ourselves and outside of us, no authentic, non-hierarchical connection among oppressed groups can take place" (Moraga and Anzaldúa 1981, 29). In this sense, empathy appears as a detonator for anger, because it pushes the writer to recognize and denounce the global powers that reiterate the subordination of the world poor. In observing the massive displacement carried out in the name of development and progress, the writer invokes collective outrage as the basis for action. By pushing others to join demonstrations and actions of protest, Roy sees empathy and anger as the basic material that allows coalitions across class and caste.

Roy's empathy stems from collective outrage, and it generates a shared commitment to justice and equality. A memorable passage in *The God of Small Things* (1997) stresses the role of anger in constructing new relations and alliances against subalternity. While traveling with their mother and uncles, the twins at the center of the story are trapped at a railway crossing in the midst of a workers' demonstration. The heated atmosphere of protest is palpable: "The marchers on that day were party workers, students, and the laborers themselves. Touchables and Untouchables. On their shoulders they carried a *keg of ancient anger*, lit with a recent fuse. There was an edge to this anger that was Naxalite, and new" (A. Roy 1997, 69; emphasis mine). Anger creates or strengthens bonds between subjects rebelling against oppression and unites Dalits to Adivasis, city dwellers to rural villagers. When acknowledged as a driving force and put to use by a group of peers, as Lorde advised, anger "births change, not destruction" (Lorde 1984, 131).

WRITING THE BODY AND THE LOSS OF SOVEREIGNTY

For Devi and Roy equally, witnessing and sharing experiences of institutional discrimination generates anger and stimulates resistance against longer histories of inequality and violence. Anger emerges in their works, as Lorde anticipated, as an "act of clarification," because it institutes a form of communication that facilitates or alters existing relations. Taking the cue from here, Ahmed and Frye invite us to think about anger itself as a speech act, whose affective force supplements language. Frye maintains that "being angry at someone is somewhat like a speech act in that it has a certain conventional force whereby it sets people up in a certain sort of orientation to each other" (Frye 1983, 88). Anger gives rise to communicative situations, which include a request for uptake from the addressee and a response to the implicit claims that underlie stimulation. As Frye shows, anger entails an act of claiming that calls for a response to feeling or being wronged and for the recognition of being rightly positioned in the world. It involves a request of acknowledgment that can be translated into a claim to domain: "Anger implies a claim to domain—a claim that one is a being whose purposes and activities require and create a web of objects, spaces, attitudes and interests that is worthy of respect, and the topic of this anger is a matter rightly within that web. You walk off with my hammer and I angrily demand that you bring it back. Implicitly, I claim that my project is worthy, that I am within my rights to be doing it, that the web of connections it weaves rightly encompasses that hammer" (Frye 1983, 87). Other scholars have noted that, to support her argument on the formation of anger, Frye refers to a controversial notion of respect, which is linked to an idea of rights and property (see Campbell 1997, 158). Indeed, the insistence on domain seems to derive from an image of the subject whose sense of control relates to the defense of private property, which is here represented by the hammer. This idea of the autonomous and free subject, who is also a private owner, is in fact deeply rooted in the tradition of Western philosophy referring back to Descartes, Hobbes, and Locke. It is also the idea of subjectivity that underpins modern citizenship.[4]

Frye's interpretation ends up stressing that anger requires the construction of a "certain sort of being" that can stand in relation to the person or structure one is angry at. It emphasizes the capacity of anger to push the subject to give a coherent and reasonable account of herself. On the contrary, the references to anger and the writing process that have emerged in my analysis of literary works on the environment and their context of production pointed me toward a different path. They encouraged me to explore the possibility of letting go of the image of the Cartesian subject, transparently represented and representable.

For Devi, anger and the act of claiming it entails coexist with the impossibility of giving a consistent account of her writing: "Wherever there is exploitation I report it immediately. I write directly to the pertinent ministerial department. I send a copy to the area; they make a mass-signature effort and go to the local authority. Each minister has one or two hundreds of my letters. I think a creative writer should have a social conscience. I have a duty towards society. *Yet, I don't really know why I do these things. This sense of duty is an obsession*" (M. Devi 1995, viii). In her angry act of writing, as contextual and bodily as a speech act, the subject is exposed to the mystery of what it is doing. Devi's obsessed "I" acknowledges that her writing process coexists with a lack of sovereignty over it. As Felman points out in relation to the speaking body, its scandal is "that the act cannot know what it is doing, that the act (of language) subverts both consciousness and knowledge" (Felman 2003, 67).

Similarly, in "Come September," Roy describes the work of writing as inescapably obscure. Being unable to explain what initiates the conception of literary pieces, whether fiction or nonfiction, Roy admits a certain lack of control over her writing.

> Writers imagine that they cull stories from the world. I'm beginning to believe that vanity makes them think so. That it's actually the other way around. Stories cull writers from the world. Stories reveal themselves to us. The public narrative, the private narrative—they colonize us. They commission us. They insist on being told. Fiction and nonfiction are only different techniques of storytelling. For reasons that I don't fully understand, fiction dances out of me, and nonfiction is wrenched out by the aching, broken world I wake up to every morning. (Arundhati Roy 2005, 11)

Stories ask to be told—narratives colonize writers. By operating this inversion of traditional subject-object relations, Roy emphasizes the context and conditions of the emergence of writing, instead of the sovereign will of the speaking subject. The aching world stimulates the bodily signs of anger, but the moment that the affect is enacted through language eludes the comprehension of the writing subject.

Elsewhere, Roy describes the complex interplay of responsibility and accountability that characterizes the work of public intellectuals as an obligation that acts of writing impose on writers: "There is an intricate web of morality, rigor and responsibility that art, that writing itself, imposes on a writer. . . . And that's not always easy. It doesn't always lead to compliments and standing ovations. It can lead you to the strangest, wildest places. . . . The trouble is that once you see it, you can't unsee it. And once you have seen it, keeping quiet, saying nothing, becomes as political as an act as speaking out. There's no innocence. Either way, you're accountable" (A. Roy 2002, 191–92).

Because art brings into the light the dark side of political and social matters, writing can be seen as a clarifying exercise. Roy does not portray the work of writing as having purely positive effects on the writing subject; rather, she highlights that writing can take readers to "strange and wild places" and emphasizes her experience of losing mastery over her scripts. Overall, Roy points to the impossibility of rejecting the responsibility of the knowledge acquired through practicing art.

Acts of writing start at the level of the skin, where, echoing Devi, anger at systems of power and oppression burns like the sun. For this affective contagion, Roy and Devi's struggles alongside the poor in the Narmada Valley and in Purulia appear as necessary and urgent as bodily needs. In relation to this, Devi often recalls that "Draupadi," one of her most famous short stories, was written overnight "out of an impetus." Writing anger implies being subjected to this bodily impetus, its urgency, and its condition of mystery. Acts of writing take place in a moment that Derrida would call "the night of the non-knowledge" and under the tyranny of the instant (Derrida 1990, 967).

Echoing Derrida on the impossibility of knowing one's act, Hélène Cixous points out that writing is dictated by an inexplicable urgency: "All I want is to illustrate, depict fragments, events of human life and death. . . . My kingdom is the instant, and of course I am not its queen, only its citizen" (Cixous 2008, xxii). The velocity with which writing is created differentiates it from philosophy, because the writer does not aim at "mastering or ordering or inventing concepts" (xxii). Involved in the unfolding of its act, the writer is a citizen inhabiting a space, through her body, where she is simultaneously exposed to fragments of human experience and forced to acknowledge the limits of her consciousness.

The sense of urgency described by Roy and Devi derives from experiencing the imperative to write making its way through their skin, in the form of anger and other affects. Writing is always generated through the body, which is an archive of relations, histories, and emotions that become text. As Cixous highlights, textual life begins in the body of the writer, which is modified and shaped by life events: "I don't begin by writing: I don't write. Life becomes text starting out from my body. I am already text. History, love, violence, time, work, desire inscribe in my body, I go where the 'fundamental language' is spoken, the body language into which all the tongues of things, acts, and beings translate themselves, in my own breast, the whole of reality worked upon in my flesh, intercepted by my nerves, my senses, by the labour of all my cells, projected, analyzed, recomposed into a book" (Cixous 1991a, 52). Brain, breasts, nerves, and senses are all equally involved in the writing process. More dramatically, Cixous further describes creative writing as a form of physical capture. Instead of a rational process controlled by the author, writing exercises a brief tyranny over the body: Writing "came to me abruptly. One day I was tracked down, besieged, taken. It captured me. I was seized. From where? I knew nothing about it. From some bodily region. I don't know where" (Cixous 1991a, 9). The body appears as a threshold where inside and outside are not separated and where relations of love, violence, and desire are continuously rewritten. In reading and writing the female body, Cixous describes the relation with the other, both within and beyond the self, as the renunciation of sovereign power.

The impossibility of giving an account of her actions as a writer stems from a deeper impossibility to grasp and translate into the disciplining code of language the opacity of the subject to itself. If the work of writing is one of the activities performed by the subject that fundamentally contributes to its constitution, then it also exposes the self to the unpredictability of the relation with the other. In *Giving an Account of Oneself* (2005), Butler reminds us that "if we are formed in the context of relations that become partially irrecoverable to us, then that opacity seems to be built into our formation and follows from our status as beings who are formed in relations of dependency" (Butler 2005, 20). The question of relationality determines the opacity of the subject to herself; but because writing, as explained so far, is also a dialogic process, it is similarly haunted by the impossibility of recovering its truthful essence. Narrating oneself is as problematic as giving an account of one's act of writing. Through the narration, the writer is forced to acknowledge her radical exposure to otherness and her entanglement in a scene of address that founds the field of ethics. This state of dependency on the other that characterizes the subject is inscribed in the act of writing. In performing this act, as I discuss further in the following section, a fundamental lack of sovereignty over writing does not necessarily mean a lack of responsibility or absence of agency.

DISLOCATING THE WRITER'S AGENCY

Agency, in relation to speech acts, is not simply intended as the possibility to act from the standpoint of one's identity, as frequently argued by postcolonial theorists. Being enacted by an embodied subjectivity, writing is not merely an act carried out by a woman, an Indian, or a middle-class subject. It emerges through relations and encounters that exceed and deconstruct fixed boundaries of identity categories. The practice of writing in contexts of marginality and the fact that Devi and Roy are materially, empathically, and ethically involved in struggles of Adivasis and poor peasants enable them to transcend a middle-class background and construct transversal alliances. Although the act of writing is carried out by a single individual, it transmits the force of a collective history of protest that calls to be divulged. In this context the subject position of the authors is constituted through the act of writing and does not precede it. Cixous poetically translates this process of creation of the author with the expression "First we feel. Then I write. This act of writing engenders the author" (Cixous 2005, 143). The relationship between the writing "I" and the sensing "we" does not present clear-cut boundaries but a continuity of positions that sustains the creation of a literary work.

Theorizing acts thus question the figure of the author as a Cartesian subject, willingly shaping new worlds with her pen. But they also pose a challenge to the idea of accountable reason and freedom of subjectivity that Gayatri Spivak sees as the location of agency: "The idea of agency comes from the principle of accountable reason that one acts with responsibility, that one has to assume the possibility of intention, one has to assume even the freedom of subjectivity in order to be responsible. That's where agency is located" (Spivak 1996, 294).

To challenge this view, one could argue that looking at political writing as an act that transgresses identity dislocates agency from good will and noble intentions to direct the spotlight onto the acts themselves. Acts and their consequences, rather than the authority of the writer or the identity of the intellectual, become the space of agency.

In her work *Excitable Speech* (1997), Judith Butler points out that the effectiveness of political resistance enacted through speech acts is not to be found in the intention of the speaker but in the process of resignification activated by speech itself (Butler 1997, 14–15). Butler rebels against the idealization of the speech act as a deed carried out by a sovereign subject. Instead of advocating for the materialization of the predictable effects of speech acts, she believes that failures in universalist discourses on being political can open up new possibilities of expressing dissent: "The resignification of speech requires opening new contexts, speaking in ways that have never been legitimated, and hence producing legitimation in new and future forms" (Butler 1997, 41).[5]

In the case of Devi and Roy, their writing repeats and modifies institutional language from the marginal position of rural villages. For Devi, embodied encounters shape a particular form of literary aesthetics, a language of "emergency" that calls for new political mobilization. Speaking on the border of the unsayable, she exposes an openness of language to citation and subversion. Her use of the idea of citizenship stands as an example: "The Indian constitution respected every citizen's fundamental right to become whatever he could by dint of his guts. The poor therefore had the right to become poorer still. A peasant today had the right to be a landless agricultural labourer tomorrow. There was no governmental agency or strong organization to stand by these men who made a living by cultivating other people's land" (M. Devi 1990, 87). Stating that the only right left to the landless is to become poorer points out a radical failure of the democratic ideals of the modern state and citizenship. With the decline of the Nehruvian centralized state unable to provide social equality to all its citizens, writing resists the perpetuation of an idealized image of democracy by supporting the proliferation of alternative narrations.

Cixous views this performative property of writing, opening up new scenarios and dimensions for thinking, as an essential element of ethics and politics. Writing is a place "that is not obliged to reproduce the system. That is writing. If there is somewhere else that can escape the infernal repetition, it lies in that direction, where it writes itself, where it dreams, where it invents new worlds" (Cixous and Clément 1986, 72).

Writing can escape the eternal repetition of hegemonic discourses and subject them to critique, to derision, or to inventive subversions. In "The End of Imagination" (1998; reprinted in *The Cost of Living* [1999]), for example, Roy opposes the fictional unity and benevolence of the government and polemically praises an atomism of the individual. She declares her secession from state rhetoric that supports big infrastructural projects, such as dams and nuclear plants. To fight the narrative equating the greater good of the nation to development policies feeding corporate capitalism, she announces her own transformation into an "independent, mobile republic": "If protesting against having a nuclear bomb implanted in my brain is anti-Hindu and anti-national, then I secede. I hereby declare myself an independent, mobile republic. I am a citizen of the earth. I own no territory. I have no flag. I am a female, but I have nothing against eunuchs. My policies are simple. I'm willing to sign any nuclear non-proliferation treaty or nuclear test ban treaty that's going. Immigrants are welcome. You can help me design our flag" (A. Roy 1999, 109). Other citizens of the earth are invited to found a state of hospitality where immigrants are welcome: They can contribute to writing its constitution and designing its flag. The anger prompting Roy's declaration of secession is a prelude to the call to construct a republic of immigrants. The apparent oxymoron of this image resonates with her general invitation, contained in "The Greater Common Good," to join the "ragged army" (A. Roy 1999, 81) of peasants, villagers, untouchables, and Adivasis fighting in the Narmada Valley for an alternative idea of national development. Writing is a way of acting together with others.

Proximity and empathy create reactions of anger that shape the form and content of Roy and Devi's interventions. In response to Spivak's warning on the central role of class and origin for the role of intellectuals, the writers speak neither as subalterns nor in the place of subalterns. Although fully aware of the imbalance of power determined by class difference, they are overtaken by the urgency of performing their acts of writing. Their exposed reflections on ethical writing show that, as Diane Elam reminds us, "responsibility to the other is excessive, although is not simply paralyzing" (Elam 1995, 235). For Elam, the recognition of the risk embedded in the act of writing, including the possibility of causing injustice besides one's intentions and claims, is necessary for the foundation of an ethical relation with the other and for thinking about the limits of the self. It does not, however, dissuade from acting.

Not only does Elam advocate caution in assuming the role of a spokesperson in contexts of oppression, but she also challenges the liberal idea of autonomy that sustains the legitimacy of speaking for oneself. First, the subject is never unconnected to others in a communicative situation. Second, language itself is irreducible to a segment of speech one can call its own; it is always inhabited by traces, echoes, and citations. As Elam affirms, remembering that "we do not even speak for ourselves is an important first moment in escaping the political dead end that lies at the conclusion of the struggle between liberal guilt and imperialist self-confidence, a step beyond the dialectic opposition between self and other" (Elam 1995, 237). An act of writing is always entangled in this double bind, but it also productively mobilizes the opposition between self and other to serve as an ethical form of engagement.

CONCLUSION

Lorde considered anger an agent of change when it is expressed and taken up in a group of peers. Against the background of Lorde's claim about the productivity of anger, Roy and Devi have rewritten the relations with activists and protesters, highlighting that the alliance of different strands enhances the possibility of success for civil struggles. What I have argued so far, referring to their acts of writing anger, suggests that they trigger new reflections on the question of authorship, touching on the fields of ethics, agency, and subjectivity.

Focusing on anger as a speech act and as an embodied form of communication opens the way to reconsidering the ethical relation between the writing subject and the collective space in which her writing emerges. The aspiration to ethical writing produces a paradoxical situation in which the achievement of justice is placed at risk by the potential obliteration of the other in the process of representation. In the practice of writing with the subaltern, one cannot eliminate the risk of rewriting the subaltern within a hegemonic narrative that displaces its subjectivity. On the other hand, performing an act means taking up this risk.

Highlighting the need to perform a risky act means revising the centrality of Spivak's idea of ethics, which draws from Levinas and Derrida's notion of the double bind. Spivak places the impossibility of ethics in the imperative of imagining the other as insurmountably different from and similar to the self: "The image of the other as self produced by imagination supplementing knowledge or its absence is a figure that marks the impossibility of fully realizing the ethical" (Spivak 2012, 104). And yet, Spivak maintains, despite this paradox or double bind, one is forced to take up the burden of responsibility; one cannot be mindful of an aporia when the imperative of decision has to be faced (105). So, when writers find themselves caught in the double bind of ethics, they are simultaneously compelled to act. When Devi and Roy recall the origin of their literary acts, they emphasize that in the moment of writing, subjects are not mindful of the paradox of ethics, but they are not even careless. Moreover, despite the impetus to act being triggered by an embodied experience, their anger is not irrational. The writers do not claim sovereignty over their acts but accept the responsibility that follows from them. Acts of writing reveal that lack of mastery does not mean lack of agency.

Agency here emerges as the possibility for the subject to respond to the ethical call in unforeseen, nondeterministic ways. This focus on relationality and ethics links agency to the subject rather than emphasizes the importance of analyzing forms of collectivity. In her reflections on the notion of the subaltern, Spivak considers agency as a quality of an organized collectivity in which the individual has to synecdochize itself (see Spivak 2005, 481). Following on a Marxist idea of class, she sees the individual as subsumed under a wider group that tries to empower itself to access the field of politics. This way of creating collective associations through institutional channels aims at producing a form of resistance that is intelligible within the grammar of the nation-state. In the context of this discussion on agency, Spivak proposes to see citizenship as the condition of possibility of the singular to synecdochize itself and claim India or the nation as one's own.

Instead, the analysis of Devi and Roy's writing suggests that different images of agency and citizenship emerge when one considers the relation between the subject and a noninstitutionalized kind of collectivity. As evident in the case of Roy, who worked with the Narmada Bachao Andolan for one year and then moved on, prompting public outraged reactions, the construction of an alliance in a situation of emergency can be ephemeral and not lead to the constitution of an institutionalized group. On the contrary, Devi's activism presents a lifetime commitment to Adivasis, but her writing emphasizes the necessity to take action in particularly critical conjunctural moments. The writers' agency does not seem to lie in the possibility to synecdochize themselves within a group but in their strategic and creative acts of communicating anger. The success of the writers' political performance can be pictured as the felicitous completion of an angry speech act: Language affecting an audience cannot be considered as merely reporting personal emotions; it enhances them and contributes to the formation of a group of peers.[6]

In different instances both Roy and Devi stress the political significance of calling their audience fellow citizens. This language has indeed become intelligible against the grain of politics, because their books and their actions have fueled local and international resistance.

Stressing Devi and Roy's insertion into a web of personal and political relations, in this book I have followed their emergence as authors as a consequence of particular acts of writing. The proposed idea that the writing subject is produced by its performance and does not preexist its acts questions the fixed ontology of the Cartesian subject. Moreover, the stress on feminist angry acts as "embodied thought" (Rosaldo 1984, 143) challenges the erasure of emotions from the domain of reason. Through writing, the affective force of anger opens a way to think nondualistically about body and mind, emotions and rationality, self and other. It is only beyond these binaries that writing, stimulated by close encounters with and anger at discrimination, can be conceived as enacting political struggles.

AFTERWORD

This book was animated by accounts and images of Adivasis' struggles. In Jobat, Barwani (Madhya Pradesh), and other places where the fight against the Narmada dam, its completion, and the excavation of canals is still going on, indigenous people have fought against their present dispossession and for a more just future of global development. Adults and children have repeatedly put their bodies on the line, standing in the rising waters during the monsoons and occupying government land. With firm determination, they slept in the open air for months, covered by old and thin blankets that do not warm their bodies, in the hope of settling on a piece of soil where they can farm, feed their animals, and sustain their families. They want land and demand to be treated like dignified citizens, to be provided with access to education, hospitals, and welfare.

In the Narmada Valley and in Purulia (West Bengal), two of the battlefields described in this book, Arundhati Roy and Mahasweta Devi fought alongside Adivasis to demonstrate that social discrimination is increasingly pushing indigenous people to the margins of society. They have shown that the same nation that claims to strive for modernity and quick economic growth has condemned some of its citizens living in remote rural areas to be forgotten. They sided with nonviolent demonstrations and armed conflicts of Adivasis and untouchables against instances of injustice, which have brought into the spotlight the issues of endemic poverty and institutional discrimination. Also, they questioned the rhetoric of development and the meaning of citizenship and its entitlements.

While listening to the stories of Budhan, Bhadra, and Chuni Kotal, a girl who committed suicide after being scorned by her professors because of her tribal descent, I felt compelled to write. Seeing the determination with which tribal groups and activists claim their rights, I was inspired to act. This book was born out of my rising anger at the deadly consequences of social marginalization, and it became the means to investigate the history of alienation of indigenous people from mainstream society. The feeling of being caught in a field of struggle and being drawn to act initiated the reflections on the writing subject that constitute the core of this work. My portrayal of the writing subject as nontransparent and as both affectively and bodily caught in the field it represents also illustrates the condition of work of the scholar "doing" social research.

My phrase "acts of angry writing" tries to capture the importance of affective labor for the creation of a political text, and it abandons the idea that authors are rational subjects in full control of their writing. But I do not portray the production of literature as just a nebulous impulse; nor do I reduce it to its content and context. In this book I demonstrate that the aesthetics of writing and the texture of a literary work are shaped by the circumstances of their creation and by the affective state of the writer. Writing is a bodily act; its way of "doing things with words" is saturated with affects. The aesthetics and the content of political writing equally emerge at the limit between the body and the external world. Aesthetics and ethics appear interdependent.

Together with anger, as the subtitle of this book emphasizes, orientalism and citizenship are two focal concepts in my investigation. I approached the history of denotification of tribal communities after meeting Mahasweta Devi. Her novels and short stories stimulated me to try to find the roots of a long-lasting prejudice against tribals' social organization and nomadism. As explored in the first part of the book, a form of orientalism that relegated Adivasis to the state of nature was inscribed in colonial ideology and colonial laws, such as the Criminal Tribes Act, which criminalized some Indian tribes. The view that indigenous people are naïve and dangerous still persists in popular culture and underpins the language of citizenship of the constitution, which endorsed the colonial nomenclature of denotified and scheduled tribes and backward castes.

Devi's creative works challenge this form of orientalism, presenting the political acts through which Adivasis reclaim their place in the nation. They also denounce the misrepresentation of indigenous customs that supported colonial orientalism and reinforced contemporary discrimination. In my analysis the lack of private property in indigenous communities emerged as a key element contributing to their condition of marginalization. Because of the lack of a cash economy and private property in their communities, Adivasis are effectively excluded from the dominant image of a neoliberal, progressive nation. Although indigenous people are formally equal citizens, there is no space for them in India's technologically advanced modernity. Although setting them apart from mainstream society, Devi and Roy similarly believe that Adivasis' liminal position, inside the nation and against the neoliberal predicament, enables them to interrogate the material success of the egalitarian and democratic ideals that animated decolonization and the construction of the nation.

In the second part of this book I showed that Arundhati Roy, like Devi, is well aware that the enduring postcolonial discrimination of Adivasis and untouchables derives from economic orientalism, also defined as "capitalocentric orientalism" (Chakrabarti and Dhar 2010, 33), which portrays Adivasis as out of sync with modernity. Roy's work questions the primary role of private property in the definition of citizenship and its discriminating effects; then, by referring to the aesthetics of storytelling, Roy challenges individual authorship as a form of private property. Her rhetorical use of speech acts to respond to the normative power of national politics multiplies existing versions of truth about what constitutes the common good of the nation.

Roy and Devi's portrayals of tribal struggles do not fall into the orientalist trap of romanticizing indigenous people or essentializing their culture. In this respect, Pal's autobiography, to which I dedicated the third part of this book, is different from the work of the other two writers. *Warrior in a Pink Sari* presents a much more stereotypical image of a single heroine, Sampat Pal, who combats women's exploitation in the region of Bundelkhand. Despite this bias, in several works published on the Gulabi Gang, anger at oppression powerfully emerges as Pal's motivation to found the gang in 2006 and becomes the affective glue that sustains their collective work. The gang's acts of violence are spontaneous outbursts of anger at exploitation.

In different forms, through essays, short stories, and autobiographical novels, Devi, Roy, and Pal point to the gap between formal citizenship and substantial equality. These women's writing and activism rearticulate people's claims to rights to food, land, and gender equality and create a language for existing or upcoming struggles. But with the expression "acts of writing," which resonates with Isin's theorization of acts of citizenship, I have tried to communicate my interest not only in the rights these writers claim but also in how their claims are actualized. As Zivi points out in her investigation of the process of claiming rights, "Even a claim to very specific economic, social and political rights, is never a singular utterance. . . . It is, instead, a series of activities that should be analyzed for the varied effects it has on the world" (Zivi 2012, 11). In the cases of Devi, Roy, and Pal, the subversive potential of their acts is to be read in conjunction with their legal activism, participation in marches, and support for violent resistance. By joining rallies and violent protests, activist writers mobilized well-known repertoires of collective action to express their anger at injustice. Also, making their claims nearby orientalized and marginalized subjects, they positioned millions of Indian citizens living at the margins of the modern nation at the center of the political arena.

Acts of rights claiming perform a social change by bringing into being new demands and forms of inclusion. In India, although much of the recent global discourse has focused on women as victims of rape, activist writers have highlighted that lower castes, indigenous people, and women continuously rewrite the social text through acts of disobedience, insubordination, and resignification of laws and customary practices. Not only has literary writing created a language to articulate those acts without repeating orientalist stereotypes, but it also has produced a space to reflect on who is a citizen and what it means to be a citizen. This language subversively repeats the laws that should grant social and legal equality, pointing to their misfire. Felman demonstrated that misfire is not mere failure; the statements of law are not simply ineffective, but they can act in unforeseen ways. In the case of citizenship, the Indian model of class-differentiated citizenship, designed to protect minorities, entrenched divisions and reinforced a politics of identity. Against communalism, identity struggles, and the persisting stigmas of backwardness and criminality, literary activism gave rise to new alliances and relations of solidarity across castes and classes.

NOTES

INTRODUCTION

1. In 2013 Arundhati Roy was invited to participate in the Annual Anil Sinha Memorial Lecture and to speak on the theme "Mapping Anger: Spontaneous Protests and Complicit Silences." Held as an open conversation with journalist Amit Sengupta, the lecture touched on several issues, including peasants' protests, rape, and Maoist guerrillas. A recording of the event, held in Delhi on March 2, 2013, is available at www.youtube.com/watch?v=aKXAoHu1JeU (accessed January 23, 2014).
2. Using the term *Adivasi* (tribe or indigenous people) implies specific inherited cultural constructs. The commonly accepted equivalence between "tribals" and "aboriginals" is rooted in social Darwinism. It is a consequence of the belief that certain groups, living at the margins of Western, Muslim, and Hindu civilizations, were unable to progress beyond tribal organization and remained outside advancing societies. The classification of Indian tribes, carried out during imperialism, is permeated by an evolutionist bias. The word *Adivasi* literally means "original inhabitants" and signifies the isolation of tribal groups from Hindu societies and the caste system. Adivasis occupy different and faraway territories, have several languages, and are culturally diverse; hence they are far from constituting a homogeneous group. In this book I uphold David Hardiman's idea that Adivasi identity exists as a consequence of a politics of resistance. He defines Adivasis as groups "which have shared a common fate in the past century" and have generated a collective identity (Hardiman 1987, 15–16). Together with Adivasis, I also use the terms *tribes* and *tribals*, because they are widely accepted in mainstream social and academic debates. These terms define the groups that were

isolated during colonial rule and are the main addressees of antipoverty NGO and governmental actions in Indian society today.

3. An article on the event, which reports on the ceremony and the motivations for the award, can be found at www.thehindu.com/todays-paper/tp-national/yashwantrao-chavan-award-for-mahasweta-devi/article1533416.ece (accessed March 12, 2012).
4. Stephen Moss reported on interviewing Arundhati Roy on *Broken Republic* and, dismissively, highlighted that her angry tone could be an impediment to reaching a wider audience. Roy's response to such dismissal reiterated the importance of anger. Moss recalls the incident in the following way: "There is intense anger in the book, I say, implying that if she toned it down she might find a readier audience. 'The anger is calibrated,' she insists. 'It's less than I actually feel.' But even so, her critics call her shrill. 'That word *shrill* is reserved for any expression of feeling. It's all right for the establishment to be as shrill as it likes about annihilating people.'" For the full text of the interview, see www.theguardian.com/books/2011/jun/05/arundhati-roy-keep-destabilised-danger (accessed April 16, 2012).
5. Women became the symbol of the newly born nation and, as Mrinalini Sinha's *Specters of Mother India* (2006) clearly demonstrates, popular culture sanctified the image of the mother of the country, Mother India, positing it on the border between sacred and profane. However, although represented as goddesses, women were the main target of deportations, abductions, and rape (Menon and Bhasin 1998; Das 2007).
6. As Anupama Roy (2005) puts it, "The history of nationalism has largely been a history of male aspirations based on the exclusion of women" (40). If nationalism is a hegemonic narrative that creates a myth of unity, as Homi Bhabha describes it (1990; 1994), it prompts us to excise stories of belonging that undermine the homogeneous image of the nation it sustains.
7. Jayal affirms that colonial policy has infantilized tribal communities, seeking to isolate them with the objective of protecting them from the destructions of "civilization."
8. The phrase "group-differentiated citizenship" more often indicates the successes of civil rights and women's, environmental, and queer movements to obtain differentiated rights in liberal democracies.
9. Bonded labor is a system of inherited debts. Employers give high-interest loans to workers, whose entire families work at low wages to pay off the debt. Bihar and Uttar Pradesh have the highest figures of unorganized and indebted labor in India.

10. Chapter 9 contains a more detailed analysis of the importance of Derrida's ideas of performance in relation to law and literature.
11. For a report on Devi's talk, see www.dnaindia.com/node/1792445 (accessed February 1, 2015).

CHAPTER 1

1. This chapter incorporates parts of an interview with Mahasweta Devi that I recorded in her house in Kolkata on September 11, 2011; I refer to it as "my interview." The inspiration for this section of the book, though, came from a series of conversations with Devi that took place between September 2011 and January 2012.
2. Looking at Devi's long activist commitment, Arya notes that she is, in fact, "associated with about two dozen voluntary tribal welfare organizations" (Arya 1998, 70).
3. Devi's activism spread awareness of Budhan's case well beyond Purulia. A play and a theater company solely formed by denotified tribals were dedicated to Budhan and carry his name. Henry Schwarz's *Constructing the Criminal Tribe in Colonial India: Acting Like a Thief* (2010) explores the creativity of this initiative against the background of the colonial construction of criminality. Kerim Friedman and Shaswati Talukdar's documentary *Acting Like a Thief* (2005) powerfully reveals the activities of the Budhan Theatre group, composed of Chhara tribals living in Ahmedabad.
4. M. Devi, interview with the author, Kolkata, September 11, 2011.
5. My use of the word *orientalist* here follows Said and differs from its use in the "Anglicist/Orientalist debate" over Indian education. In this dispute over the British educational policy implemented in the colony, Macaulay was the biggest opponent of the Orientalists (see Zastoupil and Moir 1999).
6. With its interdisciplinary focus on textual representations of the East, Said's *Orientalism* provides a "suggestive model for trying to grasp the full 'imaginative geography' of colonial and neoliberal forms of rule" (Elmarsafy et al. 2013, 4). Elmarsafy and colleagues' recent edited collection provides new and convincing rereadings of Said's seminal book that trace the legacy of his intellectual influence but remain close to the writer's concern with literature and arts, his style, geographic focus, and political interest. On the other hand, other scholars, such as Engin Isin, maintain that "the debate [around this concept] has remained focused on representations of the Orient in occidental art and literature" (Isin 2005, 31). Isin believes that it is both important and necessary to look at how orientalism shaped

political and legal practices and influenced the construction of contemporary citizenship all over the world.

7. By "legal orientalism," I do not refer to the existing literature of comparative legal studies dealing with non-Western law. Rather, I want to stress the importance of unearthing orientalist assumptions concealed in the cultural sources of law and highlight how law disempowered colonial subjects, depriving them of their political subjectivity.

8. As Nigam notes, despite their apparent exceptionality, the founding principles of the CTA were not entirely new and this act "developed out of a number of coercive measures of different chronologies and dispersed locations which overlapped and imitated one another" (Nigam 1990, 136).

9. Despite the importance of Thugs as legal subjects in British India, information on their existence and their actions is partial and fragmentary. An archive on Thugs, codifying colonial knowledge on the subject, was created by the British administrator William Henry Sleeman. Sleeman was the district commissioner of Narsinghpur in the Saugor and Narmada Valley Territories in the 1820s and in 1835 was appointed general superintendent of the operations for the suppression of Thuggees. He firmly believed that Thug gangs were criminals who worshipped the goddess Kali and sacrificed their victims to her. They were thought to have a distinctive language, their own code of behavior, and their own religious beliefs, which made them resemble a separate caste or tribe (see Bates 1995b). The documentation contained in Sleeman's archive, mainly constituted by the writing of English politicians and colonial administrators, is the only source of information on the existence of Thugs that remains available today. Parama Roy and a number of postcolonial scholars have ultimately posed doubts on the existence of Thug gangs as distinct from more common bands of robbers that used to attack travelers journeying across rural areas. Roy stresses that the construction of Thugs as a criminal phenomenon is fundamentally founded on an absence: the absence of their confession. C. A. Bayly similarly highlights that the intensified legal focus on Thugs was accompanied by increased media attention on their case. He maintains that a sort of "information panic" stimulated the colonial representations of outlaw, which stressed the picaresque character of these gangs of murderers, of their brave and treacherous actions (see Bayly 1996, 174). These features contributed to their transformation into the "most celebrated case of orientalist myth-making." They inspired a wide variety of texts, from Philip Meadows Taylor's three-volume crime novel

Confessions of a Thug (1839) to the more recent *Indiana Jones and the Temple of Doom* (1984) directed by Steven Spielberg. Orientalism here emerges more as "a distorted mirror, rather than a purely fictional construct" (Bayly 1996, 173). Taking the cue from Bayly and Roy, Alexander Lyon Macfie, in "Thuggee: An Orientalist Construction?" (2008), specifically refers to orientalism to describe the fragmentary and often erroneous interpretation of local customs that supported the Acts on Thuggee and Suppression as well as the CTA. This inadequate and fragmentary knowledge was underpinned by widespread theories of racial superiority. Macfie writes, "Sleeman treats the thugs as a caste and their system as a 'natural pastime.' A sense of racial superiority permeates his (and other similar) remarks, which betrays a woeful lack of reasonableness. There is no evidence that the thugs constituted an exclusive social order inspired by a religion. Nor had they any cultural or regional organization. Similarly there is no justification for tracing the origins of thuggee back to times immemorial" (Macfie 2008, 391). Macfie does not totally reject the historical traces sustaining the existence of Thugs as a clearly defined criminal organization. In his literary review of anthropological and legal studies on Thugs, he supports the skepticism expressed by Kim Wagner on the positions of postcolonial scholars. After carrying out fieldwork research in Uttar Pradesh, where he became interested in the oral tales on Thugs, Wagner became convinced that "while the appropriateness of the denomination 'thug' can be discussed it seems obvious that it was a recognizable and longstanding phenomenon predating British colonial rule" (Wagner 2004, 963). Macfie considers Wagner's work convincing, but he also states that it is impossible to disconnect any understanding of this phenomenon from the orientalist legacies of Christian-Protestant-Enlightenment values that Sleeman and his colleagues carried with them.

10. The state of Jharkhand borders West Bengal to the east. The area of Ranchi is well-known to Devi from her frequent travels across the region.
11. Parama Roy's reading of the short story highlights that the use of specters, animal allegories, and nonhuman figures reveals the limit of the language of realism, because the sufferings of the poor "exceed any available language of social realism" (P. Roy 2010, 23). In my opinion, though, Devi's references to spectral visions present an aspect of the set of magico-religious beliefs that exist in rural India; they are not a digression but an integral part of the realism of her prose.
12. M. Devi, interview with the author, Kolkata, September 11, 2011; emphasis mine.

CHAPTER 2

1. M. Devi, interview with the author, Kolkata, September 11, 2011.
2. M. Devi, interview with the author, Kolkata, September 11, 2011.
3. Devi has written extensively on tribal groups and their lack of legal knowledge, highlighting how their lack of education is exploited by the authorities in cases of land disputes. Her article "Land Alienation Among Tribals" is particularly important in this respect (see M. Devi 1997, 99–113).
4. M. Devi, interview with the author, Kolkata, September 11, 2011.
5. As Bashai says, "You can go to court if the *jotedar* refused to pay your wages. But will you dare? The administration is indifferent. Will you protest? The *jotedar* is not afraid of the administration" (M. Devi 1990, 103).
6. Munda people are Adivasis based in central and eastern India and in Bangladesh. Their language is Mundari.
7. Devi's novel pays particular attention to the continuity that remains tangible during the Emergency: "The hollers like 'eliminate poverty,' 'bond labour's illegal,' 'now moneylenders' loan for agriculture is illegal' become posters and get stuck on trees and stations and bus-bodies in the remotest parts of the country. But in reality people like Chotti and Chhagan continue to get ground down. These five reigning years are dedicated to the task of making the rich richer, keeping the lower castes and the Adivasis crushed underfoot, and, above all, turning those designated hoodlums without portfolios into cannibal gods with police support" (M. Devi 2003, 190).
8. The songs collected in the novel express the point of view of the Mundas and imitate their language. One of the first songs the reader encounters contains the prophecy of a rebellion that will be guided by Chotti Munda. Chotti is a leader because his bow can scare the police and because his pleas can reach the "Gormen": "Ye raise the bow, ye hit t' target / Makes the Daroga [police officer] mighty afraid, mate— / Ye go to Gormen and tell 'em our pleas / Makes Daroga mighty afraid, mate— / So they didn' let ya play yer arrer . . . Which Munda knows t' bowspell? / Only ye, mate— / Which Munda is Gormen's buddy? / Only ye, mate— / So they didn' let ya play yer arrer" (M. Devi 2003, 66–67).
9. It was, in fact, the governor general who, according to the Criminal Tribes Act of 1871, could "declare a tribe, gang or class to be a criminal tribe" (see Act XXVII of 1871).
10. M. Devi, interview with the author, Kolkata, September 11, 2011.
11. M. Devi, interview with the author, Kolkata, September 11, 2011.

12. For Devi's talk at the 2013 Jaipur Literary Festival, see www.dnaindia.com/node/1792445 (accessed January 5, 2015).

CHAPTER 3

1. Sarkar traveled widely in Europe in the early 1920s and came into contact with modernist art, which he endorsed as a possible international language to be promoted in Bengal. Sarkar supported Gaganendranath Tagore's interpretation of Cubism and brightly reviewed his shows in Calcutta.
2. The birth of modernism in Bengal can be traced to the 1940s: "Modernism is self-consciously professed only in the 1940s, by a number of artists' groups: the Calcutta Group (formed in the shadow of the 1943 famine), the Progressive Painters' Association of Madras (1944), the Progressive Artists' Group of Bombay (1947), the Delhi Shilpi Chakra (1949), and the Triveni Kala Sangam (1951). Many of the artists were Marxists, and had links with the communist Indian People's Theatre Association and with 'progressive' writers" (Chaudhuri 2010, 948).
3. Tagore's political stance is reflected both in the thematic focus of his work, on lowly life in rural areas, and in his choice of techniques. Tagore's minimalist art anticipates modernist trends (Mitter 2007, 29); his nationalism confronted materialism and urban development, identified as Western, and his paintings expressed a longing for a mythical primitive simplicity.
4. In Hindi, although modernism developed an elitist trend with Ajneya's formalism, realism in fiction remained greatly influential. Radical political writers increasingly turned to prose in various parts of the country and, as Chaudhuri maintains, "The most striking modernist fiction was produced in Urdu, by writers like Sa'adat Hasan Manto, Ismat Chugtai, and Qurratulain Haider" (Chaudhuri 2010, 957).
5. It is important to stress that, as Chaudhuri notes, the international wave of modernism and art deco had penetrated India before Le Corbusier's intervention: "G. B. Mhatre employed art deco, and a number of architects trained in Britain, Europe, or America brought international modernism home. Habib Rahman, who had worked for Gropius, designed the West Bengal New Secretariat Building (1944–54) in Calcutta under clear Bauhaus influence, as well as the Gandhi Ghat in Barrackpore (1948)" (Chaudhuri 2010, 952).
6. To respect the local character, Le Corbusier's agreement with Nehru specified the exclusion of skyscrapers. The architect opted for a symmetric grid

plan, leaving plenty of green spaces and dividing the city into sectors, each of which had both residential and commercial areas. The architect also appointed Pierre Jeanneret to design thousands of pieces of equipment to sit inside monuments and buildings.

7. Rajewari Sunder Rajan believes that "the scandal of the state" lies in the fact that in order to be recognized as citizens, people should conform to the idea of the liberal subject. Through referring to a number of iconic cases, such as Irom Sharmila's hunger strike, Ranjan demonstrates how women who reject the paradigm of the citizen-consumer find no place for themselves in contemporary India (Rajan 2003).
8. I refer here to Devi's commitment to fight against the prejudice affecting the tribes that were notified as criminals under the British Criminal Tribes Act (1871). As I highlighted in Chapter 1, which is specifically dedicated to the history of criminalization and its aftermath, the stigma created by this law still persists today.
9. The confiscation of land initiated by the British coincided with the introduction of enclosures and legislation on private property. The legislation recognized property as the cardinal principle regulating land use, betraying the traditional customary rights of indigenous cultures. A more accurate analysis of Singh's work is featured in Chapters 5 and 6, and it relates to the contemporary enforcement of the Land Acquisition Act.
10. The laws against bonded labor are also supported by other legislation, such as the Contract Labor (Regulation and Abolition) Act (1970) and the Inter-State Migrant Workmen (Regulation of Employment and Conditions of Service) Act (1979).
11. Mohan Ramanan and Pingali Sailaja say, "Short Story writing is not new to India. As a literary form, the Indian short story, or to be precise, the 'brief' story in a variety of sub-forms, goes back to the *Kathasaritasagara*, the *Panchatantra*, the *Jataka Tales*, and to the tradition of folk-lore and legend, to the richness of which, a compiler like A. K. Ramanujan has done justice in his recent *Folk Tales from India*. In matters of strategies for storytelling, or weaving a narrative, or creating a *frisson* or generating suspense, Indians have a fine native provenance to go by and need not seek Western models. Without doubt the Indian short story is built on strong indigenous foundations" (Ramanan and Sailaja 2000, 3).
12. In "Of Other Voices: Mahasweta Devi's Short Stories Translated by Gayatri Chakravory Spivak," Tutun Mukherjee observes that Devi's prevalent use of short stories reveals the influence of traditional forms on her narrative. In this

work of criticism, short stories are considered a "form from the margins, ex-centric, not a part of the official or high-cultural hegemony" (T. Mukherjee 2000, 95).

CHAPTER 4

1. Interview with the author, December 27, 2011, Jobat, Alirajpur District, Madhya Pradesh, India.
2. As I explained in the Introduction, my idea of acts of writing echoes some fundamental elements that characterize Engin Isin and Greg Nielsen's theorization of acts of citizenship. In Isin and Nielsen's *Acts of Citizenship* (2008), citizenship is conceived not as a fixed legal status but as a process involving practices of becoming citizens (acts) through making claims and inventing possibilities of intervention on the political agenda. Rather than being merely a document or a definite status, citizenship can be seen as a practice enacted every day. Acts of claiming rights and demanding justice can destabilize the construction of citizenship as a biopolitical device linking bodies to a given national territory. An example of the disruptive and transformative acts that Isin and Nielsen consider is the Montgomery boycott initiated by Rosa Parks: an act ignited by a single subject that triggered a radical revision of rights. Actors putting citizenship on trial exercise their political subjectivity by calling into question the monolithism of juridical language, thereby opening the way for future possible articulations of a form of "citizenship to come." For an in-depth reflection on acts of writing, see Part IV.
3. The essay led to an increase in violent polemics. On July 22, 1999, as stated in the *Indian Express* the following day, the Gujarat government presented "before a three judge bench comprising Chief Justice A. S. Anand, Justice S. P. Bharucha and Justice B. N. Kirpal, several statements of NBA and the book 'The Greater Common Good' written by Roy, a portion of which dealt with the fallacy of court ruling permitting raising of the height of the dam from 80 to 85 metres." Although the judicial procedure did not progress to a better state, after a preliminary investigation the court recognized that the provided evidence, including Roy's writing, appeared to be an "attempt to undermine the dignity of the court and influence the course of justice" ("Arundhati's Remark May Invite SC Action," 1999). This was just the first of a long series of court cases in which Roy was involved as a result of her criticism of the Supreme Court's decisions to support the dam, the last of which eventually led to her imprisonment for a day in 2002.

4. Then Baviskar adds, "The essay was followed by the 'Rally for the Valley,' where urban supporters flocked to the Narmada Valley to pledge their solidarity with the anti-dam struggle. Amidst the hoopla surrounding this event and the media focus on the participating celebrities, it became important to remember another perspective on the Narmada issue" (Baviskar 2004, 240). Baviskar's pioneering work in the Narmada Valley, published in *The Belly of the River* (1994) and several articles, is an important source of information and inspiration. She expresses insightful concerns over the social class of activists and the fading activism that followed the 2000 Supreme Court judgment, both of which constitute a matter of interrogation for my research. However, during my fieldwork in the Narmada Valley, I witnessed the present activities of the NBA in both the Badwani District and the Alirajpur District, where the cooperation of activists and village people still drives the protest forward to ensure rehabilitation to the people affected by the Sardar Sarovar project. My aim here is to refocus the discussion on the ongoing activism of Adivasis associated with the NBA and on their claims, needs, and acts.
5. In her acknowledgments, Roy thanks Patrick McCully, whom, she says, "I have never met, but whose book *Silenced Rivers*, is the rock on which this work stands" (A. Roy 1999, 3).
6. In 2000, Ramchandra Guha replied harshly to the essay, accusing Roy of serious deficiencies in her account and urging her to "revert to writing fiction" (Guha 2000). Guha assumes an equality between the essay and an objective, exhaustive account of the history of modern dams. His bitter article raised a *querelle* and a significant response by Chittaroopa Palit: "One of the other things that is deeply disturbing about Guha's article is the contempt that he shows for literature. By advising Arundhati Roy to go back to creative writing, he implies that literature is not about politics. That Velutha or the way he loved or died is not a skein from the political life or the personal anguish of the Dalits in our country. (But then, he admits to not having read *The God of Small Things*, though how someone can condemn a writer so roundly without having read her work is a puzzle.) Living in a country where *Neel Darpan*, a celebrated play about the plight of the indigo planters during colonial times, inspired peasant struggles and a resistant subaltern consciousness; where the independence struggle (and many people's movements before and after) were marked by the participation of writers and artists; where authors like Gopinath Mohanty and Mahasweta Devi have held up for the nation's conscience the relentless expropriation of tribal resources and the pauperization

of the tribal communities; where Ashapurna Devi's trilogy has shown, layer by layer, what it is to be a woman in a patriarchal society; where fiction in every Indian language as well as Indian writing in English have shown us the impossible political contradictions of our times; where cultural movements like the Indian People's Theatre Association and the Kerala Sastra Sahitya Parishad have happened, to *then* suggest that art and literature is *not* about politics is—to understate it—preposterous" (Palit 2001).

7. Amita Baviskar stresses the importance of the alliance between the Andolan protesters and Chhattisgarh Mukti Morcha, industrial laborers fighting for fair employment: "Such strategic alliances and ideological stands prove that solidarities can be established across cultural difference to forge a more inclusive oppositional politics" (Baviskar 2004, 294). This openness to the other is also reflected in the history of the movement. In 1996 the NBA, together with other groups working on women's issues, Dalit struggles, and environmental preservation, gave birth to the National Alliance of People's Movement (NAPM).
8. Bavadam provides several examples of people inspired by Roy's essay: "Jyotsna, a scientist from Hyderabad, said: 'I have come to add my voice (to that of the displaced people and of the NBA).' Several participants were inspired by Arundhati Roy's essay, 'The Greater Common Good.' Manu from Thiruvananthapuram found the essay compelling. Kavita from Mumbai said that she had been aware of the Narmada issue for several years but had never really understood the details until she read the essay" (Bavadam 1999).
9. Patkar (1999) also suggests that the significance of Roy's essay has to do with its ability of "telling the tragic tale" that unfolds in the name of progress and development: "The strength of her essay is not the statistics, which she has meticulously gathered, but the vivid description of the simultaneously horrifying and tragic tale of uprooting of the tribal and rural populations."
10. Roy theorizes her own writing process: "Stories reveal themselves to us. The public narrative, the private narrative—they colonize us. They commission us. They insist on being told. Fiction and nonfiction are only different techniques of storytelling" (Anupama Roy 2005, 11). In Chapter 6 I present a more specific discussion revolving around the formal consequences of theorizing storytelling as the foundation of literature and its language.

CHAPTER 5

1. In this chapter I deal with the intersection, overlapping, and opposition of three concepts: common good, commons, and commoning. The idea of the

common good, as used by Roy, has an Aristotelian root and a Utilitarian echo; it points to the possibility that the good for the nation as a whole may be achieved only through the sacrifice of a minority. Hardt and Negri's idea of the commons, instead, refers to the common wealth; it encompasses both the natural world, which has been colonized and increasingly privatized, and the socially constructed commons, such as language, social relations, affects, and thoughts. Hardt and Negri also refer to the socially constructed commons as a process: Commoning is the sharing of social creative experiences that enables the creation of new political imaginaries. Open access to the commons is needed in order to "develop fully and put into practice the multitude's abilities to think and cooperate with others" (Hardt and Negri 2009, 309).

2. For a discussion on these themes, see also Pathak (2002) and Gadgil and Guha (1993).
3. As Crispin Bates summarizes in his article "Race, Caste, and Tribe in Central India: The Early Origins of Indian Anthropometry," the stigmatization of tribals as criminals spread throughout the Indian territory and sustained the use of special control measures against them, such as the criminalization of certain tribes, also by means of the Criminal Tribes Act of 1871. Among the affected tribes were the Maghyar Doms in Bihar, the Kunjurs and Khangars in Bundelkund, and the Ramosi, Mang, Kaikari, and Bowrie tribes in the Narmada Valley. These groups were described as habitually criminal, and adult male members of such groups were forced to report weekly to the local police (see Bates 1995b, 229). This infamous act, which officially declared some of the tribes to be outlaws, created a stigma of thievery that is hard to eradicate. In regions such as Madhya Pradesh, a few groups were formally affected by it.
4. For many rural people, and especially the poorest among them, the submergence of the commons is one of the worst losses to a reservoir. In semi-arid areas of India, for example, poor villagers collect almost all of their firewood and meet up to four-fifths of their grazing needs from common lands. Yet their losses are rarely compensated (Hardt and Negri 2000, xv).
5. Nixon describes the emerging resistance against the environmental deprivation and the appropriation of natural resources by governments and corporation as "environmentalism of the poor." He notes that deprived communities "experience environmental threat not as a planetary abstraction, but as a set of inhabited risks, some imminent, some obscurely long term" (Nixon 2011, 4).
6. Hardt and Negri are clear about the importance of the regime of property for perpetrating inequality and injustice, because the entitlement to property

cannot be disconnected from the history of slavery and white supremacy: "The rule of property is a means of creating identity and maintaining hierarchy. Property is so profoundly entangled with race" (Hardt and Negri 2009, 326).

CHAPTER 6

1. Brinda Bose (1998) explored the relation between desire and transgression in *The God of Small Things* and argued that the representation of desire in the novel has to be considered as one of the political aspects of the book.
2. One of the reactions that followed the publication of "The Greater Common Good" came from Ramachanda Guha, who bitterly exhorted Roy to go back to writing novels (see Chapter 4).
3. Mukherjee claims that the analysis of the novel "demands the application of an ecomaterialist perspective which sees environment, history and culture in their real, mutually interpenetrated condition" (U. P. Mukherjee 2010, 83).
4. My reading of Roy's work of storytelling echoes Itzhak Roeh's argument in "Journalism as Storytelling, Coverage as Narrative" (Roeh 1989).
5. At the end of his philosophical exposition, Austin realizes that the divide between the locutionary and illocutionary is blurred. In Chapter 10 I deal more specifically with the ambiguities of Austin's theory, its revisions, and the multiple readings of his work that are useful for contemporary literary criticism.
6. A similar exhortation can be found later in the text: "Nobody knows this but Kevadia colony is the key to the world. Go there and secrets will be revealed to you" (A. Roy 1999, 59).
7. Mukherjee proposes that, from an ecomaterialist perspective, the objective of criticism is to "look at how these styles and forms themselves reproduce the material environments of historical unevenness within which stories can be told" (U. P. Mukherjee 2010, 107).

CHAPTER 7

1. In this part I use the terms *gang*, *association*, and *movement* indistinctly, as they are all in use in Pal's and Khan's books.
2. The reader is not informed about the process of translation (supposedly) from French into English, and nowhere in the book is there the name of the translator.
3. See "A Group of Women Standing Up for Their Rights in a Feudal Part of India," at youtube.com/watch?feature=player_embedded&v=EXwH-kjSUSs (accessed April 25, 2015).

4. "A Group of Women."
5. Babuji is a former school teacher. Being an educated man, he has always taken care of the bureaucratic aspect of the association, including enrolling and counting members. Babuji's help enabled Pal to formally found an NGO, but their partnership also caused resistance from other villagers. Because the two lived together in the office that is the headquarters of the Gulabi Gang, their relationship was sometimes considered suspicious, if not immoral. During the last years and particularly after Pal ran for local elections, the relationship between Pal and Babuji has become increasingly tense. Kim Longinotto's documentary captures the incipient conflict between the two personalities. Babuji complains about Pal's authoritarian attitude and her way of making decisions without consulting him. Pal does not want to share her glory with anyone. The conflict escalated until March 2014, when, during a meeting in Banda presided over by Babuji, Pal was thrown out of the very association she founded and accused of serving her own personal interests. The newly elected chief is Suman Singh Chauhan, a former assistant commander of the group.
6. Karen Offen traces the history of works of philosophy and criticism that, between the seventeenth and nineteenth centuries, deployed the analogy between marriage and slavery to support what can be considered a "feminist politics" before the time. Offen shows that in the eighteenth century Mary Astell's famous line "If all men are born free, how is it that all women are born slaves?" (Offen 2007, 60) suggests that marriage is the government of women's freedom. In France the writings of Montesquieu, Madeleine de Scudéry, and Madame Dupin, among others, use the slavery analogy to highlight that women have free will and cannot be forced into subjection.
7. De Beauvoir suggests that women have been historically outside the process of recognition and that this explains both the reason for their oppression and the fact that men cast them as their absolute other (De Beauvoir 2010, 6–7).
8. I cannot help recalling here anarchist writer Emma Goldman's neat stand against marriage: "Marriage is primarily an economic arrangement, an insurance pact. . . . Its returns are insignificantly small compared with the investments. In taking out an insurance policy one pays for it in dollars and cents, always at liberty to discontinue payments. If, however, a woman's premium is her husband, she pays for it with her name, her privacy, her self-respect, her very life, 'until death doth part'" (Goldman 2004, 53).
9. In the Narmada Valley a similar enterprise was started in 1991–1992 with the establishment of the first Jeevan Shala (school of life), a school for children

of different ages run and funded by the Narmada Bachao Andolan. For an overview of the activities of these schools, see www.narmada.org/ALTERNATIVES/jeevanshalas.html (accessed April 20, 2015).

10. Guha opens the first volume of the Subaltern Studies series with his homage to Italian philosopher Antonio Gramsci: "We recognize of course that subordination cannot be understood except as one of the constitutive terms in a binary relationship of which the other is dominance, for 'subaltern groups are always subject to the activity of the ruling class, even when they rebel and rise up'" (Guha and Spivak 1988, 1). In *Habitations of Modernity* (2002), Chakrabarty helpfully summarizes the main themes of Guha's work and proposes to read "subaltern" politics as horizontal affiliations that counteracted colonial actions: "Using people and subaltern classes synonymously, and defining both as the 'demographic difference between the total Indian population' and the dominant indigenous and foreign elite, Guha claimed that there was, in colonial India, an autonomous domain of the politics of the people that was organized differently than the domain of the politics of the elite. Elite politics involved vertical organization and a greater reliance on Indian adaptation of British Parliamentary institutions and 'tended to be more legalistic and constitutional in orientation.' In the domain of subaltern politics, on the other hand, mobilization for political intervention depended on horizontal affiliations such as 'the traditional organization of kinship and territoriality, or on class consciousness.' Subaltern politics tended to be more violent than elite politics" (Chakrabarty 2002, 8).

11. Fernandes proposes a multilayered analysis of the transposition of Phoolan Devi's life in film and literature. She argues that Kapur's work revives the stereotypical image of developing world men's monstrosity and has the effect of victimizing Devi, depriving her of agency. On the other hand, its depiction of rape "subverts particular moral and social codes that govern the politics of sexuality in the Indian bourgeois public sphere" (Fernandes 2001, 68).

12. In its classical definition, rooted in German fiction, the bildungsroman is concerned with education and progress (*Bildung*) of the main character. Mullaney reflects on the importance of bildungsroman in the narration and reproduction of empires: "The psychological structure of the bildungsroman with its emphasis on cultivation, coherence and maturity often forged through the mediating structures of education, lends itself to the creation and reproduction of the justifications for imperialism" (Mullaney 2010, 30). Empires and nations depend on the reproduction of a particular world order.

In a similar way, I argue that the bildungsroman of the poor reinforces Western ideology and white supremacy.

13. Instead, as Mullaney highlights, following Ahmad, the postcolonial bildungsroman exposes "how societies are fractured, damaged and derailed by the legacies of colonialism or the competition or conflict between different political formations in the postcolonial state" (Mullaney 2010, 32). They question the coercive power of the nation and, instead of portraying the assimilation of citizens within a certain social order, show people's estrangement from their own community.
14. The introduction, like the preface, includes a commentary on the process of writing the book. It reveals the desire to tell the story of another: "The more I got to know Hiru and the more I learnt from Panchmahals and tribal life, the more tempted I became to tell the real life tale of a woman who had actually lived this life" (Parikh 2010, 3).

CHAPTER 8

1. A comparison could be drawn between Pal's conception of justified violence against oppression and the way in which Frantz Fanon sees violence as a tool of resistance against the brutal domination of colonialism. But in addition, Fanon, like Pal, considers violence an instrument of community building against the individualism of the elites: "The colonialist bourgeoisie had hammered into the native's mind the idea of a society of individuals where each person shuts himself up in his own subjectivity, and whose only wealth is individual thought. . . . The very forms of organization of the struggle will suggest him a different vocabulary. Brother, sister, friend—these are words outlawed by the colonialist bourgeoisie, because for them my brother is my purse, my friend is part of the scheme I am getting on" (Fanon 1963, 36). I expand the discussion on violence in the last section of this chapter.
2. Arendt identifies labor, work, and action as the constituent activities that determine the completeness of the *vita activa*. In *On Violence* Arendt maintains that action is the essence of political beings: "What makes a man a political being is his faculty of action; it enables him to get together with his peers, to act in concert, and to reach out for goals and enterprises that would never enter his mind, let alone the desires of his heart, had he not been given this gift—to embark on something new" (Arendt 1970, 81).
3. Because of the emphasis placed on the relation of the subject to its outside, Maurizio Passerin d'Entrèves considers Arendt's model of action as standing

somewhere in-between the heroic and the participative (Passerin d'Entrèves 1993, 65, 98, 154).

4. White and Rastogi analyze Sampat Pal's case and define the Gulabi Gang's activity as an instance of local vigilantism, which complies with all the characteristics listed by Les Johnston in his definition of vigilante activism (Johnston 1996). The characteristics include "(a) premeditation by participants; (b) private citizens whose engagement is voluntary; (c) a social movement acting without the state's authority or support; (d) the use or threat of force; (e) an established order under threat from the transgression, the potential transgression or the imputed transgression of institutionalized norms; and (f) an aim to control crime or other infractions by offering assurances of security to participants and others" (White and Rastogi 2009, 315).
5. It is important to remember that Arundhati Roy harshly criticized Shekhar Kapur's movie soon after its release. Roy openly denounced Kapur's decision to represent a living woman's rape without her permission in "The Great Indian Rape Trick" (A. Roy 1994a; 1994b), published in two parts, and in the essay "The Naughty Lady of Shady Lane."
6. In 2002 and 2003 Mayawati was charged with misappropriating funds in the controversial Taj Corridor project, which led to the discovery of assets allegedly disproportionate to her known income.
7. In his formulation of answerability as a feature of acts of citizenship, Isin refers to Bakhtin's reflections in *Toward a Philosophy of the Act* (Isin and Nielsen 2008, 28–29). Bakhtin states that theorizing an act means understanding that the "moment constituted by the performance of thoughts, feelings, words, practical deeds is an actively answerable attitude that I myself assume—an emotional-volitional attitude toward a state of affairs in its entirety, in the context of actual unitary and once-occurrent life" (Bakhtin 1993, 37).
8. The page numbers for Sen (2012) come from the PDF version of the article, which can be downloaded from the website.
9. Sundar writes, "Insurgent vigilantism by subaltern groups recognizably challenges the legitimacy of the state, but when the very groups who control the state also resort to vigilantism, the purpose is clearly something else—to escape culpability, strike terror, create a sense of helplessness or foment civil war" (Sundar 2010, 116).
10. Pratten and Sen open the introduction of *Global Vigilantes* with a quote from Mary Douglas: "All margins are dangerous" (Pratten and Sen 2007, 8). Indeed, vigilante groups often pull together individuals from the fringes

of mainstream society who react militarily to the feeling that their identity is under threat. In their book Pratten and Sen collected essays dealing with different cases of vigilantism from around the globe and accounted for the diverse activities of fanatical nationalist groups as well as separatist movements and violent forms of women's activism.

11. White and Rastogi state, "We distinguish vengeance—a wish to destroy and degrade the wrongdoer—from retribution—a wish to vindicate the value of the victim and the community as a whole" (White and Rastogi 2009, 317).
12. Arendt says, "Violence, being instrumental by nature, is rational to the extent that it is effective in reaching the end that must justify it. And since when we act we never know with any certainty the eventual consequences of what we are doing, violence can remain rational only if it pursues short-term goals" (Arendt 1970, 78).

CHAPTER 9

1. In *Must We Mean What We Say?* Stanley Cavell discusses Austin's work and proposes a more nuanced reading of the importance of intentionality in the production of artworks. Cavell believes that artworks are "intentional objects" and, even though not every bit of them is the result of a rational calculation, artists bear the responsibility of what they mean through their artworks (see Cavell 1976, 236–37).
2. As Derrida notes, performativity is that "which defines precisely the power *of* language and power *as* language, the excess of the language of power or of the power of language over constative or cognitive language" (Derrida 2002, 118).
3. Cixous reads Kafka's story in a similar way: "The law in Kafka says: 'You will not enter,' because if you do, you will discover that I do not exist. One has to do everything so that the law will be respected, so that one stays in front of the word, so that the word will be the law, as it says in all the books" (Cixous 1991b, 27).
4. It is useful to recall Derrida's brilliant definition of literarity as a characteristic of the noematic structure of a written text: "There are 'in' the text features which call for the literary reading and recall the convention, institution, or history of literature. This *noematic* structure is included (as 'nonreal,' in Husserl's terms) in subjectivity, but a subjectivity which is non-empirical and linked to an intersubjective and transcendental community" (Derrida 1992, 44).
5. Cixous writes, "Communication takes place at the level of the body. We receive, or hear, with the body; . . . This raises the question of the value of

speech, of its development, of what it carries (*fait passer*) or does not carry" (Cixous 1991b, 69).

CHAPTER 10

1. For the stress on the importance of experience for analyzing women's writing, I am indebted to the strand of feminist thought, born in the 1980s, that goes under the name of standpoint theory. In my work I keep a tight focus on how women's embodied experience influences the formation of their world of knowledge, but I combine this approach with a reflection on postmodern theories of the performativity of subject formation.
2. As Ahmed states, "Anger is creative: it works to create a language with which it responds to that which one is against, whereby 'the what' I renamed, and brought into a feminist world" (2004, 176).
3. Empathy has been rejected by feminists of color as the benevolent attitude of white feminists who, de facto, keep their racial privileges. Roy's conception of empathy, though, is different from Ann Russo's contested position in "We Cannot Live Without Our Lives: White Women, Antiracism, and Feminism" (see Caygill and Sundar 2004). Roy does not make reference to her own identity as the basis for empathy. Rather, she highlights the common conditions of subordination to capitalist and patriarchal powers. The awareness of the different ways in which people experience subordination and oppression leads to the type of coalition politics that Roy performs in the Narmada Valley. As Rosario Morales explains, "Color and class don't define people or politics. . . . Understanding racist ideology—where and how it penetrates—is important for the feminist movement" (Morales 1981, 91). In what follows I argue that, even though empathy may be an insufficient condition for coalitional work, it can also be considered, as in Roy's example, a decisive emotional element in the production of resistance.
4. Anupama Roy highlights that colonial ideology promoted a hierarchical construction of masculinity in the subcontinent and defined the possession of private property as a necessary attribute of male political subjects. Ideas of citizenship, introduced in the twentieth century, relied on this social order, which portrayed women as having a necessarily dependent relation with property and family (Anupama Roy 2005, 148). The consequence was that, to affirm their political agency and their right to vote, women had to fit into a social narrative that demanded the emergence of the image of a "unified political woman" (148), educated and "respectable." Starting from deconstructing the attribute of private property that remains implicit in discourses

on political subjectivity, I here present an argument on political acts that does not rely on the ideal Cartesian subjects defined by unity and reason.

5. Butler adds, "Contemporary forms of political agency, especially those unauthorized by prior conventions or by reigning prerogatives of citizenship, tend to derive political agency from the failures in the performative apparatus of power, turning the universal against itself, redeploying equality against its existing formulations, retrieving freedom from its contemporary conservative valence" (Butler 1997, 93).
6. In an article that starts from rereading Spelman and Austin in relation to the expression of emotions, Colombetti highlights how language can enhance affects and induce emotional experiences that would not otherwise occur. Relying particularly on Spelman, I similarly point out here that language and specific forms of writing can transform people's affective life (see Colombetti 2009).

BIBLIOGRAPHY

Agamben, G. 1998. *Homo Sacer: Sovereign Power and Bare Life.* Stanford, CA: Stanford University Press.

Ahmad, A. 1992. *In Theory: Classes, Nations, Literatures.* London: Verso.

Ahmed, S. 2004. *The Cultural Politics of Emotion.* Edinburgh: Edinburgh University Press.

Ahmed, T. 2006. *Literature and Politics in the Age of Nationalism: The Progressive Writers' Movement in South Asia, 1932–1956.* London: Routledge.

Anand, M. R. 1999. "The Sources of Protest in My Novels." In *The Indian Novel with a Social Purpose*, ed. K. Venkata Reddi and P. Bayapa Reddy, 18–29. New Delhi: Atlantic.

Anzaldúa, G. 1987. *Borderlands: The New Mestiza/La Frontera.* San Francisco: Aunt Lute Books.

Arendt, H. 1958. *The Human Condition.* Chicago: University of Chicago Press.

———. 1970. *On Violence.* New York: Harvest Book.

"Arundhati's Remark May Invite SC Action." 1999. *Indian Express*, July 23. archive.indianexpress.com/Storyold/110923/ (accessed April 25, 2015).

Arya, S. 1998. *Tribal Activism: Voices of Protest, with Special Reference to Works of Mahasveta Devi.* Jaipur: Rawat.

Austin, J. L. 1975. *How to Do Things with Words.* Cambridge, MA: Harvard University Press.

Bagchi, A. 1996. "Conflicting Nationalisms: The Voice of the Subaltern in Mahasweta Devi's *Bashai Tudu.*" *Tulsa Studies in Women's Literature* 15(1): 41–50.

Bahri, D. 2003. *Native Intelligence: Aesthetics, Politics, and Postcolonial Literature.* Minneapolis: University of Minnesota Press.

Bakhtin, M. M. 1993. *Toward a Philosophy of the Act.* Austin: University of Texas Press.

Balakrishnan, G. 2000. "Virgilian Visions." *New Left Review* 5: 142–48.

Banerjee, S. 2010. *Becoming Imperial Citizens: Indians in the Late-Victorian Empire.* Durham, NC: Duke University Press.

Barthes, R. 1977. *Image, Music, Text.* London: Flamingo.

———. 1979. "Lecture: In Inauguration of the Chair of Literary Semiology, Collège de France, January 7, 1977." *Oxford Literary Review* 4(1): 31–44.

Bates, C. 1995a. "Lost Innocents and the Loss of Innocence: Interpreting Adivasi." In *Indigenous Peoples of Asia*, ed. R. H. Barnes, A. Gray, and B. Kingsbury, 109–19. Ann Arbor, MI: Association of Asian Studies.

———. 1995b. "Race, Caste, and Tribe in Central India: The Early Origins of Indian Anthropometry." In *The Concept of Race in South Asia*, ed. P. Robb, 219–59. New Delhi: Oxford University Press India.

Bavadam, L. 1999. "A Flood of Support." *Frontline* 16(17). www.hindu.com/fline/fl1617/16171290.htm (accessed January 2, 2015).

Baviskar, A. 2004. *In the Belly of the River: Tribal Conflicts over Development in the Narmada Valley.* Delhi: Oxford University Press.

———. 2007. "Indian Indigeneities: Adivasi Engagements with Hindu Nationalism in India." In *Indigenous Experience Today*, ed O. Starn and M. D. L. Cadena, 275–303. Oxford, UK: Berg.

Baxi, U. 1994. *Mambrino's Helmet? Human Rights for a Changing World.* New Delhi: Har-Anand.

Bayly, C. A. 1996. *Empire and Information: Intelligence Gathering and Social Communication in India, 1780–1870.* Cambridge, UK: Cambridge University Press.

Benhabib, S. 2002. *The Claims of Culture: Equality and Diversity in the Global Era.* Princeton, NJ: Princeton University Press.

Benjamin, W. 1970. "The Storyteller: Reflections on the Works of Nikolai Leskov." In *Illuminations: Essays and Reflections*, by W. Benjamin; ed. H. Arendt; trans. H. Zohn, 83–110. London: Pimlico.

Bhabha, H. K. 1990. *Nation and Narration.* London: Routledge.

———. 1994. *The Location of Culture.* London: Routledge.

Biswas, Soutik. 2007. "India's 'Pink' Vigilante Women." BBC News, November 26. news.bbc.co.uk/1/hi/world/south_asia/7068875.stm (accessed December 12, 2014).

Booth, W. 1890. *In Darkest England and the Way Out.* London: International Headquarters of the Salvation Army.

Bora, R. 1997. "Outing Texture." In *Novel Gazing: Queer Readings in Fiction*, ed. E. K. Sedgwick, 94–127. Durham, NC: Duke University Press.

Bose, B. 1998. "In Desire and in Death: Eroticism as Politics in Arundhati Roy's *The God of Small Things*." *ARIEL: A Review of International English Literature* 29(2): 59–72.

Brown, R. M. 2009. *Art for a Modern India, 1947–1980*. Durham, NC: Duke University Press.

Brown, W. 2010. *Walled States, Waning Sovereignty*. New York: Zone.

Butler, J. 1990. *Gender Trouble: Feminism and the Subversion of Identity*. New York: Routledge.

———. 1997. *Excitable Speech: A Politics of the Performative*. New York: Routledge.

———. 2003. "Afterword." In *The Scandal of the Speaking Body: Don Juan with J. L. Austin, or Seduction in Two Languages*, by S. Felman, 113–23. Stanford, CA: Stanford University Press.

———. 2004. *Undoing Gender*. New York: Routledge.

———. 2005. *Giving an Account of Oneself*. Ashland, OH: Fordham University Press.

———. 2006. *Precarious Life: The Powers of Mourning and Violence*. London: Verso.

Campbell, S. 1997. *Interpreting the Personal: Expression and the Formation of Feelings*. Ithaca, NY: Cornell University Press.

Cavell, S. 1976. *Must We Mean What We Say? A Book of Essays*. Cambridge, UK: Cambridge University Press.

Caygill, M., and P. Sundar. 2004. "Empathy and Antiracist Feminist Coalitional Politics." www.feminist-reprise.org/docs/caygillsundar.htm (accessed January 2, 2015).

Chakrabarti, A., and A. K. Dhar. 2010. *Dislocation and Resettlement in Development: From Third World to the World of the Third*. London: Routledge.

Chakrabarty, D. 2000. *Provincializing Europe: Postcolonial Thought and Historical Difference*. Princeton, NJ: Princeton University Press.

———. 2002. *Habitations of Modernity: Essays in the Wake of Subaltern Studies*. Chicago: University of Chicago Press.

Chakravorty, U., S. Tanika, S. Sarkar, M. Devi, and A. Roy. 2007. "Reading Nandigram Wrongly." *Economic and Political Weekly* 42(48): 106.

Chang, J. 2012. *Inhuman Citizenship: Traumatic Enjoyment and Asian American Literature*. Minneapolis: University of Minnesota Press.

Chapman, J. 2007. "Arundhati Roy and the Narmada Dams Controversy: Development Journalism and the 'New International Public Sphere'?" *Journal of Communication* 17(2): 21–39.

Chatterjee, P. 1993. *The Nation and Its Fragments: Colonial and Postcolonial Histories.* Princeton, NJ: Princeton University Press.

Chaudhuri, S. 2010. "Modernisms in India." In *The Oxford Handbook of Modernisms*, ed. P. Brooker, Andrzej Gąsiorek, Deborah Longworth, and Andrew Thacker, 942–60. Oxford, UK: Oxford University Press.

Cixous, H. 1991a. *"Coming to Writing" and Other Essays*, ed. D. Jensen. Cambridge, MA: Harvard University Press.

———. 1991b. *Readings: The Poetics of Blanchot, Joyce, Kafka, Kleist, Lispector, and Tsvetayeva.* Minneapolis: University of Minnesota Press.

———. 2005. *Stigmata: Escaping Texts.* London: Routledge.

———. 2008. *White Ink: Interviews on Sex, Text, and Politics*, ed. S. Sellers. Stocksfield, UK: Acumen.

Cixous, H., and C. Clément. 1986. *The Newly Born Woman.* Minneapolis: University of Minnesota Press.

Collu, G. 1999. "Adivasis and the Myth of Independence: Mahasweta Devi's 'Douloti the Bountiful.'" *ARIEL: A Review of International English Literature* 30(1): 43–57.

Colombetti, G. 2009. "What Language Does to Feelings." *Journal of Consciousness Studies* 16(9): 4–26.

Das, V. 2007. *Life and Words: Violence and the Descent into the Ordinary.* Berkeley: University of California Press.

Das Gupta, A., and S. K. Panikkar. 1995. "The Transitional Modern: Figuring the Post Modern in India?" *Lalit Kala Contemporary* 41: 17–24.

De Beauvoir, S. 2010. *The Second Sex.* New York: Knopf.

Derrida, J. 1988. *Limited Inc.* Evanston, IL: Northwestern University Press.

———. 1990. "Force of Law." *Cardozo Law Review* 11(919): 921–1045.

———. 1992. *Acts of Literature.* New York: Routledge.

———. 2002. *Without Alibi.* Stanford, CA: Stanford University Press.

Devi, M. 1990. *Bashai Tudu.* Calcutta: Thema.

———. 1995. *Imaginary Maps: Three Stories.* New York: Routledge.

———. 1997. *Dust on the Road: The Activist Writings of Mahasweta Devi*, ed. M. Ghatak. Calcutta: Seagull Books.

———. 1998. *Bitter Soil*, trans. I. Chanda. Calcutta: Seagull Books.

———. 2002. "Year of Birth—1871." www.indiatogether.org/bhasha/budhan/birth1871.htm (accessed December 20, 2014).

———. 2003. *Chotti Munda and His Arrow.* Malden, MA: Blackwell.

———. 2011. Preface to and letter in *Tragic Tales from Jangalmahal*, ed. P. Kumar Roy, 1–2, 51–54. Kolkata: Deep Prakashan.

Devi, P., M. T. Cuny, and P. Rambali. 1996. *I, Phoolan Devi: The Autobiography of India's Bandit Queen.* London: Little, Brown.

Elam, D. 1995. "Speak for Yourself." In *Who Can Speak? Authority and Critical Identity*, ed. J. Roof and R. Wiegman, 231–38. Urbana: University of Illinois Press.

Elmarsafy, Z., A. Bernard, and D. Attwell, eds. 2013. *Debating Orientalism.* London: Palgrave.

Fanon, F. 1963. *The Wretched of the Earth.* London: Penguin.

Felman, S. 2003. *The Scandal of the Speaking Body: Don Juan with J. L. Austin, or Seduction in Two Languages.* Stanford, CA: Stanford University Press.

Fernandes, L. 2001. "Reading 'India's Bandit Queen': A Trans/National Feminist Perspective on the Discrepancies of Representation." In *Haunting Violations: Feminist Criticism and the Crisis of the "Real,"* ed. W. Hesford and W. Kozol, 47–75. Urbana: University of Illinois Press.

Finlay, C. J. 2009. "Hannah Arendt's Critique of Violence." *Thesis Eleven* 97(1): 26–45.

Fischer-Tine, H., and M. Mann. 2004. *Colonialism as Civilizing Mission: Cultural Ideology in British India.* London: Anthem.

Fleischmann, A. N. M., N. Van Styvendale, and C. McCarroll, eds. 2011. *Narratives of Citizenship: Indigenous and Diasporic Peoples Unsettle the Nation-State.* Edmonton, Canada: University of Alberta Press.

Fontanella-Khan, A. 2013a. "The Baddest Woman in India: Sampat Pal, Head of India's Vigilante Pink Gang." *Slate*, August 14. slate.com/articles/double_x/doublex/2013/08/sampat_pal_head_of_india_s_vigilante_pink_sari_revolution.html (accessed November 20, 2014).

———. 2013b. *Pink Sari Revolution: A Tale of Women and Power in India.* New York: Oneworld.

Foucault, M. 1984. "What Is an Author?" In *The Foucault Reader*, ed. P. Rabinow, 101–20. London: Penguin.

Freitag, S. 1991. "Crime in the Social Order of Colonial North India." *Modern Asian Studies* 25(2): 227–61.

Frye, M. 1983. *Politics of Reality: Essays in Feminist Theory.* Trumansburg, NY: Crossing Press.

Gadgil, M., and R. Guha. 1993. *This Fissured Land: An Ecological History of India.* Berkeley: University of California Press.

———. 1995. *Ecology and Equity: The Use and Abuse of Nature in Contemporary India.* London: Routledge.

Ghosh, B. 2009. "The Bigamous Body of India's Bandit Queen." In *States of Trauma: Gender and Violence in South Asia*, ed. P. Chatterjee, Minali Desai, and Parama Roy, 23–51. New Delhi: Zubaan.

Ghosh, R., and A. Navarro Tejero. 2009. *Globalizing Dissent: Essays on Arundhati Roy.* New York: Routledge.

Goldman, E. 2004. "Marriage and Love." In *Feminisms and Womanisms: A Women's Studies Reader*, ed. A. Prince, S. Silva-Wayne, and C. Vernon, 53–58. Toronto: Women's Press.

Guha, R. 2000. "The Arun Shourie of the Left." *The Hindu*, November 26. www.thehindu.com/2000/11/26/stories/13260411.htm (accessed April 18, 2015).

Guha, R., and G. C. Spivak. 1988. *Selected Subaltern Studies.* New York: Oxford University Press.

Haldar, P. 2007. *Law, Orientalism, and Postcolonialism: The Jurisdiction of the Lotus Eaters.* Abingdon, UK: Routledge-Cavendish.

Hardiman, D. 1987. *The Coming of the Devi: Adivasi Assertion in Western India.* Delhi: Oxford University Press.

Hardt, M., and A. Negri. 2000. *Empire.* Cambridge, MA: Harvard University Press.

———. 2006. *Multitude: War and Democracy in the Age of Empire.* London: Penguin.

———. 2009. *Commonwealth.* Cambridge, MA: Harvard University Press.

Hobsbawm, E. J. 1959. *Primitive Rebels: Studies in Archaic Forms of Social Movement in the 19th and 20th Centuries.* Manchester, UK: Manchester University Press.

hooks, b. 1995. *Killing Rage: Ending Racism.* London: Penguin.

Isin, E. F. 2005. "Citizenship After Orientalism: Ottoman Citizenship." In *Challenges to Citizenship in a Globalizing World: European Questions and Turkish Experiences*, ed. F. Keyman and A. Icduygu, 31–51. London: Routledge.

———. 2009. "Citizenship in Flux: The Figure of the Activist Citizen." *Subjectivity* 29: 367–88.

———. 2012. *Citizens Without Frontiers.* New York: Continuum.

Isin, E. F., and G. M. Nielsen. 2008. *Acts of Citizenship.* London: Zed.

Isin, E. F., and M. Saward, eds. 2013. *Enacting European Citizenship.* Cambridge, UK: Cambridge University Press.

Jaggar, A. 1989. "Love and Knowledge: Emotions in Feminist Epistemology." In *Gender/Body/Knowledge: Feminist Reconstructions of Being and Knowing*, ed. A. Jaggar and S. Bordo, 145–71. New Brunswick, NJ: Rutgers University Press.

Jain, R. K. 2002. *Between History and Legend: Status and Power in Bundelkhand.* Hyderabad: Sangam.

Jameson, F. 1981. *The Political Unconscious: Narrative as a Socially Symbolic Act.* London: Methuen.

———. 1986. "Third World Literature and the Era of Multinational Capital." *Social Text* 15: 65–88.

Jayal, N. G. 2013. *Citizenship and Its Discontents: An Indian History.* Cambridge, MA: Harvard University Press.

Johnston, L. 1996. "What Is Vigilantism?" *British Journal of Criminology* 36(2): 220–36.

Kapur, G. 2000. *When Was Modernism: Essays on Contemporary Cultural Practice in India.* New Delhi: Tulika.

Kapur, J. 2013. *The Politics of Time and Youth in Brand India: Bargaining with Capital.* London: Anthem.

Kasturi, M. 1999. "Rajput Lineages, Banditry, and the Colonial State in Nineteenth-Century 'British' Bundelkhand." *Studies in History* 15(1): 75–108.

Katyal, A. 2002. "The Metamorphosis of Rudali." In *Muffled Voices: Women in Modern Indian Theatre*, ed. L. Subramanyam, 194–214. New Delhi: Har-Anand.

Kelly, J. 2012. "The Anthropology of Nehru's Interventions: Swaraj, Hill Tribes, Comintern, the UN, and Bandung." www.columbia.edu/cu/societyoffellows/kelly.pdf (accessed December 13, 2014).

Kennedy, G. 2000. *Just Anger: Representing Women's Anger in Early Modern England.* Carbondale: Southern Illinois University Press.

Kim, S. J. 2013. *On Anger: Race, Cognition, Narrative.* Austin: University of Texas Press.

Klein, N. 2004. "Arundhati Roy: Word Warrior." In *The Checkbook and the Cruise Missile: Conversations with Arundhati Roy*, Arundhati Roy and D. Barsamian, vi–xii. London: South End Press.

Klingensmith, D. 2007. *One Valley and a Thousand: Dams, Nationalism, and Development.* New Delhi: Oxford University Press.

Kothari, S. 1996. "Whose Nation? The Displaced as Victims of Development." *Economic and Political Weekly* 31(24): 1476–85.

Kumar Roy, P., ed. 2011. *Tragic Tales from Jangalmahal.* Kolkata: Deep Prakashan.

Locke, J. 1948 [1690]. *The Second Treatise of Civil Government, and A Letter of Toleration,"* ed. J. W. Gough. Oxford, UK: Basil Blackwell.

Lombroso, C. 2006 [1876]. *Criminal Man*, trans. Mary Gibson and Nicole Hahn Rafter. Durham, NC: Duke University Press.

Longfellow, B. 2002. "Rape and Translation in *Bandit Queen*." In *Translating Desire: The Politics of Gender and Culture in India*, ed. B. Bose, 238–55. New Delhi: Katha.

Loomba, A. 2005. *Colonialism/Postcolonialism.* London: Routledge.

Lorde, G. A. 1982. "How I Became a Poet." In *Zami: A New Spelling of My Name—A Biomythography*, by G. A. Lorde, 31–34. Berkeley, CA: Crossing Press.

———. 1984. "The Uses of Anger: Women Responding to Racism." In *Sister Outsider: Essays and Speeches*, by G. A. Lorde, 124–33. Berkeley, CA: Crossing Press.

Ludden, D. 1993. "Orientalist Empiricism." In *Orientalism and the Postcolonial Predicament: Perspectives from South Asia,* ed. C. Breckenridge and P. Van Der Veer, 25–278. Philadelphia: University of Pennsylvania Press.

Macaulay, T. B. 1862. *Macaulay's Minutes on Education in India Written in the Years 1835, 1836, and 1838.* Calcutta: C. B. Lewis.

Macfie, A. L. 2008. "Thuggee: An Orientalist Construction?" *Rethinking History* 12(3): 383–97.

Maine, H. J. S. 1861. *Ancient Law: Its Connection with the Early History of Society, and Its Relation to Modern Ideas.* London: Murray.

Mayhew, H. 1851. *London Labour and the London Poor: Cyclopedia of the Condition and Earnings of Those That Will Work, Those That Cannot Work, and Those That Will Not Work.* London: George Woodfall & Son.

Mayhew, H., and J. Binny. 1862. *The Criminal Prisons of London and Scenes of Prison Life.* London: Frank Cass.

McCall, S. 2002. "Mahasweta Devi's Documentary/Fiction as Critical Antidote: Rethinking Bonded Labour, 'Women and Development,' and the Sex Trade in India." *Resources for Feminist Research* 29(3–4): 39–58.

McCully, P. 2001. *Silenced Rivers: The Ecology and Politics of Large Dams.* London: Zed.

Menon, R. 2004. *No Woman's Land: Women from Pakistan, India, and Bangladesh Write on the Partition of India.* New Delhi: Women Unlimited.

Menon, R., and K. Bhasin. 1998. *Borders and Boundaries: Women in India's Partition.* New Delhi: Kali for Women.

Mill, J. S. 1955 [1869]. "The Subjection of Women." In *The Rights of Woman [by] Mary Wollstonecraft; The Subjection of Women [by] John Stuart Mill*, 219–66. London: J. M. Dent.

Miller, J. H. 2001. *Speech Acts in Literature.* Stanford, CA: Stanford University Press.

———. 2005. *Literature as Conduct: Speech Acts in Henry James.* New York: Fordham University Press.

Mitter, P. 2007. *The Triumph of Modernism: India's Artists and the Avant-Garde, 1922–1947.* London: Reaktion.

Mohanty, C. T. 2003. *Feminism Without Borders: Decolonizing Theory, Practicing Solidarity.* Durham, NC: Duke University Press.

Mohanty, S. P. 2011. *Colonialism, Modernity, and Literature: A View from India.* New York: Palgrave Macmillan.

Moraga, C., and G. Anzaldúa, eds. 1981. *This Bridge Called My Back: Writings by Radical Women of Color.* New York: Kitchen Table.

Morales, R. 1981. "We Are All in the Same Boat." In *This Bridge Called My Back: Writings by Radical Women of Color*, ed. C. Moraga and G. Anzaldúa, 91–93. New York: Kitchen Table.

Morrison, T. 1970. *The Bluest Eye.* New York: Holt, Rinehart & Winston.

Morrison, T. 1987. *Beloved.* New York: Random House.

Mukherjee, T. 2000. "Of Other Voices: Mahasweta Devi's Short Stories Translated by Gayatri Chakravory Spivak." In *English and the Indian Short Story: Essays in Criticism*, ed. M. Ramanan and P. Sailaja, 94–105. New Delhi: Orient Longman.

Mukherjee, U. P. 2010. *Postcolonial Environments: Nature, Culture, and the Contemporary Indian Novel in English.* Basingstoke, UK: Palgrave Macmillan.

Mullaney, J. 2002. *Arundhati Roy's* The God of Small Things*: A Reader's Guide.* New York: Continuum.

———. 2010. *Postcolonial Literatures in Context.* London: Continuum.

Nehru, J. 1955. "The Tribal Folk." In *The Adivasis*, ed. J. Nehru, 1–8. Delhi: Ministry of Information and Broadcasting.

Nigam, S. 1990. "Disciplining and Policing the 'Criminals By Birth,' Part 1: The Making of a Colonial Stereotype—The Criminal Tribes and Castes of North India." *Indian Economic and Social History Review* 27: 131–64.

Nilsen, A. G. 2010. *Dispossession and Resistance in India: The River and the Rage.* London: Routledge.

Niranjana, T. 1992. *Siting Translation: History, Post-Structuralism, and the Colonial Context.* Berkeley: University of California Press.

Nixon, R. 2011. *Slow Violence and the Environmentalism of the Poor.* Cambridge, MA: Harvard University Press.

Offen, K. 2007. "How (and Why) the Analogy of Marriage with Slavery Provided the Springboard for Women's Rights Demands in France, 1640–1848." In *Women's Rights and Transatlantic Antislavery in the Era of Emancipation*, ed. K. K. Sklar and J. B. Stewart, 57–81. London: Yale University Press.

Oomen, B. 2004. "Vigilantism or Alternative Citizenship? The Rise of Mapogo A Mathamaga." *African Studies* 63(2): 153–71.

Osborne, J. 1994. *Look Back in Anger.* Genoa: Cideb.

Pal, S., and A. Berthod. 2010. *Sampat Pal, Warrior in a Pink Sari: the Inside Story of the Gulabi Gang as Told to Anne Berthod.* New Delhi: Zubaan.

Palit, C. 2001. "The Historian as Gatekeeper." *Frontline* 17. www.hindu.com/fline/fl1726/17261160.htm (accessed April 25, 2015).

Parikh, S. K. 2010. *And Still My River Flows: Story of a Tribal Woman from the Hinterlands of Gujarat.* Ahmedabad: Navbharat Sahitya Mandir.

Passerin d'Entrèves, M. 1993. *The Political Philosophy of Hannah Arendt.* London: Routledge.

Pateman, C. 1988. *The Sexual Contract.* Cambridge, UK: Polity.

Pathak, A. 2002. *Law, Strategies, Ideologies: Legislating Forests in Colonial India.* New Delhi: Oxford University Press.

Patkar, Medha. 1999. "The Narmada Valley as a Symbol." *Frontline* 16(14) (July 3–16). www.narmada.org/archive/hindu/files/fline.fl1614.16141150.htm.

Peirce, C. S. 1991. *Peirce on Signs: Writings on Semiotic*, ed. J. Hoopes. Chapel Hill: University of North Carolina Press.

Pink Gang. 2010. Directed by E. Bisi. La Sarraz Pictures. Documentary.

Pink Saris. 2010. Directed by K. Longinotto. Women Make Movies. Documentary.

Prasad, R. 2010. "Banda Sisters." In *Women of the Revolution: Forty Years of Feminism*, ed. Kira Cochrane, 329–32. London: Guardian.

Pratten, D., and A. Sen. 2007. "Global Vigilantes: Perspectives on Justice and Violence." In *Global Vigilantes*, ed. D. Pratten and A. Sen, 1–21. New York: Columbia University Press.

Rabinowitz, Peter J. 1995. "Speech Act Theory and Literary Studies." In *The Cambridge History of Literary Criticism*, ed. R. Selden, 8: 347–74. Cambridge, UK: Cambridge University Press.

Radhakrishna, M. 2001. *Dishonoured by History: "Criminal Tribes" and British Colonial Policy.* Hyderabad, India: Orient Longman.
Rajan, R. S. 2003. *The Scandal of the State: Women, Law, and Citizenship in Postcolonial India.* Durham, NC: Duke University Press.
Ramanan, M., and P. Sailaja. 2000. *English and the Indian Short Story: Essays in Criticism.* New Delhi: Orient Longman.
Ramirez, R. K. 2007. *Native Hubs: Culture, Community, and Belonging in Silicon Valley and Beyond.* Durham, NC: Duke University Press.
Roeh, I. 1989. "Journalism as Storytelling, Coverage as Narrative." *American Behavioral Scientist* 33(2): 162–68.
Rosaldo, M. Z. 1984. *Knowledge and Passion: Ilongot Notions of Self and Social Life.* Cambridge, UK: Cambridge University Press.
Roy, Anupama. 2005. *Gendered Citizenship: Historical and Conceptual Explorations.* New Delhi: Orient Longman.
Roy, Arundhati. 1994a. "The Great Indian Rape: Trick I." www.sawnet.org/books/writing/roy_bq1.html (accessed April 2, 2014).
———. 1994b. "The Great Indian Rape: Trick II." www.sawnet.org/books/writing/roy_bq2.html (accessed April 2, 2014).
———. 1997. *The God of Small Things.* New Delhi: IndiaInk.
———. 1999. *The Cost of Living.* New York: Modern Library.
———. 2002. *The Algebra of Infinite Justice.* London: Flamingo.
———. 2004. *Public Power in the Age of Empire.* New York: Seven Stories Press.
———. 2005. *An Ordinary Person's Guide to Empire.* London: Penguin.
———. 2008. *The Shape of the Beast: Conversations with Arundhati Roy.* New Delhi: Penguin.
———. 2009. *Field Notes on Democracy: Listening to Grasshoppers.* New Delhi: Hamish Hamilton.
———. 2011. *Broken Republic: Three Essays.* New Delhi: Hamish Hamilton.
Roy, Arundhati, and D. Barsamian. 2004. *The Checkbook and the Cruise Missile: Conversations with Arundhati Roy.* London: South End Press.
Roy, P. 1998. *Indian Traffic: Identities in Question in Colonial and Postcolonial India.* Berkeley: University of California Press.
———. 2010. *Alimentary Tracts: Appetites, Aversions, and the Postcolonial.* Durham, NC: Duke University Press.
Said, E. W. 1978. *Orientalism.* London: Routledge.
Sain, K. 1978. *Reminiscences of an Engineer.* New Delhi: Young Asia.
Sangvai, S. 2002. *The River and Life: People's Struggle in the Narmada Valley.* Mumbai: Earthcare.

Schwarz, H. 2010. *Constructing the Criminal Tribe in Colonial India: Acting Like a Thief.* Oxford, UK: Wiley-Blackwell.

Searle, J. R. 1969. *Speech Acts: An Essay in the Philosophy of Language.* Cambridge, UK: Cambridge University Press.

Sedgwick, E. K. 1990. *Epistemology of the Closet.* London: Penguin.

———. 2002. *Touching Feeling: Affect, Pedagogy, Performativity.* Durham, NC: Duke University Press.

Sen, A. 2009. "Reflecting on Resistance: Hindu Women 'Soldiers' and the Birth of Female Militancy." In *States of Trauma: Gender and Violence in South Asia*, ed. P. Chatterjee, M. Desai, and P. Roy, 257–92. New Delhi: Zubaan.

———. 2012. "Women's Vigilantism in India: A Case Study of the Pink Sari Gang." Online Encyclopedia of Mass Violence, December 20. www.massviolence.org/Article?id_article=574 (accessed April 26, 2015).

Sharma, R. N. 1979. *Criminology and Penology.* Meerut: Rajhans Prakshan Mandir.

Singh, C. 1986. *Common Property and Common Poverty: India's Forests, Forest Dwellers, and the Law.* Delhi: Oxford University Press.

Singha, R. 1993. "'Providential' Circumstances: The Thuggee Campaign of the 1830s and Legal Innovation." *Modern Asian Studies* 27(1): 83–146.

———. 1998. *A Despotism of Law: Crime and Justice in Early Colonial India.* Calcutta: Oxford University Press.

Sinha, M. 2006. *Specters of Mother India: The Global Restructuring of an Empire.* Durham, NC: Duke University Press.

Spelman, E. 1989. "Anger and Insubordination." In *Women, Knowledge, and Reality: Explorations in Feminist Philosophy*, ed. A. Garry and M. Pearsall, 263–73. Boston: Unwin Hyman.

Spivak, G. C. 1981. "'Draupadi' by Mahasweta Devi." *Critical Inquiry* 8(2): 381–402.

———. 1987. *In Other Worlds: Essays in Cultural Politics.* New York: Methuen.

———. 1988. "Can the Subaltern Speak?" In *Marxism and the Interpretation of Culture*, ed. C. Nelson and L. Grossberg, 66–111. Urbana: University of Illinois Press.

———. 1990. "Woman in Difference: Mahasweta Devi's 'Douloti the Bountiful.'" *Cultural Critique* 14: 105–28.

———. 1996. *The Spivak Reader: Selected Works of Gayatri Chakravorty Spivak*, ed. Donna Landry and Gerald MacLean. New York: Routledge.

———. 2005. "Scattered Speculations on the Subaltern and the Popular." *Postcolonial Studies* 8(4): 475–86.

———. 2012. *An Aesthetic Education in the Era of Globalization.* Cambridge, MA: Harvard University Press.

Srivastava, N. 2002. "Multiple Dimensions of Violence Against Rural Women in Uttar Pradesh." In *The Violence of Development: The Politics of Identity, Gender, and Social Inequalities in India*, ed. K. Kapadia, 235–92. London: Zed.

Sundar, N. 2010. "Vigilantism, Culpability, and Moral Dilemmas." *Critique of Anthropology* 30: 113–21.

Talukdar, S., and M. Devi. 2001. *Mahasweta Devi: Witness, Advocate, Writer.* DER. Documentary.

Taylor, C. 1989. *Sources of the Self: The Making of the Modern Identity.* Cambridge, UK: Cambridge University Press.

Taylor, P. M. 1839. *Confessions of a Thug.* London: Eyre & Spottiswoode.

Thomas, B. 2007. *Civic Myths: A Law-and-Literature Approach to Citizenship.* Chapel Hill: University of North Carolina Press.

Tickell, A. 2007. *Arundhati Roy's* The God of Small Things. London: Routledge.

Trinh, T. M. H. 1991. *When the Moon Waxes Red: Representation, Gender, and Cultural Politics.* London: Routledge.

Trivedi, N. 2006. "Biopolitical Convergences: Narmada Bachao Andolan and Homo Sacer." *Borderlands* 5. www.borderlands.net.au/vol5no3_2006/trivedi_biopolitical.htm (accessed April 21, 2015).

Venkata Reddi, K., and P. Bayapa Reddy. 1999. *The Indian Novel with a Social Purpose.* New Delhi: Atlantic.

Wagner, K. A. 2004. "The Deconstructed Stranglers: A Reassessment of Thuggee." *Modern Asian Studies* 38(4): 931–63.

Wandor, M. 1987. *Look Back in Gender: Sexuality and the Family in Post-War British Drama.* London: Methuen.

Wenzel, J. 1998. "Epic Struggles over India's Forests in Mahasweta Devi's Short Fiction." *Alif: Journal of Comparative Poetics* 18: 127–58.

White, A., and S. Rastogi. 2009. "Justice by Any Means Necessary: Vigilantism Among Indian Women." *Feminism and Psychology* 19(3): 313–27.

World Commission on Dams. 2000. *Dam and Development: A New Framework for Decision-Making.* London: Earthscan.

Yadav, K. 2003. *Tribals in Indian Narratives.* Shimla, India: Indian Institute of Advanced Studies.

Zastoupil, L., and M. Moir. 1999. *The Great Indian Education Debate: Documents Relating to the Orientalist-Anglicist Controversy, 1781–1843.* Richmond, UK: Curzon.

Zivi, K. 2012. *Making Rights Claims: A Practice of Democratic Citizenship.* New York: Oxford University Press.

INDEX

www.ingramcontent.com/pod-product-compliance
Lightning Source LLC
LaVergne TN
LVHW010353080826
844660LV00004B/264
9780814340578